The Engineering Leadership Playbook

Strategies for Team Success and Business Growth

Raphael Neves

Apress®

The Engineering Leadership Playbook: Strategies for Team Success and Business Growth

Raphael Neves
Alenquer, Portugal

ISBN-13 (pbk): 979-8-8688-0139-6 ISBN-13 (electronic): 979-8-8688-0140-2
https://doi.org/10.1007/979-8-8688-0140-2

Copyright © 2024 by Raphael Neves

This work is subject to copyright. All rights are reserved by the Publisher, whether the whole or part of the material is concerned, specifically the rights of translation, reprinting, reuse of illustrations, recitation, broadcasting, reproduction on microfilms or in any other physical way, and transmission or information storage and retrieval, electronic adaptation, computer software, or by similar or dissimilar methodology now known or hereafter developed.

Trademarked names, logos, and images may appear in this book. Rather than use a trademark symbol with every occurrence of a trademarked name, logo, or image we use the names, logos, and images only in an editorial fashion and to the benefit of the trademark owner, with no intention of infringement of the trademark.

The use in this publication of trade names, trademarks, service marks, and similar terms, even if they are not identified as such, is not to be taken as an expression of opinion as to whether or not they are subject to proprietary rights.

While the advice and information in this book are believed to be true and accurate at the date of publication, neither the authors nor the editors nor the publisher can accept any legal responsibility for any errors or omissions that may be made. The publisher makes no warranty, express or implied, with respect to the material contained herein.

    Managing Director, Apress Media LLC: Welmoed Spahr
    Acquisitions Editor: Shiva Ramachandran
    Development Editor: James Markham
    Coordinating Editor: Shaul Elson

Cover designed by eStudioCalamar

Distributed to the book trade worldwide by Apress Media, LLC, 1 New York Plaza, New York, NY 10004, U.S.A. Phone 1-800-SPRINGER, fax (201) 348-4505, e-mail orders-ny@springer-sbm.com, or visit www.springeronline.com. Apress Media, LLC is a California LLC and the sole member (owner) is Springer Science + Business Media Finance Inc (SSBM Finance Inc). SSBM Finance Inc is a **Delaware** corporation.

For information on translations, please e-mail booktranslations@springernature.com; for reprint, paperback, or audio rights, please e-mail bookpermissions@springernature.com.

Apress titles may be purchased in bulk for academic, corporate, or promotional use. eBook versions and licenses are also available for most titles. For more information, reference our Print and eBook Bulk Sales web page at http://www.apress.com/bulk-sales.

Any source code or other supplementary material referenced by the author in this book is available to readers on GitHub (https://github.com/Apress). For more detailed information, please visit https://www.apress.com/gp/services/source-code.

If disposing of this product, please recycle the paper

To God for guiding me on this creative path and keeping me aware of my story. To my beloved wife, Camila, whose unwavering patience and support sustained me through the journey of writing this book. And to my precious children, Isaac, Victor, Elisa, João, Laura, and Isabel, who fill my heart with love and inspiration every day.

Table of Contents

About the Author xiii

Introduction xv

Chapter 1: Principles to Become an Effective Engineering Leader 1

Lead by Example 2
    Role Modeling: Leading Through Action 3
    Setting the Bar: Demanding Excellence Through Standards 4
    Promoting Positivity: Enabling Teams to Thrive 5
    Exemplifying Accountability: How You Should Own Mistakes 6
    Walking the Talk: Aligning Your Words and Behavior 8
    Upholding Integrity: Remaining True to Your Principles 9

Develop Emotional Intelligence 10
    Understanding Emotional Intelligence (EQ) 11
    Components of EQ 11
    Practical Strategies for Improving Your EQ 17

Empower Your Team 23
    Know Your People: The Key to Unlocking Their Potential 23
    Frequent Communication and Feedback 24
    Positivity Fuels Empowerment 25
    Set Them Free 25

Embrace Feedback 26
    Unpacking Feedback: The Positive and the Critical 26
    Crafting Constructive Conversations: The Feedback Blueprint 27

TABLE OF CONTENTS

- From Tension to Trust: An Engineering Feedback Tale 28
- Hold a Growth Mindset 30
  - Beyond a Fixed Mindset 30
  - The Importance of Reflection for Sustainable Growth 31
  - The Grace of Unlearning 32
  - Value the Process over the Outcome 33
  - Cultivating Your Growth Mindset 34
- Tame Your Time and Effort 36
  - Time Beyond Money: Why It Matters Most 36
  - Time and Effort Mastery: The Perfect Match 37
- Communicate Clearly 41
  - The Influence of Clear Communication on Leadership 41
  - Crafting Your Message: Delivery and Design 42
  - The Role of Empathic Listening in Effective Communication 43
  - Practical Strategies for Enhancing Clear Communication 45
- Takeaways 46
- Time to Practice 49

Chapter 2: Leadership Styles and Situational Leadership 51
- Autocratic Leadership: Decisiveness in Motion 52
  - The Benefits of Decisive Direction 53
  - The Challenges of Autocratic Leadership 54
  - Autocratic Leadership Versus Other Leadership Styles 56
  - An Autocratic Leader in Action 58
- Transformational Leadership: Inspiring Innovation and Growth 60
  - The Four 'I's of Transformational Leadership: The Formula for Inspiring Innovation and Growth 61
  - How Transformational Leadership Stands Apart 63

TABLE OF CONTENTS

    Mastering Transformational Leadership's Pitfalls 64
    Transformational Leadership Restoring a Struggling Tech Company 65
Servant Leadership: Empowering and Enabling Others 68
    Cultivating the Servant Leader Mindset: Core Characteristics 68
    Implementing Servant Leadership: Key Principles 69
    Navigating Criticisms and Challenges of Servant Leadership 71
    Comparing Servant Leadership to Complementary Styles 73
    Servant Leader: Revitalizing a Broken Culture 76
Democratic Leadership: Fostering Collaboration and Inclusion 78
    The Democratic Leader's Toolbox: Core Characteristics 79
    Principles for Practicing Democratic Leadership 80
    Avoiding the Pitfalls of Democratic Leadership 82
    Comparing Democratic Leadership to Other Styles 84
    Democratic Leadership in Action 86
Laissez-Faire Leadership: Nurturing Autonomy and Ownership 89
    Empowering Through Autonomy: The Guiding Principles of
    Laissez-Faire Leaders 89
    The Shadow Side of Freedom: Accounting for the Risks 92
    The Nuances of Laissez-Faire Leadership 94
    Unlocking Potential: A Case Study of Laissez-Faire Leadership 95
Situational Leadership: Adapting to the Constant Changes 98
    First Things First: Identifying the Readiness Level 99
    The Compass Within: Navigating Situational Leadership Styles 101
    Situational Leadership and Its Intrinsic Challenges 103
    The Making of an Engineer: A Situational Leadership Case Study 104
Choosing the Right Leadership Style for Your Team 107
Takeaways 108
Time to Practice 110

TABLE OF CONTENTS

Chapter 3: Collaboration and Team Dynamics 113

Uncovering the Individuality Within Your Team 114

    Forging Authentic Leadership Connections: A 4-Session Framework 115

    Illuminating Inner Motivations: Unearthing Hidden Values and Evolving Principles 121

Cultivating Trust Through Accountability, Integrity, and Restorative Leadership 124

    Leading By Example: The Catalyst of Trust 126

    Cultivating Accountability, Earning Trust 127

    Restoring Trust After It's Broken 129

Navigating the Minefield: Mastering Conflict Management 130

    The Most Common Shades of Conflict 131

    Fostering Open Dialogue to Resolve Conflicts 132

    Mediating Disputes and Facilitating Constructive Dialogue 133

Embracing Customer-Centricity Within Engineering Teams 137

    Strategies to Foster a Customer-Centric Culture 138

    Overcoming Roadblocks to Customer-Centricity 143

Collaborating with Product Teams 146

    Defining the Product and Engineering Roles 147

    Dispelling Ownership Misconceptions 148

    Aligning on What Comes Next: Product and Engineering Partnering on the Roadmap 151

Leading Remote Teams: Adapting to the New Normal 154

    Surpassing Key Challenges of Leading Remote Teams 155

    Ensuring Transparency and Clarity on Goals and Expectations 158

    Bridging Office and Remote Employees 161

One-on-One Meetings: An Essential Leadership Tool 163

    The Purpose of One-on-Ones: Strengthening Bonds and Communications 163

    Conducting Impactful One-on-Ones: Preparation, Collaboration, and Accountability 165

    Optimizing One-on-One Consistency, Frequency, and Scheduling 167

    Avoiding Common One-on-One Pitfalls 171

  Takeaways 172

  Time to Practice 178

Chapter 4: The Art of Mentoring 181

  Understanding the Nuances Between Coaching and Mentoring 183

  Reaping the Rewards of Mentorship 185

    The Benefits for Mentees 186

    The Benefits for Mentors 188

  Cultivating a Mentor Mindset 190

  Mentorship Program Structure: A Blueprint to Success 193

    Phase 1: Matching and Orientation 195

    Phase 2: Profiling 198

    Phase 3: Developing and Learning 202

    Phase 4: Closing and Celebrating 207

  Crafting Impactful Individual Development Plans 208

    SMART Goals and OKRs: Uncovering the Foundation 209

    OKR + SMART: A Personalized Approach to Growth 212

  Takeaways 216

  Time to Practice 219

Chapter 5: Fostering Growth and Innovation 221

  Cultivating a People-Centric Culture 223

  Turning the Ship Around: A New Era at Microsoft 225

  Pillars for Creating an Engineering Culture Rooted in Growth and Innovation 227

TABLE OF CONTENTS

    Craft a Compelling Strategic Vision 228

    Psychological Safety 232

    Collaboration and Knowledge Sharing 236

    Growth Mindset 239

    Autonomy and Empowerment 241

Creating an Environment to Support Growth and Innovation 243

    Centralize Knowledge to Avoid Reinvention 244

    Cultivate Creativity Through Idea Portals 245

    Leverage Sandboxes to Safe Experimentation 246

    Support Creativity with Processes and Governance 247

    Foster Innovation Through Diverse and Unbiased Hiring 248

Embedding Innovation Through Purposeful Rituals 266

    Sparking Innovation Through Hackathons 267

    Embedding Customer Obsession Through Collaborative Design Sprints 269

    Standardizing Innovation Recognition with Quarterly All-Hands Meetings 271

    Accelerating Innovations Through Early Feedback 273

    Fueling Growth Through Learning Days 274

    Learning from Stumbles to Reach New Heights 276

Embracing Continuous Change 278

    Modeling Adaptability and Growth as a Leader 279

    Driving Change Through Transparent Leader-Team Collaboration 281

    Squandering Seeds of Innovation 283

Shepherding Growth and Innovation-Oriented Cultures 287

Takeaways 289

Time to Practice 291

TABLE OF CONTENTS

Chapter 6: Evaluating and Developing Your Team 295

Using the 9-Box Model to Support Talent Calibration 298

Performance and Agility: A Customized Approach to the 9-Box Model 299

Assessment Definitions: Unlocking the Essence of Performance and Agility 302

Putting It All Together: Evaluating Talent with the 9-Box Model 303

Performance Reviews: The Arc for Success.. 314

Cadence: As Important As the Structure.. 315

Structure: A Blueprint for Performance Reviews.. 319

Performance Improvement Plan: Revitalizing Potential 326

What Exactly Is a Performance Improvement Plan (PIP)? 327

Why Should I Adopt a Performance Improvement Plan? 328

Setting the Foundation for Performance Improvement 329

A Blueprint for Performance Improvement Plan.. 331

Terminations: A Necessary Evil 339

The Role of Performance Improvement Plans on Terminations................... 340

Don't Wait Too Long 341

Don't Make the Call Unilaterally 341

Lead with Heart During Hard Goodbyes... 343

Takeaways 344

Time to Practice 346

Index... 347

xi

About the Author

As a passionate and customer-centric engineering leader, **Raphael Neves** excels at fostering collaboration between engineering and cross-functional teams to create innovative and value-driven products. He embraces that people are the main motto for driving any business to success and directly contributes to making engineering leaders less tech-centric and more human-oriented. With extensive experience across various industries, he brings to his debut book the secret ingredients to develop a strong leadership character, build high-performing teams, drive continuous improvement, create a rock-solid engineering culture, and align engineering efforts with business objectives.

Raphael dedicated more than half of his professional journey to leadership roles, growing teams, developing people, and fostering a customer-centric and human-oriented culture in his engineering teams.

Introduction

As technologists, we glorify the figure of the lone coding genius, the pioneering inventor, the brilliant engineer who revolutionizes industry armed only with caffeine and clever algorithms. This archetype dominates our industry's lore—the heroic programmer who spends epic nights drinking coffee after coffee to solve impossible problems. The geek superhero whose powers lie in mastery of elegant and high-performance application design, design patterns, and clean code—whatever this is. They inspire jargon and expire low cycles of complexity but inevitably succumb when faced with some derivative of kryptonite, which many call "business value."

This false definition of efficiency often leads us to spend too much time looking for unicorns to satisfy the immediate needs of our teams to the detriment of culture, collaboration, and the group. While many of us intrinsically express the desire to become the next hero, this mythology obscures a greater truth: innovation does not arise from the efforts of one person but from teams inspired and united by trust, passion, and purpose.

Ten years ago, I learned this lesson in a challenging and frustrating way while leading a team that performed complex systems integration for a major Brazilian government agency. The project required interfacing multiple datasets and algorithms into a robust real estate management application to optimize the valuation of state properties throughout Brazil. Our mission was to interconnect multiple data sets—property deeds, ownership records, tax information, geographic coordinates—into a unified system that could analyze the data and accurately estimate real estate valuation on a large scale.

INTRODUCTION

The implementation required us to revamp the current system architecture to enable the asynchronous process of ingesting terabytes of disjointed data in various formats and states of degradation into a specific data lake. We then needed to develop proprietary algorithms to synthesize the inputs and process data that could quickly generate property value assessments aligned with the unique characteristics of the land, buildings, and location.

Despite the complexity and unknowns, the team collaborated seamlessly, overcoming technical hurdles after technical hurdles. I saw junior engineers adopting an attitude that I had never seen in senior engineers. They were hungry for success! As the end approached, a nontechnical roadblock arose: we had to ingest data from the Brazilian Army's geographic database for precise terrain measurements and assessments. Our progress depended on getting access to integrate the application with this data.

The deadline for delivering the system was approaching, and despite countless demands to gain access and complete the integration, our leader stated that Army approval would come soon and insisted that we should proceed with simulated data. Trusting your word, we come together to align the final efforts and perform some tests before the deadline. When the day of delivery arrived, the team was buzzing with anxiety and nervousness; everything looked ready for customer demonstration and delivery. Then came the punch in the gut: there was still no approval for access to the Army database. In the absence of these geographic coordinates, an essential part of the system's functionality was completely disabled, rendering the application useless. Despite all our efforts, we were unable to deliver the project as promised.

The team was completely frustrated because the solution, despite being well-designed, did not deliver the expected value to our customers. We failed. Our leader, instead of acknowledging their unchecked assurances and supporting us, exploded with blame and toxic abuse. He criticized me in front of astonished customer representatives, decimating my credibility by falsely accusing me of incompetence and mishandling the entire initiative.

Back at the office, he continued his tirade, publicly embarrassing our team in front of the entire company despite our tireless work and dedication. His duplicity and aggressiveness completely destroyed our morale and confidence. From that moment on, I realized that a good engineering leader is not one who has the greatest technical knowledge but rather one who is capable of inspiring people to achieve remarkable results collectively through care and compassion. Someone with enough humility to recognize their mistakes and learn from them. A leader who takes responsibility, especially when things get off track.

It doesn't matter how beautiful the solution your team builds, how many hours they dedicate, or how much effort they put into their work if they don't have someone to inspire them, to set an example, to remove obstacles, to help them understand the intricacies of whys behind every business need. Understand that, as a leader, you can make or break your team. Forget the familiar analogies that many companies preach as part of their culture. This is nonsense to attract candidates. Instead, view your team as a professional sports team. Understand that your players will have good and bad days, excellent skills, and many opportunities for improvement. They will train day after day and will commit to pushing each other to deliver their best. They will prepare daily to improve their skills to achieve the ultimate goal: winning the championship. Sometimes they will win, and sometimes they will fail. But this is trivial because they were forged in a culture of mutual support, where the success of some depends on the success of others. Still, there is no magic ingredient to make this happen. They need a maestro to maintain their pulse, control over priorities, and the desire to succeed and overcome obstacles. They need you!

INTRODUCTION

I hope these pages inspire you to reject the mythology of the hero engineer and the common misconception that successful engineering leaders are those who carry strong technical knowledge. However, my greatest hope is that my experience and practical advice will contribute to your journey in adopting an empowering, human-centered approach tailored to our industry. Keep an open mind, and I promise you that at the end of this immersion, you will realize that taking a people-focused approach is just as important and impactful as your technical knowledge.

Who Should Read This Book?

This book is designed primarily for engineering leaders looking to challenge the status quo of traditional technical leadership and adopt an approach where people are the catalyst for business success and growth. Regardless of your industry or experience or whether you lead a small team or an entire department, this book will provide valuable insights, strategies, and practical tools to enhance your skills, optimize your collaboration with cross-functional partners, and help your team members thrive.

Furthermore, it is also relevant for senior engineers who aspire to leadership roles or who seek to become more influential in their teams. The concepts of delivering feedback, communicating effectively, being a mentor and mentee, understanding how to contribute sustainably to the team's success, fostering group dynamics, and promoting a culture of innovation and continuous learning are fundamental for any experienced engineer. If you want to go beyond code, this book is for you.

However, the principles and strategies discussed in the following pages are universally applicable and transferable across sectors and functions. So, if you want to understand how to impact your business by placing people as the main driver of change and success, this book is a practical and enlightening resource for your leadership journey.

INTRODUCTION

How This Book Is Structured

This book was created using personal models forged throughout my career, with the intention of serving as a reference guide and personal roadmap to support you in your career growth. Some chapters are interconnected, and following the suggested order can make it easier to immerse yourself in the next subjects. However, despite this logical connection, each chapter adds value individually, and you can jump from one to another to address a specific topic. Also, at the end of each chapter, you will find the most significant conclusions, followed by practical exercises to help you connect the content of this book with your reality.

In Chapter 1, we will explore the principles that I have focused on throughout my career path to become an effective leader. These skills are the foundation for everyone who wants to become more influential on their teams, from individual contributors to senior leaders. We begin to explore the importance of leading by example and establishing that you are the living model for how your team will behave and perform. A strong leader does not shy away from difficult challenges and sees adversity as an opportunity for growth, embodying a positive attitude, being responsible, defending their integrity regardless of the situation, and honoring their words with actions. Next, we will discuss the importance of developing emotional intelligence and empowering high-performing individuals. People don't like following orders for the sake of following orders, but rather, they need context and clarity about their impact on the overall objective; they need purpose and autonomy. Additionally, accepting feedback and maintaining a constructive mindset are important principles to enable your long-term growth. The chapter ends with strategies for adopting clear communication and managing your time efficiently—topics often overlooked by engineering leaders.

Next, we will cover different leadership styles, highlighting their benefits, pitfalls, and main characteristics. It's about demystifying the misconception of the one-size-fits-all approach that we intrinsically

INTRODUCTION

carry in our minds. It's okay to prefer adopting one leadership style over another, but acting as an autocratic leader when the situation requires more collaboration or adopting the mentality of extreme delegation when your team requires close guidance may not be as effective as you think. You will finish this chapter with a new perspective and a desire to adapt your leadership style based on the situation, each individual's level of confidence, and competence.

Moving forward, you will be exposed to the most significant aspects of improving your team dynamics and collaboration with cross-functional partners. You will learn techniques for creating meaningful one-on-one connections and recognizing strengths, areas for improvement, and the true ignitors of each team member or colleague with whom you nurture a relationship. We'll explore the importance of embracing a customer-centric culture as your core motto and how you can collaborate with Product teams to craft impactful roadmaps forged in reality. This chapter also offers a modern approach to supporting the new normal of leading remote and hybrid teams supported by diversity and trust. Last but not least, I'll share my framework for running one-on-one meetings that really matter.

As a leader, one of the most essential activities in your daily routine will be to unleash the potential of others through mentoring and coaching. I will equip you with the tools to build mentoring programs adapted to the needs and realities of your team members, allowing you to create relevant and concrete Individual Development Plans covering technical skills and soft skills.

Additionally, we will discuss the importance of fostering growth and innovation, creating a culture of creativity and experimentation that views change as a positive factor for business growth. However, it is necessary to use practical strategies to launch these new ideas and find the right stakeholders and decision-makers to bring them to fruition. You'll understand how to properly manage stakeholder relationships, advocate for your team's needs, align them with company values and mission, and optimize your hiring process to balance technical skill with culture and diversity.

Finally, we will discuss different definitions of success and metrics, with the aim of helping you adopt practical strategies to establish reward cycles and handle promotions and performance reviews fairly and efficiently.

CHAPTER 1

Principles to Become an Effective Engineering Leader

Leadership is a journey of continuous growth that requires dedication, patience, and an openness to learn. For engineering leaders, while technical expertise may help you step into a management role, foundational leadership principles shape your capacity to guide and inspire teams.

This chapter will explore the core principles contributing to authentic, effective engineering leadership. These include leading by example, where leaders become living models of the standards they set by displaying integrity, fostering work ethics, and matching words with actions.

We will also discuss the importance of emotional intelligence (EQ) in handling your own emotions and understanding the feelings of others, enabling more transparent communication and empathy-driven decisions, and fostering a collaborative environment where team members feel valued and understood.

Also, we will cover empowering your team by gaining a deep understanding of their aspirations and abilities. This empathetic leadership allows you to unlock their potential by providing growth opportunities, open communication channels, and recognition.

Creating a feedback culture is also imperative, where bidirectional, nonjudgmental feedback facilitates continuous improvement and trust. This principle is complemented by the growth mindset, where challenges become opportunities to learn and adapt rather than failures to avoid. Finally, we will explore time management strategies that enhance focus and prevent burnout and communication techniques that elucidate complex concepts, align objectives, and build robust connections.

Although not a checklist, these principles offer guideposts to help engineering leaders cultivate team environments where innovation and excellence can thrive. Leadership demands lifelong learning, but you will be well-equipped to make a meaningful impact with an open mind and concerted effort.

Lead by Example

Leadership hinges on authenticity and action, and true leaders embody the values they advocate, consistently demonstrating innovation, customer-centricity, and a balanced work ethic. By setting realistic standards, they foster excellence within their teams, always emphasizing co-creation and mutual growth. Besides that, a leader's optimism and resilience, especially during challenges, shape team morale, while their transparency and accountability bolster trust and open communication.

Leaders invite feedback and introspect to ensure alignment between their words and actions for continual growth. At the heart of transformative leadership lies integrity, where ethical choices prevail over fleeting benefits, building a legacy of trust, respect, and principled decisions.

CHAPTER 1   PRINCIPLES TO BECOME AN EFFECTIVE ENGINEERING LEADER

Role Modeling: Leading Through Action

Leading by example means role modeling desired behaviors and attitudes so your team can mirror them. It goes far beyond voicing values—you must become a living, breathing embodiment of what you advocate. Moreover, role modeling deals intimately with your persona, character, and disposition. Your everyday conduct, tackling challenges, and responding to successes and failures form the blueprint your team will consciously and subconsciously follow.

Do you want to cultivate bold innovation? Don't just say it—demonstrate it. Tackle stagnant processes yourself; brainstorm with other teams—pilot cutting-edge tools. Making innovation tangible through your efforts lays the foundation for your team to reflect that inventive spirit. Or suppose you aim for relentless customer-centricity; make it real for your team. Share customer pain points, invite users to discuss experiences, and spend time interacting with frontline staff to gain empathy. When you live the commitment to understanding customers, your team will weave that perspective into all they do.

Great role models embrace and live their words. Take leaders who advise work-life balance but email at midnight; those mixed signals breed cynicism and eroding influence. Authenticity is key; when you live the behaviors you endorse, the impact amplifies exponentially, and trust and respect flourish.

Still, role modeling has challenges, making perseverance and self-awareness vital. You must consistently self-assess—"Do my actions align with the values my team needs?" But the rewards outweigh the work. By embedding desired behaviors, you imprint excellence into their identity, transforming your team's achievements and who they become.

To master role modeling, identify a few core behaviors integral to your team's success. For example, if agility and continuous learning are critical, demonstrate your appetite for new skills, processes, and tools. Or, if creativity and out-of-the-box thinking are essential, share stories of how you broke old rules and tried unconventional approaches to spark new ideas. Your willingness to defy the status quo will embolden your team to do the same, so make your learning journey transparent to motivate others.

Of course, no one exhibits ideal behaviors all the time. Admit your mistakes and share lessons learned from occasional lapses. Your transparency will build trust and reassure your team that growth, not perfection, is the goal.

Setting the Bar: Demanding Excellence Through Standards

As a leader, establishing ambitious yet realistic performance standards is essential. Your precise expectations regarding quality, effort, and excellence send powerful messages about the behaviors you demand from your team. Suppose you uphold elevated standards personally and provide the mentoring, training, and resources to help your team reach them. In that case, you cultivate an environment where stellar achievements become the norm rather than the exception—setting the bar high stimulates your team members to unleash their fullest potential.

However, your set standards must align directly with your team's capabilities. Boldly proclaiming the need for revolutionary innovation will ring hollow if your team lacks foundational creative thinking, design, or experimentation skills. You must ensure standards are grounded in a realistic appraisal of strengths and developmental areas.

When establishing exact performance benchmarks and rubrics, involve your team directly in framing what success looks like at each level; people hate to be told what to do without clarity on the benefits and impact of doing it. Co-creating quality standards together breeds intrinsic motivation and ownership, driving more extraordinary dedication, whereas standards erected as top-down mandates from leadership often produce resentment or apathy. Enable your people to stretch themselves beyond their comfort zone safely. Once you set these precise standards, reference them frequently when providing developmental feedback, coaching, and recognition. Consistently reinforcing priorities gives your team tangible targets to chase, cementing a culture of excellence rather than settling for mediocrity.

Just as crucial, hold yourself equally accountable to the high expectations you outlined. As the leader, casually dismissing or rationalizing sloppy work, missed deadlines, or half-efforts can severely damage your credibility and signal that your standards are arbitrary rather than sacrosanct. Remember, you set the ceiling for what your team believes is possible—so reach for the sky.

Although elevated standards appropriately scaffold success, you must keep expectations from becoming suffocating. Provide space for iteration, exploration, failure, and course correction with ample guidance; let your bars stretch capabilities to new levels, not impose rigid, unrealistic limitations.

Promoting Positivity: Enabling Teams to Thrive

As an engineering leader, maintaining an upbeat, optimistic mindset and modeling resilience—even in great adversity—is essential. Your attitude significantly sways team morale, motivation, and performance. When faced with setbacks, demonstrating composure and persisting with a solutions-focus shows your team how to reframe obstacles as opportunities. Your ability to remain positive in challenging moments motivates them to embrace change.

Genuine positivity means tackling even complex issues eagerly, extracting learnings from failures. Balance constructive feedback with celebrating wins—big and small—and make reflecting on past failures a regular habit. Your resilience in bouncing back from defeats will inspire your team to view them as springboards.

In engineering, complexity and tight deadlines are the norm, and as a team leader, all eyes turn to you when pressure mounts. Demonstrating grace under stress and responding eagerly with solutions, not panic, it's essential to set the tone and motivate your team to mirror your unflappable attitude amid challenges.

Nurture a culture where people voice concerns openly, propose solutions freely, debate respectfully, and acknowledge anxiety; regular touchpoints prevent problems from being buried. Recognize achievements, contributions, and growth consistently, not just upon major milestones—value mainly when your team demonstrates a positive attitude in the face of adversity. Employees regularly affirmed for improvements feel valued and outdo themselves.

Express confidence in your team's abilities continuously, especially when challenges arise. Your unwavering belief in their potential to analyze, brainstorm, and succeed together as a unit powerfully motivates them to attempt feats they would never have imagined possible without your buoyant faith.

Promoting enduring positivity requires mindfulness, empathy, resilience, and authenticity from leaders. But the immense gains in team loyalty, creativity, and fulfillment make it worthwhile. Your leadership sets the emotional tone—so let optimism and community shine through.

Exemplifying Accountability: How You Should Own Mistakes

Accountability must be paramount to you as someone working on the front line. You must take responsibility for mistakes and model transparency. However much you aim for flawless execution, errors are inevitable, but how you own your missteps reveals your integrity. Rather than trivializing failures, you should demonstrate accountability by readily admitting and absorbing lessons from mistakes. This ownership signals your commitment to truth and fallibility—that you are equally human and imperfect as a leader.

Displaying accountability for errors sets a powerful precedent for your team, yielding several benefits:

First, it fosters open communication and trust. Taking ownership of errors signals that despite the high standards you've set for your team, you don't demand perfect execution, and this attitude cultivates a transparent environment where people voice concerns freely, enabling collaborative problem-solving. Second, you earn team-wide respect by holding yourself to the same standards as everyone else. Your accountability displays that universal expectations bind *all levels*, not just junior members. Third, you promote resilience by treating missteps as opportunities for improvement rather than punishments, and your team develops the capacity to recover from setbacks, not rationalize them away. Finally, when you demonstrate accountability, you implicitly empower your team to take responsibility for their acts rather than pass on blame. This ownership significantly boosts their engagement, dedication, and performance.

Of course, no leader implements accountability flawlessly. Sometimes denial, frustration, or pride obstructs your objectivity. But introspection, humility, and self-correction help you own mistakes graciously.

Rather than upholding an illusion of infallibility, accountable leaders like yourself reveal their humanity. With patience and courage, view errors through a growth mindset. Let accountability strengthen trust, respect, and collective ownership on your team. Work through mistakes openly. The rewards of credibility and cohesion are immense.

CHAPTER 1   PRINCIPLES TO BECOME AN EFFECTIVE ENGINEERING LEADER

Walking the Talk: Aligning Your Words and Behavior

As an engineering leader, your words have power, but your actions speak volumes, and you must embody and exemplify the values and principles you advocate vocally in your behaviors. When your words and deeds form a unified message, it builds immense credibility and trust with your team.

This alignment demands constantly evaluating whether your acts mirror your stated values and vision; regular self-reflection allows you to spot inconsistencies between what you say and what you do. When those gaps emerge, correct your behaviors to realign with your words. Invite candid feedback directly from your team members on how they perceive your behaviors versus your speeches and stated priorities. Respond graciously to this feedback by implementing changes to strengthen alignment between your words and actions once these external insights help to expose your blind spots.

Practice radical transparency with your team by openly discussing your decision-making process, successes, and most significant challenges. Sharing the behind-the-scenes journey demonstrates authenticity and reinforces your messaging.

Look for opportunities to reinforce your stated values and priorities through your behaviors consistently: arrive early to meetings to demonstrate respect for others' time and take courageous or decisive moves when a situation calls for it, underscoring boldness and responsibility at critical moments. These small acts help cement your values and priorities beyond lofty speeches or vision statements. When the occasional misstep happens, acknowledge the mistake openly and transparently as part of your growth process. These authentic reflections on your gaps further humanize you as a leader, strengthening trust and bonds with the team.

Whenever you notice misalignment between your words and actions, dig deeper into the roots of that gap. Do you genuinely lack some of the skills needed to execute what you preach fully? Are unrealistic expectations or poor planning clouding your vision? This type of introspection, coupled with targeted corrections, will gradually enhance your ability to walk the talk consistently as a leader.

Part of leading means asking yourself daily, "Are my words, priorities, and vision aligned with my actual behaviors and actions?" With constant dedication and commitment to personal growth, you'll find that the gap between your speech and deeds will continue to narrow over time. Your authenticity and character as a leader will become a source of inspiration for your team. Despite challenging, cultivating true values alignment ultimately uplifts and transforms teams to reach new heights.

Upholding Integrity: Remaining True to Your Principles

Integrity forms the bedrock of your identity as a leader. You carry a unique set of principles, values, and ethics that govern your perception of right versus wrong, and maintaining integrity demands navigating situations thoughtfully and preserving your core beliefs as challenges arise.

Leaders often face predicaments that force negotiating between professional success and personal values. Those who choose convenient or rewarding paths over ethical ones in these pivotal moments reveal their true priorities. However, influential leaders know where the boundary rests, and regardless of the consequences, they choose integrity.

Making the harder but morally sound choice tells your team what you stand for. When you uphold principles with conviction, you set an example for others to do the same in future dilemmas, building an environment where ethical, transparent behavior becomes the norm. Naturally, the path of integrity is often rigorous and will require sacrifice once opportunity costs always exist. Still, integrity means playing the long game, not compromising future trust and credibility for fleeting gain. When you make values-driven decisions, you take your team two steps forward, even if you must step back as an individual.

Begin by identifying your personal values and moral standards. This clarity provides an ethical framework when faced with murky situations. It also allows communicating expectations for principled leadership throughout your organization. Then scrutinize your choices under the lens of integrity. Ask yourself: Does this align with my values? Does it feel right deep down? Is there any nagging doubt? The answers help reveal the wise path forward.

Rest assured that no leader is perfect; demonstrate a willingness to renew your commitment going forward, and make ethics and transparency central, not supplementary, in all you do! Remarkable leaders inspire not just through accolades but also character. Integrity builds trusting, principled teams who admire you for what you do and who you are.

Develop Emotional Intelligence

In an industry where technical expertise often serves as the primary measure of success, a critical yet frequently overlooked component carries considerable weight in engineering leadership: Emotional intelligence (EQ). EQ—the ability to comprehend, utilize, and manage your emotions positively—is pivotal in relieving stress, communicating effectively, empathizing with others, surmounting challenges, and defusing conflict. As leaders in software engineering, understanding that emotions can significantly influence our behavior and interpersonal relationships is essential.

This awareness allows us to manage our feelings and those of our team members, particularly during high-pressure situations. By leveraging EQ, you can foster a collaborative environment where each member feels valued and understood, improving productivity and innovation. In the ensuing sections, we will explore strategies to enhance your EQ and integrate it effectively into your role as an engineering leader.

Understanding Emotional Intelligence (EQ)

EQ is the keystone of effective leadership regardless of the industry. However, it holds particular significance in engineering leadership, where leaders frequently navigate diverse teams, mediate conflicts, negotiate trade-offs, and drive innovation—all tasks requiring high emotional awareness and understanding.

A leader with high EQ can recognize their emotional state and the feelings of others, making informed decisions that consider not just the technical or logical aspects but also the human elements. The most effective solutions often come from balancing these elements, further underscoring the importance of EQ as a principle to becoming an influential leader. This ability is crucial to effective communication, a productive work environment, and a team-oriented culture.

Components of EQ

Emotional Intelligence comprises several key components, each integral to understanding and application. Firstly, self-awareness involves understanding one's emotions, strengths, and weaknesses and recognizing how they impact our actions and decisions. Then there's self-regulation, which is about controlling or redirecting potentially disruptive emotions and impulses, all while upholding standards of honesty and integrity. On the other hand, motivation isn't just about achieving goals; it's about being passionately driven to achieve for the very sake of achievement. Equally important is empathy, which calls for a keen consideration and understanding of others' feelings, especially when making decisions. Lastly, adept social skills revolve around managing relationships, forging strong networks, seeking common ground, and fostering rapport.

CHAPTER 1   PRINCIPLES TO BECOME AN EFFECTIVE ENGINEERING LEADER

Self-awareness

To grasp the nature of self-awareness, you must first explore its components. In emotional intelligence, self-awareness represents consciously recognizing your emotions, strengths, limitations, motivations, principles, and ambitions. It's an innate compass steering your reactions to circumstances, individuals, and occurrences.

This element is indispensable in cultivating comprehension of how your emotions and actions can affect those around you. It prompts introspection on your responses and critically evaluating how you might influence your team. This insight catalyzes more measured actions and reactions, contributing meaningfully to a healthier and more prolific work setting.

Self-aware pioneers are more liable to be genuine in their interactions and transparent about their capabilities and limitations, and this authenticity can profoundly sway team dynamics, engendering trust and regard when members feel valued and more apt to share ideas and insights.

Consider a software engineering team facing a severe bug before a major product launch. As the leader, you undergo tremendous stress owing to the situation's urgency and potential fallout if unresolved. A leader lacking self-regulation may feel overwhelmed by anxiety and make reckless decisions in the heat of the moment. They could thoughtlessly demand the team work endless overtime, aggressively micromanage their tasks, and harshly blame individuals for the coding error. This authoritarian approach could rapidly deteriorate team morale, trust, and performance at such a high-stakes juncture. Exhausted, frustrated engineers are more liable to produce sloppy work. Relations may become strained beyond repair.

However, with self-awareness, you recognize that these primal urges stem from stress. Despite the formidable pressure, you make a conscious choice to respond judiciously. Instead of letting raw emotion dictate your actions, you pause, gather your thoughts, and proceed strategically. You understand that calm, focused teamwork is essential to diagnose and fix this bug methodically. Panic and blame will only deepen the crisis. You cut yourself some slack for feeling anxious given the stakes but resolve to lead the team responsibly through this challenge, no matter how daunting. This mindset shift enables a more composed, reasoned response.

Self-regulation

Self-regulation, EQ's second pillar, represents controlling or redirecting disruptive urges and emotions. This skill entails embracing ambiguity and change comfortably, an indispensable ability as a software engineering leader. It focuses on responding, not just reacting, to emotions and scenarios, thereby engendering an environment mirroring this composed, considered, and adaptive approach.

As a software engineering leader, you frequently tackle shifting landscapes and must regulate emotional responses. As the team looks to you for stability and guidance, your conduct and reactions can profoundly influence team dynamics. When you can effectively govern your emotions, you are better equipped to make sound, impartial choices and tackle stress and adversity adeptly, becoming a model for your teams.

Consider a scenario where your software engineering team just completed a major project that missed key objectives. This failure deals a harsh blow to team morale. The customers make their disappointment abundantly clear, ruthlessly highlighting all the product's shortcomings. Blindsided by the intense backlash, your team feels deeply discouraged and embarrassed, and a climate of uncertainty, frustration, and self-doubt takes hold. Team members begin insidiously blaming each other for the defeat, pointing fingers about who contributed to the issues; the once cohesive team unravels into factions deadlocked in bitter recriminations and finger-pointing.

CHAPTER 1   PRINCIPLES TO BECOME AN EFFECTIVE ENGINEERING LEADER

Meanwhile, as the leader, you wrestle with your complicated feelings about the situation. Part of you is also shocked and disappointed things veered so off-course. However, you recognize that succumbing to these negative emotions only exacerbates the team's distress. Leaders lacking self-regulation may reactively spew their frustration on the team, harshly highlighting all their mistakes in excruciating detail. They might hastily decide to overhaul the team composition or processes without considering long-term consequences, allowing their emotions to dictate their actions. This knee-jerk response would likely further shatter morale and trust, breeding hostility, resentment, and dysfunction.

As an emotionally intelligent leader, you demonstrate self-regulation by responding differently to this crisis. Rather than venting your frustration, you intentionally calm yourself before determining your next steps and recognize that scolding the team will only breed resentment and further damage morale. Instead, you gather the demoralized group and acknowledge the disappointment but frame it as a shared learning opportunity. You highlight that failure, while difficult, presents a chance to identify areas for improvement and emerge stronger. Although mistakes were made, you emphasize that no single person is to blame—it was a team effort, and you shoulder responsibility as well.

You facilitate an open, nonjudgmental dialogue where each member can voice their frustrations, concerns, and suggest process refinements; you actively listen and empathize with their discouragement but continually reinforce that the regrettable setback offers invaluable lessons; you inspire the team to avoid dwelling on what went wrong and instead channel their energy toward brainstorming ways to avoid future pitfalls.

Rather than dictate severe changes in response to disappointment, you prudently consider measured tweaks to tools, training, and team organization. You double down on rallying the team together rather than breaking their spirit further. This composure and solutions reinvigorate their motivation to excel, where your calm but optimistic response in adversity demonstrates exemplary self-regulation while upholding team morale.

Motivation

In tech, intricacy and adversity are the norm, so motivation is not just desirable for you as an engineering leader; it is fundamental. Unlike extrinsic motivation fueled by tangible rewards or fear of consequences, EQ's motivational element is intrinsic—achieving for achievement's inherent sake, driven by a passion for the work or a broader purpose.

Cultivating intrinsic motivation empowers you to persist when projects become convoluted, deadlines loom, and team morale plummets. Your motivation becomes a contagion that infuses your team with meaning and zeal, inspiring them to exceed limitations and demonstrate resilience despite obstacles. For instance, consider a scenario where your team reaches an impasse on a high-stakes project. Progress stalls, frustration mounts, and team cohesion fray as members question whether success is possible.

A leader lacking motivation might withdraw or displace blame, further deteriorating team confidence and performance. However, you recognize that this crucial juncture demands you to step up and rally the team. You immerse yourself in analyzing the obstacles while driving home this project's broader purpose and potential impact. You reiterate that though the path is murky, you have utmost faith in the team's ability to illuminate the way forward together. Your hands-on involvement and inspirational rhetoric reignite the team's diminished motivation, pushing them to remarkable breakthroughs against the odds.

Empathy

Regarding engineering leadership, empathy is paramount. Empathy entails attuning yourself to others' sentiments, grasping their mindsets, and letting that understanding orient your actions. Discussing this human-focused aptitude seems unusual in a field renowned for technical prowess. However, it's this unique fusion that makes empathy so indispensable for engineering leaders.

CHAPTER 1   PRINCIPLES TO BECOME AN EFFECTIVE ENGINEERING LEADER

At its essence, engineering is problem-solving, and the most efficacious problem-solvers genuinely comprehend the people they're solving issues for and with. So, empathy provides you with insight to pinpoint and tackle human needs through your initiatives, enabling superior products, user-friendly software, and impactful solutions. Regarding your team, empathy breeds a more supportive, inclusive, and collaborative climate; an empathetic engineering leader will appreciate members' efforts, grasp their challenges, and address their needs effectively, and this mentality forges stronger interpersonal bonds, enhances communication flows, and nurtures mutual respect and understanding.

For instance, consider a scenario where a key team member seems withdrawn and disengaged. Rather than dismissing it, you approach them with patience and care as an empathetic leader, and through active listening, you learn they are struggling with imposter syndrome and self-doubt. Having recently been promoted, they feel anxious about measuring up technically and fear exposing their shortcomings. Meanwhile, they hesitate to ask for help due to pride, isolating them from the team and making their work suffer without proper guidance.

You gain critical insight into their struggles by grasping their emotional state and inner conflict; you provide validation that it's normal to feel unsure when stretching into new responsibilities and highlight times their expertise has shone despite their self-doubts. With this approach, you create safe opportunities for them to ask questions and request mentorship without shame.

Rather than frustration at their lack of engagement, you react with empathy and give them the tools to overcome their roadblocks. Your tailored support, such as coaching/training, nurtures their technical skillset and self-assurance, helping them reframe mistakes as learning opportunities, not evidence of inadequacy.

Your empathy transforms a withdrawn, insecure team member into a confident, empowered contributor. Their renewed motivation enhances team morale, productivity, and cohesion. This showcases emotional intelligence at its finest.

Social Skills

Social skills like lucid communication, conflict resolution, and team collaboration are vital for engineering leaders. Unlike individual contributors, leaders must coordinate diverse teams, unify them toward shared goals, and cultivate an optimal work climate. These responsibilities mandate engaging empathetically and effectively with your teams, an ability enabled by sturdy social skills.

Moreover, competently channeling a team's collective aptitude through social interaction can spell the difference between success and failure. Engineering leaders boasting polished social skills are better positioned to inspire, influence, and secure buy-in for their visions. This stems from adeptly connecting with others, comprehending differing mindsets, and communicating ideas persuasively. You may need to convince leadership about a new project's feasibility, negotiate resourcing with other departments, or rally your team behind your vision to guarantee alignment and motivation.

In these situations, robust social skills empower you to progress key interactions, distinguishing you as an authoritative leader. Additionally, you will likely be more capable of constructing expansive internal and external networks, accelerating your career ascent.

Practical Strategies for Improving Your EQ

As we delve into the practical strategies for improving emotional intelligence (EQ), we must understand that this is not a one-off task. Developing EQ is a continuous process, requiring resilience and persistence. Just like any other skill, it is something that you have to work on consistently, gradually honing and improving over time.

CHAPTER 1   PRINCIPLES TO BECOME AN EFFECTIVE ENGINEERING LEADER

Remember that progress may take time to be apparent, and feeling frustrated or like you're not making any headway is normal. However, it's vital not to let these feelings deter you; persistence is the key. The transformations you aim for are profound and will take time to manifest. When you feel frustrated, remember that this is a sign of growth and learning.

It's also crucial to set your own pace in adopting these strategies. EQ works and delivers value differently for each person, shaped by their experiences, strengths, and areas of development. It's okay to take your time to internalize and apply these strategies.

Lastly, developing EQ requires stepping out of your comfort zone and into your growth zone. You'll need to explore unfamiliar territories of self-perception and self-expression, which can sometimes be uncomfortable. Still, keep an open mind and embrace this discomfort as a part of your growth process.

Now, let's explore these practical, doable strategies that will help you boost your EQ in all five fundamental areas: self-awareness, self-regulation, motivation, empathy, and social skills.

Building Self-awareness

1. **Introspection and Reflection:** This practice is essential as it allows you to internalize your feelings and understand their triggers. You can implement it by dedicating a few quiet moments each day to self-reflection. Think about the day's events and your emotional response to them. Over time, this practice can help you recognize emotional patterns and manage your reactions better, resulting in heightened self-awareness and allowing you to make more emotionally intelligent decisions.

2. **Solicit Feedback:** Regular feedback can provide an outside perspective on your actions and their impact. You can ask your peers, superiors, and subordinates for constructive feedback. This strategy helps you understand the gap between your intended and perceived impact, enabling you to take corrective measures. Remember, receiving feedback can sometimes be challenging. It's crucial to approach it with an open heart and the intent to learn and grow.

3. **Keep a Journal:** Journaling allows you to track your emotions and reactions over time. Write about the day's significant events and how they made you feel. Review these entries periodically to identify emotional patterns and understand your triggers. Over time, you'll likely notice improved emotional control and understanding.

Enhancing Self-regulation

1. **Mindfulness Practices:** Techniques such as meditation or yoga are proven to reduce stress and improve emotional regulation. Schedule regular mindfulness sessions into your routine. Over time, this practice can boost your ability to stay composed during challenging situations, making you a steadier presence for your team.

2. **Take a Pause:** When faced with a challenging situation, take a moment to process your feelings instead of immediately reacting. This pause allows you to formulate a response rather than react

impulsively. Implement this by consciously taking deep breaths or counting to ten when confronted with a stressful situation. This will likely lead to more measured responses and fewer regrets.

3. **Adaptability Exercises:** Embrace new challenges regularly to become more comfortable with change. This could be learning a new programming language or taking on a different type of project. You'll become more adaptable by constantly pushing your comfort zone, making handling the rapid changes in the tech industry easier.

Motivation

1. **Set Personal Goals:** Goals aligning with your interests and values can keep you focused and driven. Write down your goals and review them regularly to ensure your daily actions align with them. This practice can maintain your motivation levels, even when projects get tough.

2. **Celebrate Milestones:** Regularly acknowledging and celebrating progress can cultivate a positive outlook and drive to achieve. Celebrate these achievements, whether a minor project completion or reaching a significant target. This practice not only boosts your motivation but can also foster a positive team culture.

3. **Cultivate Passion:** Cultivating a passion for your field can feed your intrinsic motivation. Stay updated on industry trends, learn new technologies, and encourage your team to do the same. Your passion will likely inspire your team, fostering a collective drive to excel.

Cultivating Empathy

1. **Active Listening:** Active listening allows you to understand the speaker's perspective deeply. Practice active listening in your conversations by focusing on the speaker and asking clarifying questions. This practice can strengthen your empathy, enabling you to respond more effectively to your team's needs.

2. **Encourage Openness:** Cultivate a team culture that values the open sharing of thoughts and feelings. This approach will provide insights into your team members' experiences, allowing you to respond empathetically. Remember, creating a relaxed environment requires demonstrating openness yourself. Share your experiences and feelings to encourage your team to do the same.

3. **Walk in Their Shoes:** Try to see situations from others' perspectives. This practice helps you understand their feelings and reactions, enabling more empathetic responses. Regular exercise can lead to stronger team relationships and a more inclusive work environment.

CHAPTER 1   PRINCIPLES TO BECOME AN EFFECTIVE ENGINEERING LEADER

Strengthening Social Skills

1. **Communication Skills Training:** Strong communication skills enhance your ability to express yourself clearly and understand others. You can improve these skills by attending workshops or online courses. As your communication skills improve, you'll likely find it easier to build relationships and gain support for your ideas.

2. **Networking:** Networking allows you to interact with a variety of individuals, helping to enhance your social skills. Attend industry events, webinars, and social activities. This exposure can broaden your understanding of people and strengthen your ability to connect with diverse individuals.

3. **Conflict Resolution:** Addressing conflicts proactively, rather than avoiding them, strengthens your ability to navigate difficult conversations—practice resolving disputes by addressing issues directly but empathetically. Over time, this practice can lead to a more harmonious work environment.

Remember, improving your EQ is a journey of continuous learning and growth. Implement these strategies with patience and persistence, and you'll likely see a significant impact on your leadership style and team dynamics.

Empower Your Team

The first step toward empowerment is getting to know your team members at a fundamental level. While reviewing their skills and experiences provides part of the picture, you must dig deeper once each individual on your staff brings a unique blend of aspirations, strengths, weaknesses, passions, and perspectives.

Know Your People: The Key to Unlocking Their Potential

Take time to understand the human elements that drive your team, and schedule regular one-on-one conversations focused on their goals, interests, challenges, and visions for how they want to grow professionally. Open up about your story to encourage vulnerability and demonstrate genuine care for their welfare. Although initial meetings may seem stilted, your empathy and listening will gradually cultivate an openness, revealing each person's motivations.

This holistic comprehension allows you to nurture their journey, enabling you to gain clarity on which team members thrive creatively but need support overcoming tunnel vision, whereas others may demonstrate analytical talents but hesitate to propose unconventional ideas. When developmental gaps become apparent through close observation and feedback, address them through training and coaching. Importantly, it also recognizes innate strengths and gives opportunities to share gifts like mentoring emerging talent, leading brainstorms, or presenting confidently.

Even though you may lean on the expertise of senior engineers at first, ensure not to neglect developing junior team members; empower them with stretch assignments that align with their capabilities but also push boundaries, paired with your guidance to help them navigate new

CHAPTER 1   PRINCIPLES TO BECOME AN EFFECTIVE ENGINEERING LEADER

waters. For example, an intern could be responsible for assessing and recommending innovative debugging tools if aligned with their interests. Such empowerment through accountability significantly builds skills and self-assurance.

Look also for latent talent across departments eager to expand abilities, and offer to mentor cross-departmental individuals with leadership potential or invite them to collaborate on special engineering projects. This inclusive empowerment breaks down organizational silos while diversifying perspectives.

Frequent Communication and Feedback

As you progress to the following principle, *Embrace Feedback*, we will discuss that consistent, bidirectional feedback facilitates growth by aligning expectations and surfacing developmental gaps, directly impacting how efficiently you empower your team.

Establishing open channels where your team can share concerns, propose process enhancements, and exchange perspectives freely will allow you to gain a pulse on underlying issues before they escalate while providing critical insights to enhance your leadership approach. Equally vital in empowerment is providing ongoing constructive feedback focused on improvement rather than just evaluation. Frame critiques as opportunities for advancement, not punishment for imperfect work, and ask sincerely for their input on strengthening team processes and standards. This open, continuous feedback exchange cements trust between your staff and enables you to course-correct your approaches based on their input rather than relying solely on top-down mandates.

Empowerment requires a foundation of transparent, compassionate communication where you know your team's thoughts and express their contributions matter. Consistent feedback aligned with this spirit allows your staff to spread their wings fully.

Positivity Fuels Empowerment

As explored in the "Lead by Example" section, maintaining an upbeat, optimistic attitude as an engineering leader is pivotal. Your positive mindset and resilience in facing challenges set the tone for your team, and this principle holds immense significance in empowering your people. Regardless of size, celebrating wins reinforces the desired growth behaviors and motivates your team to persist. People accomplish incredible feats when their leader notices incremental improvements along the journey rather than just the end destination.

Highlight minor daily victories publicly—an ingenious solution, an efficient new process, or a junior engineer's first significant solo project completion. Although major achievements deserve extensive celebration, empowerment means recognizing progress through each stage, not just grand finale milestones, and your gratitude for these smaller-scale successes fuels your team with positivity and validation.

Each person you empower wants to make you proud by reaching new capabilities, and shining a light on their gradual daily growth will make them push themselves to new heights to delight you continually.

Set Them Free

Finally, the most crucial step in empowerment is granting autonomy. Once you provide the tools for success through training, feedback, and access to resources, step back. Avoid micromanaging execution or second-guessing their approach to new responsibilities. Trust their emerging skills. Mistakes will happen during this empowered independence, but treat them as learning opportunities when handled calmly, not causes for reprimand.

Leading through empowerment takes dedication, empathy, and patience. While challenging at times, the rewards of seeing each individual advance from uncertainty to mastery are immense. You may begin believing you must have the solutions. However, empowerment means asking the right questions to unlock potential. By uplifting others, you gain far more than you give. With an open heart, you will experience empowerment's incredible reciprocal power.

Embrace Feedback

Feedback is pivotal for personal and professional growth because it offers a unique perspective, allowing us to understand and reflect on the broader implications of our actions on others and the business. Recognizing that a genuine feedback culture is more than just about managers providing feedback to their reports is crucial. It's centered on fostering bidirectional interactions, where team members confidently share their insights and concerns without fear of retaliation.

Unpacking Feedback: The Positive and the Critical

Feedback is essential to strengthening the bonds between leaders and team members, cultivating an environment of mutual trust, and propelling change and innovation, and it comes in two principal flavors—positive and critical. Each serves a vital purpose on your journey as an engineering leader.

Positive feedback is the celebratory fuel for your team's engine. It loudly proclaims, "You're on the right track!" When you commend an engineer's innovative solution during a retrospective or praise your team for flawless execution on a tight deadline, you illuminate success, and your applause sets the tone of what behaviors and performance you value, affirming, "This is what excellence looks like around here." It becomes the North Star guiding your staff toward greatness.

Positive feedback is a motivational rush that releases dopamine, leaving your team hungry for more. However, resist making positive feedback a sugar rush, and balance it with critical feedback's unsweetened power to transform.

Conversely, critical feedback is more than just a tool for pointing out flaws; it unpacks growth opportunities. When presenting essential insights, it's paramount to remain objective, timely, and emotionally balanced. These discussions can be challenging and may stir emotions, but you must embrace them as a leader, ensuring they're constructive and lead to improvement.

Crafting Constructive Conversations: The Feedback Blueprint

Regardless of its nature, feedback should be clear, structured, and constructive. Before initiating a feedback conversation, be prepared for an engaging dialogue. Equip yourself to address three pivotal questions:

1. **What prompted this feedback?** Link it directly to behavior, action, or performance. No matter what, it must link to something tangible.

2. **Why is it crucial to share this feedback?** Offer your perspective on the action's implications, whether positive or negative.

3. **Could there be a different approach?** Share insights on potential improvements or alternative strategies.

If there's any uncertainty regarding these questions, take a moment to reflect. Only proceed when you're confident in your stance.

Feedback is a two-way street; it's a conversation. Listen with intent, engage in discussions, and aim for mutual understanding. While feedback plants the seeds of growth, nurturing those seeds takes time. After your dialogue, draft a clear action plan, ensuring commitment from all sides. Periodically revisit this plan, guiding your team through challenges and supporting them in their growth journey.

From Tension to Trust: An Engineering Feedback Tale

To truly grasp the intricacies of delivering and receiving feedback, especially critical, let's unpack a scenario where a leader noticed a lousy behavior and decided to act upon it. This story underscores the importance of the principles we've discussed and offers a tangible illustration of how you can approach, manage, and utilize feedback for growth.

At Acme Co., the sprint retrospective meetings were always a collaborative space where team members discussed the progress of ongoing projects, what went wrong, the lessons learned, and what was fueling the team. During one such meeting, a junior developer, Mia, suggested an alternative approach to a feature that James, a seasoned software engineer, had been working on. Feeling his expertise was being questioned, James responded curtly, dismissing Mia's idea without consideration and disparagingly. The room grew tense, momentarily disrupting the collaborative spirit. As the manager, you noticed the shift in dynamics and recognized the need to address the situation.

Let's use the blueprint discussed in the previous section to unpack this situation and understand how you could deliver critical feedback to James:

1. **What prompted this feedback?** The immediate trigger was James' unprofessional behavior during the meeting. His inability to handle a differing opinion and his dismissive attitude toward Mia was a tangible concern, affecting team cohesion and potentially stifling open communication.

2. **Why is it crucial to share this feedback?** Collaboration and open dialogue are essential in a team-driven environment like software development. If such incidents go unaddressed, it could lead to a toxic work culture where team members hesitate to voice their opinions or share innovative ideas. Addressing James' behavior is vital to maintaining a healthy team dynamic and upholding company values and standards.

3. **Could there be a different approach?** James could empathetically listen to Mia's perspective to understand her concerns and suggestions. Based on his experience, James could lead an open discussion of the benefits and drawbacks of Mia's approach, embracing a growth mindset and fostering an environment of mutual respect and diversity where feedback and collaboration thrive.

Recognizing the need for direct intervention, you set aside time for regular one-on-one sessions with James over the next few weeks, focusing on discussing effective communication strategies, understanding team dynamics, and exploring ways to handle disagreements constructively. By sharing your experiences and insights as a leader, you aim to guide James toward becoming a more effective communicator and team player. Additionally, you recommend that James take some time for self-reflection by journaling his thoughts and feelings to understand better his reactions and how he can handle similar situations.

You initiate a conversation with James, emphasizing the importance of maintaining professionalism and fostering a positive team environment. You discuss the incident, ensuring you listen to his side of the story, and then outline your plan for the one-on-one sessions and the importance of self-reflection. James, realizing the impact of his actions, appreciates the constructive feedback and the opportunity for growth. He commits to the sessions and self-reflection, and over time, with consistent guidance and introspection, James evolves into a more effective communicator, fostering a more inclusive and collaborative environment at Acme Co.

Hold a Growth Mindset

To better understand the importance of this principle for engineering leaders, we must know where we are coming from. In the past, we believed that human nature couldn't acquire new abilities and that our intelligence was static and unchangeable. This belief made us live in a bubble of fear, avoiding challenges for too long. People stuck in this way of thinking embrace a *static mindset* and believe they can't change, which is often their most significant impediment. In 2006, psychologist Carol Dweck challenged this perception and introduced the refreshing idea that a person could get any ability or talent if they dedicate the right amount of effort, perseverance, strategy, and time, exploring that we can change and adapt our thinking to different situations. People began to call it a *growth mindset*.

A growth mindset is a conviction that our potential is not predetermined and that through dedication and continuous learning, we can expand our skills, overcome obstacles, and achieve greater mastery. This perspective encourages curiosity, resilience, and a proactive approach to successes and failures. We see each experience as an opportunity to learn, adapt, and evolve.

Beyond a Fixed Mindset

As an engineering leader, you're often called upon to evolve beyond a fixed way of thinking, and you must understand that your responsibility is beyond making technical decisions. You're a linchpin for your team and partners on diverse matters, and believing that one cannot change will hamper your progress and stifle the growth of those you guide.

The essence of adopting a growth mindset is more than personal evolution but rather an edge in the competitive landscape. This mindset reframes failures as formative lessons and paints each challenge as a learning opportunity, whether a setback or triumph. As a leader, your behavior sets a precedent, and when you exhibit a growth mindset, it benefits your development and molds the culture of your team, where they embrace challenges and innovation thrives.

Consider this: You step into an unfamiliar market after a success streak in a different company. It's all new—technologies, patterns, dynamics. While your past experiences give you confidence, can you truly succeed by mirroring your previous strategies? Reliance on past success is perilous because every context is unique, and replicating a one-time system may not guarantee success elsewhere.

A growth mindset propels leaders to be adaptable and receptive instead of resting on past laurels. It's about breaking free from old habits and obsolete beliefs that confine you to your comfort zone. Leaders imbued with this dynamic mindset not only grasp their influence but also recalibrate their practices to fit the current situation. Yet, recognizing areas for growth demands introspection and a willingness to challenge the status quo.

The Importance of Reflection for Sustainable Growth

For genuine growth, assessing our current state, evaluating past actions, and envisioning future possibilities are essential. Analyzing our decisions lets us extract lessons from our experiences and plan for what lies ahead.

Maintaining a balance between introspection and growth is crucial for enduring personal and professional development. A growth mindset propels us to embrace challenges and extend our limits. In tandem, reflection ensures that our growth is purposeful and well-directed, driving us to identify behavioral patterns, appreciate our achievements, and gain insights from setbacks, acting as a guiding compass.

We transform challenges into opportunities by seamlessly merging introspection with a growth perspective. Those proficient in reflection can pinpoint the roots of obstacles and understand the reactions they trigger. With a clear understanding and a growth-oriented outlook, hurdles evolve into platforms for advancement, and over time, this equilibrium fosters significant progression in both personal and professional spheres.

Balancing active learning with self-reflection requires effort and persistence. Initial attempts might seem daunting, but with consistency, they become intuitive. This commitment not only unveils our potential but also refines our worldview, enhancing resilience and adaptability in leadership roles and helping us discern obsolete practices and beliefs.

The Grace of Unlearning

We've all heard it: "Change is the only constant." Nowhere is this truer than in engineering. Yesterday's solutions forge today's innovations, but clutching to them mindlessly can hinder tomorrow's progress. We must discern what's essential to keep and what's necessary to abandon.

Consider unlearning as strategic decluttering. Imagine a closet brimming with summer clothes, yet winter is knocking. You need to make space for jackets, scarves, and boots. How can your wardrobe adapt to the chilly days ahead if your wardrobe remains packed with summer attire?

In leadership, the act of unlearning stands shoulder to shoulder with learning. Let go of avoiding difficult conversations; abandon the notion that leadership means being the hero constantly; release the belief that you must always be in the limelight or have control over every detail; understand that your team doesn't need omnipresence or omniscience to excel. And sometimes, it's perfectly fine to admit, "I don't know *yet*."

Embrace this: unlearning carves out space for fresh, relevant insights. When you balance the thirst for growth with the art of discarding outdated beliefs, you craft an environment ripe for transformative change—exactly what every impactful leader needs.

Value the Process over the Outcome

Embracing this principle opens the gates for all other concepts covered in this chapter. The more you strive and surmount, the hungrier you become for progress. Ambition ignites, and setting goals becomes second nature. But remember, a growth mindset isn't solely about reaching the summit—it's about cherishing and absorbing lessons from the climb.

We delved into the growth mindset's foundation earlier: persistence, dedication, time, and strategy are its cornerstones. But sometimes, despite efforts, desired outcomes elude us, spawning feelings of disillusionment. Yet, recognizing tangible shifts demands patience and perseverance.

Let's get this straight: Growth transcends mere favorable results, and how you chart your development—your decisions and demeanor—holds more weight than the finish line. If leadership excellence is your aim, buying ten leadership books without imbibing their wisdom is fruitless. Start cultivating a reading habit; define your rhythm, maintain consistency, relish the process, and entertain diverse viewpoints. Carve out dedicated slots for reading and learning; grapple with distractions, juggle priorities, and fan the flames of motivation. Then, lay the groundwork for applying newfound knowledge; admit your novice status, wrangle with impostor feelings, and accept missteps.

Furthermore, honoring the journey equips you with insights into your triumphs—discerning the reasons and the strategies for future endeavors. Always weigh the significance of your chosen route. In moments of doubt, pause. Reflect on a past victory and inquire: What drove this success? The answer, invariably, lies in your actions and approach, whether facing headwinds or tailwinds.

CHAPTER 1   PRINCIPLES TO BECOME AN EFFECTIVE ENGINEERING LEADER

Cultivating Your Growth Mindset

As an engineering leader, you must make lifelong learning and continuous self-improvement paramount to reach your full leadership potential. Let's explore several practical strategies to help ingrain an adaptive, progress-oriented mindset:

1. **Seek an Accomplished Mentor:** Identify an engineering executive who embodies the growth mindset within or outside your company. Meet 1:1 frequently to understand how they overcame obstacles like failed product launches through relentless self-reflection. Examine how they challenged assumptions and pushed beyond their comfort zone. Let their real-world experiences motivate you to emulate their hunger for self-improvement.

2. **Conduct In-Depth Failure Analysis:** Rather than gloss over a botched product release, do a substantive postmortem review. Gather all teams to analyze the root causes while emotions remain fresh. Facilitate an open, nonjudgmental dialogue by asking, "How did unclear objectives contribute to team friction? How might better coordination have prevented defects?" Resist the temptation to blame. This brutally honest event report will illuminate areas where process and leadership need improvement.

CHAPTER 1   PRINCIPLES TO BECOME AN EFFECTIVE ENGINEERING LEADER

3. **Maintain a Rich Milestone Journal:** Growth and improvement as an engineering leader accumulate slowly. Note successes like "My patience listening first rather than solving empowered my team to tackle issues themselves." But also diligently log behaviors needing improvement, like micromanaging others' projects. Review this journal monthly to celebrate progress and critically assess your leadership trajectory.

4. **Proactively Request Candid Feedback:** Ask trusted peers and team members for constructive critiques focused on your blind spots, not just strengths. This harsh but vital feedback, even anonymized, provides the self-awareness to get better. Don't be defensive—be grateful. Follow up by outlining how you will improve.

5. **Approach Problems with a Beginner's Mind:** Resist assumptions and conventional solutions when facing a technical challenge. Revert to asking foundational questions to expand possible approaches. Maintain intellectual humility no matter your experience level. This mental flexibility leads to unexpected but ingenious insights.

6. **Challenge Outdated Perspectives:** Growth requires identifying unexamined biases and beliefs that limit your leadership. Be willing to research and adopt more progressive mindsets around change management, consensus building, psychological safety, and conflict resolution. A great leader never stops evolving.

CHAPTER 1   PRINCIPLES TO BECOME AN EFFECTIVE ENGINEERING LEADER

Commit to a new self-improvement technique like the above each quarter. Concrete steps enable growth, whether it's a mentoring partnership, anonymized feedback channel, or journaling practice. As an engineering leader, you set the standard, so pursue mastery not for yourself but to empower your team to reach new heights.

Tame Your Time and Effort

Time management stands as a pivotal skill to become effective and efficient, but truly mastering your hours and energy demands thoughtful prioritization of your efforts to ensure you work on responsibilities that align with your core goals and the organization's strategic mission.

As a leader, your responsibilities expand beyond technical oversight, and you are tasked with guiding teams, thinking strategically about the future, fostering innovation, continuous self-improvement, and enabling your staff to excel. With such a diverse portfolio, scattered focus risks diluting your efficacy across these critical realms.

Cultivating the ability to manage your limited time and mental bandwidth wisely is imperative. Mastering these two resources helps you determine where to channel your energies each day—when to tackle complex challenges, collaborate openly, or recharge your senses. This competency enables you to remain balanced and forward-thinking amid infinite demands.

Time Beyond Money: Why It Matters Most

Time is the currency of life, our most precious and nonrenewable resource; you can't reclaim it once spent. Therefore, effective time management enables wisely investing your hours with intent rather than dissipation across endless obligations.

Mastering your schedule keeps you focused on immediate duties while maintaining a future-oriented strategic vision. It bridges chaotic reactivity and tranquil purpose, preventing burnout and sustaining passion for your leadership craft. Furthermore, effort management deals with your vitality—the mental clarity, energy levels, and engagement you bring to your tasks. Not all responsibilities demand equal focus from leaders, and you must distinguish activities requiring deep thinking versus those needing transparent communication or collaboration.

Understanding yourself allows you to align your limited efforts and energies to the day's needs, driving peak performance. As demands vie for your attention, discerning where to channel your time and energy makes you an active leader who creates meaningful impact amid infinite requests. As a role model, your mastery conveys powerful messages to your team about balance, priorities, and valuing personal well-being. Yet, despite its immense benefits, this skill remains challenging in your overarching role; juggling diverse obligations can leave you time-pressed, prompting rushed decisions that erode trust.

But take heart. The following sections will uncover proven, tangible techniques to master your hours and efforts and will help reclaim control, enhance productivity, and ensure you lead with purpose while avoiding burnout.

Time and Effort Mastery: The Perfect Match

Inevitably, as an engineering leader, you shoulder significant responsibilities that span strategic oversight, stakeholder management, and enabling your team. With such a vast portfolio, scattered focus and mismanaged efforts can swiftly derail your productivity and leadership efficacy.

Therefore, cultivating your ability to manage time and channel effort purposefully emerges as a pivotal competency. Mastery in these spheres helps you discern where to invest your precious time and work on what matters most. Even though your journey is unique, proven techniques exist to help reclaim control over how you spend your days.

Let's explore six tangible strategies to transform you into a master of time and effort.

The Power of Strategic Scheduling

Make time blocking an everyday practice to take control of your demanding schedule. Carve out designated time slots throughout your day for focused work, open collaboration, strategic thinking, and rejuvenating breaks.

Although this structured approach requires forethought and discipline initially, it enhances productivity long-term by dedicating targeted time to distinct activities. Furthermore, blocking off chunks of the day for "deep work" reduces multitasking's harmful effects, allowing you to tackle complex challenges with refreshed vigor.

Using blocks for deliberate breaks is equally valuable, where you completely disengage from work. These intermittent mental resets become oases that replenish your ability to concentrate on upcoming tasks. Although you may feel pressed for time as responsibilities mount, resist the urge to eliminate recharging breaks. Their restorative effects enhance the quality of subsequent work blocks. Time blocking grants you control over your agenda, aligns efforts to priorities, and creates windows for renewal.

The Power of Strategic "No"

An endlessly open calendar is synonymous with strong, available leadership—being ready to assist your team anytime they need you. However, discernment in choosing where to invest your limited time and mental energies is a defining hallmark of influential engineering leaders.

Not every meeting request or obligation warrants your full attention and focus, no matter how critical or urgent they may appear on the surface. As countless demands vie for your mindshare daily, you must regularly step back and ask yourself, "Is this aligned with my core goals and priorities?"

With rigorous discernment, you can avoid diffusing your efforts into peripheral activities that yield minimal tangible value. Attending optional status meetings unrelated to your projects and providing feedback on low-stake documents are examples of obligations that may not justify the investment of your precious time.

Exercising a strategic yet kind "no" safeguards your most valuable and nonrenewable asset—time. It reserves these precious hours for business-critical challenges and opportunities that align with your leadership objectives and propel the organization forward. It also signals your team that you respect their time and energies equally, shielding them from getting pulled into superfluous meetings and minor tasks that divert from mission-critical work.

Deploying "no" strategically also means communicating your declines respectfully and providing alternative solutions. For example, you might respond, "I can't attend the full meeting due to other commitments, but I am happy to connect beforehand to share my perspectives on this topic."

With discernment and care, you can prioritize your team's time for work that moves the needle while modeling healthy work–life boundaries.

Delegation and Elevation

Burdening yourself with executing every task stunts your and your team's growth. Handing responsibilities to team members optimizes resources and builds trust and accountability. Delegation signifies acknowledging your team's diverse capabilities and strategically utilizing them for organizational success. However, you must pair delegated work beyond prescribing tasks with robust training, frequent check-ins, and developmental support.

Approach delegation as elevating your team by entrusting them with responsibilities that stretch their skills and decision-making. Well-planned delegation paired with caring guidance becomes a conduit for professional and personal growth, allowing you to focus on responsibilities demanding your full strategic attention.

The Restoration of Power Breaks

Our brains aren't designed for prolonged, intense cognitive exertion. Unbroken hours of mentally demanding work inevitably sap focus and spark fatigue. Counteract this decline by deliberately scheduling brief breaks to punctuate your work blocks, whether 5-minute walks or 20-minute power naps. These intermittent resets allow you to return to complex challenges with renewed acuity.

Treat breaks as essential for peak performance, not luxuries reserved for lighter days. Short but frequent breaks enhance mental clarity over back-to-back meetings or work marathons, even on the busiest days, and you must guard these sacrosanct times fiercely, disconnect completely, and let your mind recharge. The work left upon your return will benefit profoundly from the revitalized senses these brief yet restorative breaks provide.

Carving Out Time for Growth

Effective engineering leadership rests upon continuous learning and skill development, and managing time for your own growth stands as a pivotal skill in effective engineering leadership, but truly mastering your hours and energy demands thoughtful prioritization of your efforts to ensure you work on responsibilities that align with your core goals and the organization's strategic mission.

As a leader, your responsibilities expand beyond technical oversight, and you are tasked with guiding teams, thinking strategically about the future, fostering innovation, continuous self-improvement, and enabling your staff to excel. With such a diverse portfolio, scattered focus risks diluting your efficacy across these critical realms.

Cultivating the ability to manage your limited time and mental bandwidth wisely is imperative. Mastering these two resources helps you determine where to channel your energies each day—when to tackle complex challenges, collaborate openly, or recharge your senses. This competency enables you to remain balanced and forward-thinking amid infinite demands.

Communicate Clearly

Communicating with clearness is a fundamental skill that holds immense importance in the context of this chapter and various aspects of your life. Communication goes beyond mere words; it encompasses gestures, posture, and even the expressions in your eyes. Compelling communication involves aligning and harmonizing these various methods to convey a powerful and impactful message, whereas neglecting these aspects can lead to misunderstandings, ambiguities, and misconceptions. Misaligned communication can lead to damaged relationships, missed opportunities, and unproductive collaborations.

The Influence of Clear Communication on Leadership

In leadership, understanding the profound impact of communication is pivotal for fostering deeper collaboration among your team members, stakeholders, and connections. When you craft your message with clarity and adapt it to your audience, you empower them to grasp the essential elements of your message. This clarity ensures understanding and transparency and sets the tone for positive outcomes.

Creating meaningful connections is paramount to achieving success in a leadership role. As a leader, you catalyze change and directly influence the value chain connecting your team with various domains' partners. A company's collective efforts are directed toward a shared vision supported by common objectives. As a leader in engineering, your ability to communicate these objectives to your team is crucial. Your task involves translating complex business jargon and unfamiliar concepts into digestible information, enabling your team to understand their contributions to overall business growth.

Equally vital is your capability to translate technical complexities to nontechnical individuals. Consider a scenario where your product manager envisions a feature that relies heavily on collaboration with other teams or necessitates background work for scalability and reliability. Explaining these intricacies using technical language or jargon can hinder productivity and lead the group astray. Instead, adapting your communication to your audience is critical. When addressing a product-oriented audience, elucidate how technical limitations impact the evolution of the feature, the associated risks, and the inherent complexities. For an executive audience, tailor your message to explain how these technical factors can influence the company's objectives and growth. For instance, if you're delivering a feature that could disrupt overall application performance due to high parallel transactions and database access, you could explain to them that poor performance might lead to a negative user experience, risking downtime due to excessive resource consumption. This, in turn, could elevate the churn rate and negatively impact revenue.

Crafting Your Message: Delivery and Design

Irrespective of your audience, the structure and design of your message significantly impact its reception. A well-structured message, presented thoughtfully, can shed new light on a topic in engaging ways. Central to this approach is the inclusion of factual and objective statements. These statements serve as anchors, grounding your message in truth and bolstering its credibility. This approach minimizes room for ambiguity or misinterpretation.

However, it's essential to distinguish between a well-structured and comprehensive message versus an overly explanatory one. Despite the noble intention of clarifying and providing extensive information, inundating your communication with excessive details can overwhelm your audience. Paradoxically, it might obscure the core message, making it difficult to discern the main point and leading to disengagement. Remember, a concise message can often be more impactful.

Beyond verbal communication, a significant portion of message delivery occurs through nonverbal cues. A nod, a gesture, or a pause can convey volumes, adding depth to the spoken words.

The Role of Empathic Listening in Effective Communication

One of the most underestimated yet essential aspects of communication for a leader is the art of listening. While communication is often associated with influencing others, becoming accurate involves understanding. People communicate with the intent to persuade, inform, or guide; it's crucial to comprehend the expectations of your audience, their intentions with your message, and how they will process the information.

Unfortunately, many leaders listen not to understand but to respond. Your team requires more than hurried advice to resolve issues; they seek dialogue and actions that cater to their immediate needs and concerns. This level of understanding is only attainable through empathic listening.

Before delving into practical advice, it's important to grasp the types of listening and their impact on communication:

1. **Ignoring Listening:** This involves listening without genuine interest in the conveyed information. You already believe you possess all the answers and consider the information irrelevant.

2. **Pretending Listening:** This entails nodding or occasionally saying "Yeah" or "I understand," but you're disengaged. You can shift the conversation away from the current topic.

3. **Selective Listening:** Here, you only pay attention to what matters to you, dismissing the rest as irrelevant.

4. **Empathic Listening:** As a leader, embracing empathic listening is paramount. This approach involves using your ears and seeing and feeling with your heart. Communication experts estimate that only 10% of communication stems from words, 30% comes from sounds, and 60% derives from body language.

Leading effectively demands meticulous attention to detail and a genuine commitment to understanding others. Empathic listening breaks down barriers to effective communication because it's not about using a one-size-fits-all message. Instead, it's about understanding emotions, behaviors, and meanings to adapt your message and achieve effectiveness.

Incorporating empathy and attentive listening into your skill set empowers you to guide your team effectively, establish clear objectives, elucidate complex concepts, and cultivate meaningful relationships. As we progress through this section, let's explore practical strategies to enhance your communication skills.

CHAPTER 1   PRINCIPLES TO BECOME AN EFFECTIVE ENGINEERING LEADER

Practical Strategies for Enhancing Clear Communication

Once the significance of empathic listening is recognized, it's essential to acknowledge that achieving a reasonable level of clear communication requires practice and persistence. Open-mindedness and perseverance are crucial traits that will yield fruitful results in the long run. Once mastered, these skills will benefit your career as a leader and enhance various aspects of your life.

1. **Simplify Your Message:** Sometimes, less is more. Structure your message based on context to ensure clarity and effectiveness.

2. **Attend to Nonverbal Cues:** Maintain eye contact, observe body language, and be mindful of tone. Adapt your delivery to engage and facilitate understanding. Align verbal and nonverbal communication.

3. **Pause and Reflect:** Incorporate pauses between sentences to gather your thoughts before sharing them. Ensure your ideas are factual and relevant to the conversation. This approach helps you control emotions, exude confidence, and deliver accuracy.

4. **Self-reflection:** Dedicate time to evaluating your daily interactions and identifying areas for improvement. Analyze instances where empathic listening was lacking and strive to understand why. This practice allows you to eliminate biases and recognize negative communication patterns.

5. **Seek Feedback:** Request feedback from a trusted individual to enhance your communication skills. Actively listen to the input you receive.

CHAPTER 1   PRINCIPLES TO BECOME AN EFFECTIVE ENGINEERING LEADER

6. **Reverse Feedback:** Encourage your audience to explain your message back to you. This ensures alignment and minimizes ambiguity. While this approach is valuable, exercise caution to avoid becoming overwhelming.

Incorporating these strategies into your communication toolkit will equip you with the skills to guide your team effectively, set clear objectives, unpack intricate concepts, and cultivate meaningful relationships. However, dear reader, as an engineering leader, know that this chapter is but a foundation and a framework. The beauty of leadership is that it is as dynamic as the technologies you work with; it demands adaptability, creativity, and a yearning for growth.

Therefore, I urge you not to view this chapter as an end but as a commencement—the beginning of a continuous journey of development and discovery. Engage in self-reflection, be open to feedback, seek growth opportunities, and be the catalyst for positive change within your team and organization.

In a continuously changing world, particularly engineering, your leadership can serve as a guiding beacon that illuminates the path through uncertain terrain. Recognize the significant responsibility entrusted to you and embrace it with grace, composure, and unwavering dedication.

As you forge ahead, remember that leadership is akin to mastering an instrument; it demands patience, practice, and passion. May the notes you play resonate, inspire, and lead to symphonies of success and innovation.

Takeaways

1. Lead by example through integrity, work ethic, and aligning words with actions. Role model desired behaviors daily.

CHAPTER 1   PRINCIPLES TO BECOME AN EFFECTIVE ENGINEERING LEADER

2. Set ambitious yet realistic performance standards. Involve the team in defining rubrics for success.

3. Maintain an optimistic mindset. Turn setbacks into opportunities and persist through challenges.

4. Take accountability for mistakes. Be transparent to build trust and empower the team.

5. Ensure your words and behaviors align. Invite feedback and course-correct when gaps emerge.

6. Uphold integrity and ethics, even when inconvenient. Make values-driven choices to earn respect.

7. Develop self-awareness, self-regulation, motivation, empathy, and social skills—the core of emotional intelligence.

8. EQ enables managing stress calmly, decision-making with empathy, and fostering collaboration.

9. Know your team's aspirations and abilities deeply. Celebrate strengths and develop weaknesses.

10. Involve all levels in decisions to tap diverse perspectives and build ownership.

11. Give timely, constructive feedback to align expectations and enable growth.

12. Celebrate small daily wins to boost morale, not just significant milestones.

13. Embrace collective intelligence. Enable open collaboration beyond hierarchy.

14. Adopt a growth mindset that views challenges as opportunities to improve.

CHAPTER 1   PRINCIPLES TO BECOME AN EFFECTIVE ENGINEERING LEADER

15. Reflection and introspection balance continuous learning to extract insights and identify behavioral patterns.

16. Balance continuous learning with self-reflection to extract insights.

17. Let go of outdated assumptions and beliefs that limit progress.

18. Focus on the learning process, not just favorable outcomes.

19. Use time blocking to enhance productivity, reduce multitasking, and prevent burnout.

20. Strategically delegate tasks to optimize resources and develop team capabilities.

21. Power breaks avoid fatigue. Disconnect fully after work hours.

22. Carve out time for continuous personal growth and learning every week.

23. Communicate clearly. Structure messages concisely based on audience needs.

24. Listen empathetically to understand needs before responding.

25. Encourage open sharing of thoughts and feelings to gain insights.

26. Simplify complex concepts. Use factual statements to add credibility.

27. Align verbal and nonverbal cues like gestures and tone with the message.

CHAPTER 1   PRINCIPLES TO BECOME AN EFFECTIVE ENGINEERING LEADER

28. Pause before responding. Seek feedback. Explain messages to ensure clarity.

29. Leadership demands lifelong learning. Absorb these principles as a starting point.

Time to Practice

1. Reflect on when you maintained composure during a high-stress situation at work. What self-regulation strategies did you leverage in that moment? How might you continue building this capability (see "Develop Emotional Intelligence" section)?

2. Think of a past instance where your actions didn't fully align with your stated values or priorities. What were the reasons for this misalignment? How can you recognize and reconcile these gaps in the future (see "Lead by Example" section)?

3. When have you sought constructive feedback on your blind spots rather than just strengths? How did it feel to discuss those critique points openly? What benefits did it yield (see "Embrace Feedback" section)?

4. Recall a moment when you operated with a fixed mindset rather than a growth mindset. What limited beliefs held you back? How can you shift your perspective to see challenges as learning opportunities (see "Hold a Growth Mindset" section)?

5. Reflect on your schedule and efforts over the past month. Were you focused on the most high-leverage activities? How might you refine your time blocking to achieve greater task balance and prioritization (see "Tame Your Time and Effort" section)?

CHAPTER 2

Leadership Styles and Situational Leadership

Engineering leaders face a landscape of twists, turns, peaks, and valleys. To navigate it requires adaptability—not just a single rigid style, but a versatile set of leadership approaches for the many situations you will encounter. Should you take the high road of inspiration or the low road of top-down direction? Do you move ahead by empowering teams or seizing control? Which approach should you use and when?

This chapter will equip you with that versatile leadership skillset by illuminating the nuances within diverse styles. We will explore prominent approaches like the unwavering direction of autocracy, the enthusiastic inspiration of transformational leadership, the empathy and service of servant leadership, the consensus-building of democratic leadership, and the autonomy granted through laissez-faire leadership.

Situational leadership is the framework to match these approaches to your team's needs, providing the model to diagnose your team members' specific developmental levels and adapt your style accordingly—directing novices, supporting the growing, and empowering experts—based on your situational awareness and adaptability level.

CHAPTER 2   LEADERSHIP STYLES AND SITUATIONAL LEADERSHIP

The terrain ahead will challenge you to assess your team's needs amid the twists and turns. But armed with perceptiveness and a repertoire of leadership styles, you will keep progress smooth while developing your team's capabilities. Fasten your seatbelt, and let's begin this journey by exploring the autocratic leadership style.

Autocratic Leadership: Decisiveness in Motion

Autocratic leadership's roots are traced throughout human history, as kings, emperors, and conquerors dictated inflexible terms to their subjects and seized control of resources and plans. With this top-down approach, they mobilized their troops to follow a meticulous plan on their behalf supported by a culture of fear, administering consequences to those who dared to oppose them.

Despite the historical oppressiveness and the association with tyrants and dictators, the principles of autocratic leaders found a new home in management. You mobilize development teams rather than armies; the stakes may not involve kingdoms or empires, but the market share and the business growth; punitive measures have given way to hunger competition and shorter lead times.

While the variables differ in this modern era, the core tenet remains the same: You take complete command of what and how to do, independently determine the team's direction and workload distributions, and provide explicit instructions without extensive consultation or collaborative planning. You foster top-down communication flows and convey expectations and responsibilities, leaving little room for questioning or feedback. Ensure the team understands that your decisions are final and that you expect them to align precisely with your strategic vision. Finally, you maintain tight control over operations—monitoring progress closely and rapidly correcting courses when needed.

CHAPTER 2   LEADERSHIP STYLES AND SITUATIONAL LEADERSHIP

The Benefits of Decisive Direction

Although autocratic leadership carries strong and often unpopular characteristics, its decisive momentum can excel in the right circumstances. For instance, when time is scarce and bold action is needed to thrive, adopting an autocratic style streamlines the decision-making process, preventing delays from lengthy debates.

You demonstrate a tight grip to dictate the course and define what and how to establish a crystal-clear chain of command once you oversee the delegation of duties, ensuring each team member understands what you expect from them, removing any ambiguity about priorities along the way. This cohesion drives productivity by eliminating confusion over responsibilities and simplifying identifying the sources of success or failure. Your dominance over schedules, methods, and tracking compels laser-like focus on achieving objectives, ensuring your team members understand what is urgent, important, and irrelevant. With well-defined timelines, the group knows what and when to deliver and adjusts the pace to fulfill your expectations. Consequently, milestones are reached rapidly under your close supervision, even on high-pressure projects with tight deadlines or convoluted requirements.

However, you understand that being an autocratic leader does not mean neglecting the human element. Through regular check-ins and setting clear expectations, you keep team members aligned with the broader vision and invested in the end goal. You celebrate incremental wins and highlight how each person's contribution furthers shared objectives, and with selective transparency, you share the reasoning behind your decisions. This balance of human connection and centralized power preserves team cohesion even amid top-down authority.

Although excessive control has risks, prudent autocratic leadership achieves results through clarity of purpose and relentless progress monitoring. You walk a fine line between exercising authority and stifling creativity but understand that autocracy's firm direction excels at steering

CHAPTER 2   LEADERSHIP STYLES AND SITUATIONAL LEADERSHIP

teams through adversity when applied judiciously. Your ability to drive decisions empowers your team to execute efficiently in demanding environments.

The Challenges of Autocratic Leadership

Despite the benefits this leadership approach may bring to achieving goals and effectively managing projects, especially when time is of the essence, this single-minded focus can become problematic, leading to internal challenges in your team if misapplied or taken to the extreme. Let's understand the most common challenges autocratic leaders face and how they impact the team's performance.

Stifling Innovation and Motivation: With all decision-making power resting in one leader, autocratic leadership provides minimal opportunities for team members to contribute ideas or shape plans; individuals feel undervalued when you neither solicit nor welcome their input. You expect your team to follow your predetermined orders with little autonomy, damaging morale for many once very few people like to execute their tasks without clarity of their impact on the greater goal or having space to share feedback. This stifling of creativity from below causes issues requiring fresh thinking and innovation, as the organization misses out on the synergies that emerge from collaborative work. It also risks severely harming intrinsic motivation over time, breeding passive-aggressive behaviors or intentional disengagement.

Impeding Development: By prescribing tasks and decisions to the smallest detail, you leave little room for team members to exercise critical thinking, problem-solving, or independent judgment, as you limit their chances to interpret complex issues, weigh tradeoffs, and devise creative solutions. This behavior fosters an environment where a static mindset reins and hampers individual and organizational agility and resilience.

Delaying Awareness: With predominantly top-down communication, autocratic leadership often remains unaware of brewing troubles until they escalate into crises. Your team lives in a culture of silence rather than openness and avoids sharing candid feedback and essential concerns about emerging challenges, fearing unwelcome reactions. The blend of limited communication and fear within your team drastically compromises the long-term capability to react faster to adversities.

Breeding Resentment: By adopting a centralized overall attitude and ignoring any other perspectives or feedback than yours, you foster an environment of frustration and resentment, risking your team to adopt a provoking behavior as people find ways to regain some autonomy. Over time, the trust your team once had in you erodes, sabotaging the team's cooperation, commitment, and performance, creating a toxic environment.

Burdening the Leader: In their zeal for control, autocratic leaders overload themselves by personally directing everything. No single leader can optimize every decision, and the cognitive burden leads to fatigue, delays, and poorer judgment over time. It also wastes opportunities to leverage the total intellectual capacity of the organization through participation and inclusion.

Autocratic Leadership Versus Other Leadership Styles

As mentioned earlier, autocratic leaders dictate the team's pace and strategy, providing little space for collaboration and different perspectives, resulting in unilateral decisions. Still, thoughtfully integrating complementary leadership styles to the essence of autocracy mitigates the risks of applying this style and increases your influence as a leader. Let's explore the contrast between autocratic leadership and the other leadership styles mentioned in this chapter and understand how prudent integrating select qualities can balance autocracy's dominance with more inclusive, supportive, or inspirational traits.

Servant Leadership: While autocratic leaders consolidate authority and drive execution through top-down mandates, servant leaders invert this dynamic by striving to empower teams through bottom-up participation, nurturing individual growth. Remember, servant leaders champion ethical service, not control. Yet, integrating aspects of servant leadership helps mitigate autocracy's risks. For instance, you counterweigh autocracy's potential in stifling engagement by showing genuine care for your team's development needs and communicating the rationale behind decisions. Combining selective transparent explanation and individual support with your unwavering drive retains focus while building trust and goodwill.

Transformational Leadership: Transformational leaders motivate by connecting work to a higher purpose and intellectually stimulating followers to exceed expectations. You, too, aim to propel teams ambitiously ahead as an autocrat, but through firm control rather than inspiration. However, reiterating your directives' greater mission and meaning and occasionally recognizing small achievements will help you to improve your influence while nurturing the team's engagement and effort.

Laissez-Faire Leadership: Laissez-faire adopters believe in the power of delegation to achieve a greater good, with minimal top-down involvement, which could lead to poor coordination and lack of clarity on significant goals. As an autocrat, you tightly grip control and ensure people follow your plan, meticulously elaborated and free from ambiguities. However, increased autonomy, within defined guardrails, blended with autocracy, focuses efforts by fully utilizing your top performers' capabilities while sustaining coordination on priorities, catalyzing productivity and better results.

Democratic Leadership: While democrats emphasize consensus-building by soliciting extensive team input when shaping decisions, you, as an autocratic leader, recognize that endless discussion risks inaction without decisiveness, and you compensate for the lack of decision power by dictating plans unilaterally. However, occasionally requesting focused feedback, even while maintaining authority over final decisions, helps identify potential improvements you may miss independently. Consequently, you foster some sense of inclusiveness, which you can benefit from and expand your insights.

An Autocratic Leader in Action

Now that we've navigated the essence, benefits, and challenges of adopting an autocratic leadership style, let's blend everything and analyze Sarah's journey, which illustrates a startup team in a hurry to release important features to the market after succeeding in a considerable investment round.

Sarah recently became the Head of Engineering at Acme Corporation, a startup developing cutting-edge AI products. The company just secured a significant round of funding and now needs to scale up engineering to accelerate product development quickly. Given the urgent timeline and complex coordination required to achieve ambitious goals, Sarah immediately adopted an autocratic leadership style; she independently created a detailed project plan identifying all key milestones, resource needs, and technical specifications required for the following product releases and provided everyone with clear instructions on their assignments, expectations, and deadlines. Questions were allowed during daily standups, but only about execution details, not strategy debates. Sarah monitored progress closely through status reports, meetings, and code reviews, promptly correcting the team for any deviation from her original plan.

CHAPTER 2   LEADERSHIP STYLES AND SITUATIONAL LEADERSHIP

With Sarah's close eyes on the delivery process and plan execution, her team operated with extreme focus and coordination, executing their tasks as dictated and overcoming obstacles rapidly under her support, propelling the complex project forward. Consequently, they hit a milestone over milestone flawlessly. However, fatigue emerged among some engineers who felt stifled by Sarah's centralized control and lack of input opportunities as the deadline neared. A few privately wondered whether her demanding timelines were even feasible.

Recognizing these risks of diminished morale, Sarah began selectively integrating some bottom-up participation, actively listening to concerns and clarifying why certain top-down decisions were necessary for the greater good during one-on-one sessions with her staff. She also celebrated small wins and highlighted how each person's contribution mattered for every successful release. This balance preserved team cohesion amid her directiveness, keeping her momentum and influence.

Ultimately, the engineering team released all commitments on time and without major issues, pleasing the investors and the customers and preparing the ground for a new round of investments and business growth.

Sarah's blend of autocratic control and selective inclusive leadership during a demanding project proved essential. However, she ensured to clarify that this directive style was temporary. When the imminent pressure passed, Sarah eased back into control. She transitioned to a more collaborative leadership style focused on nurturing her team's capabilities, restoring the damages of a stifled group.

This example illustrates how prudent autocratic leadership can drive results in high-stakes situations while balancing risks through limited inclusive traits. Sarah determined that her team needed commanding direction but tempered the burdens through transparency and encouragement. Her adaptability and perspective sustained team success and contributed directly to the business growth and the company's reputation.

CHAPTER 2   LEADERSHIP STYLES AND SITUATIONAL LEADERSHIP

As an autocratic leader, your tight grip on decisions and operations compels coordination amid complexity. Your team trades freedom for focus, embracing your decisive direction to push ahead decisively to achieve rapid results. However, autocracy risks demoralization by stifling participation and innovation; you must walk a fine line to avoid disengagement and, with astute situational awareness, selectively blend in transparency and encouragement to temper autocracy's burdens while retaining its benefits.

Remember, no single style suits all scenarios, and different circumstances demand different leadership. But the autocrat wields a vital toolset when urgency necessitates centralized power to seize the reins and steer resolutely forward. So, as challenges warrant unwavering direction, leverage your ability to drive execution through decisive authority. Yet, it also cultivates the perceptiveness to ease control appropriately. Lastly, understand when autocracy provides indispensable focus and when participation and empowerment better serve your team's long-term interests. With that discernment, you master this influential leadership style's nuances.

Transformational Leadership: Inspiring Innovation and Growth

As a transformational leader, you recognize that fostering a culture of bold innovation is critical to pushing boundaries and pioneering transformative technologies. Still, driving accurate and consistent innovation requires more than simply demanding creative ideas from your team; you must awaken your passion and commitment to growth. This is where transformational leadership shines.

Transformational leadership stands out for its unparalleled ability to catalyze change by forming deep individual connections with team members. By adopting this style, you articulate an ambitious yet shared vision that explores people's aspirations and fosters an environment where they feel compelled to push boundaries and develop capabilities. Your approach focuses on establishing empathetic relationships, where you take a genuine interest in each person's goals, strengths, and areas for growth. You act as a mentor and motivator, recognizing unique talents and potential within the team and providing inspiration and support to encourage them to reach new heights and make their development a reality.

The Four 'I's of Transformational Leadership: The Formula for Inspiring Innovation and Growth

To efficiently adopt this leadership style, you must understand its fundamental components, which brings us to the Four 'I's of Transformational Leadership—Inspirational Motivation, Intellectual Stimulation, Individualized Consideration, and Idealized Influence. Each element is instrumental and offers unique value to your journey, but executing them in harmony builds a potent framework to unleash your team's potential and business growth.

Inspirational Motivation: Architecting Aspirations

Inspirational motivation centers on your ability as a leader to articulate an ambitious yet unified vision for the future, requiring you to move beyond sterile mission statements and infuse your communication with vivid metaphors, captivating storytelling, and contagious optimism that brings the vision to life. You paint a picture of a future that explores people's highest aspirations and ties their work to a grand purpose.

Your role is to elevate tasks from mundane obligations to vital steps toward the dream and energize teams to push past perceived limitations and embrace the vision as their own. This approach forges an emotional bond between individuals and organizational goals, driving them to surpass expectations in pursuing shared ambitions and transforming your teams from task-oriented to purpose-driven.

Intellectual Stimulation: Catalyzing Collective Intelligence

With Intellectual stimulation, you act as an intellectual catalyst, challenging your team to think critically and creatively, and you seek to disrupt complacency and spark fresh thinking by posing challenging questions and complex problems. Your role is to ignite their potential into innovative solutions and to push them to unravel intricacies, find novel resolutions, and reimagine paradigms. Rather than providing answers, you actively engage your team's intellect to elevate problem-solving abilities, transforming their collective brainpower into an innovation engine.

Individualized Consideration: Sculpting Potential

Your leadership role reappears as you traverse the realm of individualized consideration; now, you are a sculptor of human potential. This approach transcends allocating tasks based on skill set; instead, it's about recognizing that your team is not a monolithic entity but a mosaic of unique talents, aspirations, and needs.

Through nuanced understanding and targeted communication, you foster an environment where each individual feels valued, heard, and inspired to contribute their best. By recognizing the specific needs of each team member, you acknowledge and celebrate their individuality. Your tailored approach becomes the chisel that brings out the masterpiece hidden within each block of marble, transforming raw potential into refined performance. This personalized attention amplifies your leadership influence, creating a resonance of trust and commitment that permeates your entire organization.

Idealized Influence: Becoming the Moral Compass

With idealized influence, your actions speak louder than words, and you firmly establish yourself as a behavioral role model by embodying the values and vision you promote. When adversity strikes, or critical decisions loom, you consistently exemplify steadfast commitment to ethical principles.

As discussed in the "Lead by Example," principle, integrity, accountability, and altruism are fundamental to shaping a solid leadership character, and here, you are the living moral compass to role model your team; you eschew double standards and hold yourself to the same high bar expected of others.

When conflicts arise and decisions are fraught with ambiguity, your firm commitment to ethical principles provides a clarifying light, guiding you and your team toward the right course of action. Far from a burden, this moral responsibility amplifies your influence, making it as pervasive as it is enduring. Your team follows you not due to your title or authority but a more potent form of power born out of respect, integrity, and the collective desire to emulate your example.

How Transformational Leadership Stands Apart

As we solidify the understanding of the traits and how this leadership style affects your relationship with your team and company, it's essential to recognize its primary differences when compared to the autocrat, democrat, servant, and laissez-faire leaders.

Autocratic Leadership: You inspire teams toward a shared vision, unlike autocratic leaders who dictate unilaterally. While autocrats control tightly and decree decisions, you motivate through accountability and high standards. Autocratic leaders lead by formal authority, whereas you lead by moral authority derived from ideals people aspire to follow.

Democratic Leadership: Democratic leaders build consensus through lengthy deliberation and integrate diverse views through participation. You ignite action from an animating vision, making decisive calls but inviting feedback. While democratic leadership fosters inclusion, over-reliance on consensus risks inertia. Blend it with transformational leadership to benefit from both collaboration and vision.

Laissez-Faire Leadership: Laissez-faire leaders offer broad guidance but allow autonomy, risking fragmentation as teams drift apart. You provide structured mentorship focused on continuous growth and unifying everyone behind a coherent vision while encouraging ingenuity. Laissez-faire can empower experienced teams but leave others directionless.

Servant Leadership: Servant leaders focus on fulfilling needs and supporting holistically. You inspire teams to push past limits toward visionary goals. While the focus of servant leadership is to nurture, transformational leadership galvanizes. Alone, servant leadership risks complacency. Combined with transformational motivation, the two create a nurturing yet energizing environment.

Mastering Transformational Leadership's Pitfalls

Transformational leadership's immense power comes with potential pitfalls that can undermine its efficacy if left unaddressed promptly, and mastering this style requires anticipating and mitigating these hazards proactively.

First, managing overwhelming expectations requires walking a fine line between inspiration and attainability. While high expectations fuel growth, impossibly high ones discourage it. You must balance lofty visioning with incremental, morale-boosting wins. Setting ambitious yet realistic milestones will maximize your team's potential.

Second, maintaining momentum over the long term is challenging. This leadership style demands constantly rallying teams behind the mission, which risks fatiguing even the most dedicated leader. You can reinforce momentum by sharing motivational responsibilities, taking personal timeouts, and utilizing tools like training and incentives.

Additionally, preventing organizational fragmentation requires aligning all activities to strategic goals once pursuing varied innovation risks fracturing into misaligned silos. To preserve cohesion, you must continually realign to the core vision, eliminating deviant initiatives and celebrating shared wins.

Finally, complacency represents an ever-present threat. Continually hold teams accountable to standards, be proactive about emerging problems, and balance aspirations with pragmatic delivery. Avoid solely focusing on the future by staying vigilant about present performance.

Transformational Leadership Restoring a Struggling Tech Company

Consider the scenario of a once-dominant tech company that has fallen behind the times. They led the industry ten years ago, but failure to innovate left them floundering while nimbler competitors captured market share. Their flagship product feels dated, driving the engineering talent to flee for sexier opportunities in rivals. The company culture grew insular and political, stifling creativity. They are hemorrhaging customers and profits. Analysts predict irrelevance looms without swift change.

CHAPTER 2   LEADERSHIP STYLES AND SITUATIONAL LEADERSHIP

In this turbulent context, the Board appoints Paula, a transformational leader in essence, as the new company's CEO, hoping her approach can spark a turnaround. She assesses challenges and opportunities and crafts a vision for resurgent innovation, mapping a roadmap back to dominance. Yet, Paula knows realizing this requires developing new products in a vacuum, recapturing the organization's imagination, reconnecting people to a shared purpose, and reconstructing the cultural DNA to unlock ingenuity.

Her inspirational vision resonates at all-hands meetings, reminding people of past glories now within reach again. She urges teams to think disruptively, dissolve orthodoxies, and pursue moonshot ideas aligning with the roadmap, fostering autonomy but expecting accountability through defined goals. Her charisma and conviction electrify once-demoralized engineers.

Paula supports her group at every step, redirecting resources to support skills elevation and continuous learning and fostering an environment where the staff is prepared to face adversity. She incentivizes internal mobility and experimentation to break rigid thinking. Paula practices individualized consideration through regular small-team meetings, mentoring engineers, discussing their goals, advocating work-life balance, and welcoming dissenting views. People feel energized by her accessibility and interest in their growth.

Results follow steadily. A team develops an innovative algorithm that unlocks new capacities, and another reimagines the UX, delighting users again. As a leader, she ensures credit and rewards are broadly shared, cementing an ethos of unity.

Yet, skeptics remain, and Paula faces second-guessing from some board members. She stands firm in her vision and principles, and as momentum builds, she ensures urgency doesn't lead to unethical shortcuts. Of course, risks lurk amid progress. Some teams lose focus, requiring realignment to core goals. She acts promptly to counter fragmentation through inclusive brainstorming sessions and reminds people how each contributes to the larger vision.

CHAPTER 2 LEADERSHIP STYLES AND SITUATIONAL LEADERSHIP

After two years of inspired dedication, product launches re-establish the company as an innovation pioneer, again leveling up the company as a key market player. Paula's transformational leadership restored belief, momentum, and purpose, rejuvenating a workforce hungry to excel again. While challenges arose, her resilience, empathy, and focus uplifted everyone's performance. Paula led with heart and vision, revitalizing the company and preparing it to ascend new heights for years.

The transformational leader's journey is a monumental yet profoundly personal one. Your success hinges not on genius stratagems or magic formulas but on your ability to form human connections that resonate on a profound level, shining light on the intricacies of inspiration, growth, and human potential.

Execute it with authenticity, and its influence will ripple through your organization. Demonstrate small acts of leadership—a conversation, a coaching session, a moment of encouragement—and you will trigger a snowball into an avalanche of progress. However, the future will twist and turn, bringing trials and triumphs. When you face difficult crossroads, remember your principles; when motivation lulls, rekindle your inspirational flame, stay fixed on the vision that pulled you forward, and stay responsive to emerging opportunities. Lead by lifting others.

Transformational leadership exposes our shared yearning to be part of something grand, our latent talents awaiting excavation, and our potential to elevate each other. Unlocking this generates an upwelling of human energy more potent than any strategy or technology alone. Lead boldly, but lead compassionately. Therein lies the key that unlocks innovation, unshackles creativity, and catalyzes transcendence. Your leadership will transform your teams, your company, and yourself.

Servant Leadership: Empowering and Enabling Others

If you're seeking more meaningful and empowering ways to lead, exploring servant leadership offers massive potential for you and your team's growth. This people-centered philosophy directly defies the conventional management model by defining a leader's role as serving others first. Although ancient wisdom and traditions espoused servant leadership ideals for millennia, the modern servant leadership movement emerged in the 1970s through Robert Greenleaf's seminal works. Greenleaf coined the term "servant leadership" and emphasized that, unlike authoritarian methods, servant leaders derive satisfaction from empowering people, not controlling them.

At its core, servant leadership flips the hierarchy and power dynamic upside down. Rather than viewing leadership as an opportunity to consolidate authority, you adopt a mindset of empowering others through ethical service, shifting your motivation from self-interest to collective benefit. You lead by listening, building trust, and uplifting teammates, not wielding top-down control.

Cultivating the Servant Leader Mindset: Core Characteristics

Adopting a servant leadership mentality requires developing and embodying specific core characteristics. Even though you can learn a new skill set, these characteristics stem from intrinsic values and mindsets, and anchoring your approach around these attributes is essential for transformative service.

Empathy forms the foundation of servant leadership. You must cultivate deep compassion for your team and tune in to understand their needs and struggles at a profoundly human level. Leadership is ultimately about uplifting shared experiences, not just driving tasks and efficiency. You must foster emotional intelligence by appreciating colleagues' diverse challenges professionally and personally.

Equally vital is *humility*. The servant leader mindset means discarding ego and ambition in favor of selfless support. Be willing to work alongside your team in the trenches, not just direct from the top; actively seek out their ideas, and remember you can learn as much from them as they can from you. Leading with humility builds trust and community.

Servant leaders also hone the ability to *listen deeply*. Rather than just issuing orders, pause to actively hear your team's inputs, concerns, and ideas. Listening demonstrates respect and creates space for others to offer creative solutions. You must strive to understand fully before seeking to be understood.

Lastly, cultivate *foresight*. Anticipate challenges on the horizon, make decisions with your team's long-term interests, and prepare them for future success beyond immediate needs. Adopt a broad perspective that weighs both goals and cultural impact.

While embodying these characteristics occurs over a lifetime, making them your guiding lights illuminates the direction to becoming a great servant leader. With empathy, you support each person's journey; with humility, you invite new voices; with deep listening, you gain collective wisdom; with foresight, you sustain growth. Anchoring in these attributes allows you to unlock your team's greatest potential.

Implementing Servant Leadership: Key Principles

Even though cultivating the right mindset and characteristics is crucial, servant leadership truly comes alive through principles in action. As a servant leader, you must translate values into behaviors to serve and empower your team meaningfully.

Prioritizing your team members' growth and well-being represents a central principle. Rather than viewing them as a means to an end, make nurturing them intrinsically rewarding. You must invest time as a mentor and provide opportunities tailored to help individuals advance professionally, allowing your team members to thrive in their areas of excellence but primarily to support their growth in weaker areas.

You must also actively empower and enable team members by sharing authority and autonomy. Solicit and implement their ideas, replace micromanagement with macro support—resources, training, mentorship. Grant ownership of projects based on trust, not control to nurture leadership skills in others. After all, your role is to facilitate, not command.

Furthermore, servant leaders cherish community building. Promote camaraderie, human connections, transparency, and inclusivity to prevent siloed thinking. Tend to the team's emotional spirit, celebrate wins of all sizes, and facilitate open communication and constructive conflict. Your mission is to shepherd a collective sense of purpose beyond tasks and targets.

Finally, upholding strong ethical principles represents a key commitment, and you must make considerations around integrity, sustainability, and social impact central to decisions. Be guided by a moral compass, even if it means sacrificing short-term gains, and set an expectation that ethics matter as much as results. Your legacy endures through whom you empower and the principles you instill.

Of course, bridging vision and implementation remains challenging, and progressing meaningfully requires commitment, patience, and reflection. But steadfastly translating servant leadership ideals into action is rewarding, especially when you build trusted teams that outperform expectations, uplift one another, and make moral choices. The juice is well worth the squeeze.

Navigating Criticisms and Challenges of Servant Leadership

Implementing any leadership approach inevitably faces criticisms and challenges that you must face. By adopting the servant leadership mindset, you will likely encounter obstacles as you aim to empower your team through ethical service.

Critics may claim that servant leadership's emphasis on empowerment risks decreasing efficiency or eroding authority, while some may see servant leaders as too soft or indecisive. Misconceptions around servant leadership as abdicating responsibility rather than redefining leadership may arise, and proactively addressing these criticisms is crucial for successfully transitioning to this participative, people-centric style. Each challenge highlights areas requiring your discernment. You can reinforce servant leadership principles by anticipating and preparing for objections while acknowledging valid concerns.

> **Balancing Authority with Servitude:** A significant challenge is striking the right equilibrium between service and authority. Servant leaders aim to involve team members democratically but still require the capacity for decisive direction when appropriate. You must discern when consensus-building and autonomy will foster growth versus when clear leadership is necessary to maintain focus and progress. Involve your team sincerely in shaping solutions, but don't allow endless debate to stall important decisions; grant independence for collaborators to create freely but intervene with constructive guidance when efforts stray off-course; nurture, empower, and develop your team while still guiding firmly toward key goals when required.

Risk of Inefficiency: Servant leadership's inclusive process can seem slower than a top-down decree. Taking time to listen, build trust, and gain buy-in may sacrifice some short-term efficiency. However, while empowerment might have upfront costs, it drives much greater engagement, ownership, and innovation later on. Remain patient as you involve team members meaningfully in decisions and projects; explain how their inputs and growth matter, not just immediate results; keep important initiatives progressing by incrementally empowering, not micromanaging.

Counterarguments and Misconceptions: Some common counterarguments and misconceptions about servant leadership also arise. For instance, it does not mean total abdication of power but rather the moral stewardship of authority. Servant leadership is still leadership, redefined with service at the core. If you adopt this leadership style, critics may tag you as a soft leader. However, empathetic leaders can still be courageous, visionary, and results-focused once they ground themselves in ethical human considerations while aiming boldly ahead. Blend compassion with conviction intelligently to correct this misconception.

Communicate these distinctions clearly and lead by example to adopt this leadership style effectively, and with perseverance and reflection, your team will grow as empowered, values-driven individuals and an integrated community, achieving results and a culture where they can thrive.

CHAPTER 2   LEADERSHIP STYLES AND SITUATIONAL LEADERSHIP

Comparing Servant Leadership to Complementary Styles

As an engineering leader embracing servant leadership, you gain an immense advantage by understanding how this approach compares and can blend with the other leadership styles covered in this chapter. Let's explore how pure servant leadership philosophically differs from other prominent styles and how it can be integrated intelligently based on circumstances. With mastery of this nuanced integration, you can amplify your influence as a servant leader and help your team to succeed at a breakneck speed.

Autocratic Leadership: Autocratic leaders follow a top-down, directive leadership that commands productivity through rigid control, whereas servant leadership inverts this dynamic by empowering teams through ethical service. Autocrats consolidate authority and drive tasks through mandates. Conversely, servant leaders share power and cultivate engagement by meeting needs. While autocracy provides direction, it risks stifling the morale and innovation that servant leadership unlocks. Blending aspects of decisive direction from autocracy with servant leadership's compassion enables responsive, values-driven, and ethical leadership.

Transformational Leadership: Transformational leadership aims to rally teams behind a bold, shared vision by igniting their motivation and intellectual capabilities, and like servant leadership, both approaches value developing people and engaging intrinsic motivation. However, at its core, transformational leadership seeks to compel teams to exceed expectations in achieving the leader's vision. On the other hand, servant leadership addresses individual needs to nurture their well-being and growth; while the former propels ambition, the latter provides support. Blending aspects of transformational leadership's inspirational motivation with servant leadership's humanistic approach creates a robust framework that allows you to achieve inspired performance and fulfillment.

Laissez-Faire Leadership: Laissez-faire leadership represents a highly hands-off approach, granting teams near-total independence and autonomy with little leader involvement, and unlike servant leadership's commitment to service and support, laissez-faire risks poor cohesion, direction, and nurturing. Although laissez-faire leadership allows maximum freedom, it provides minimal coaching, mentorship, or developmental feedback to help team members reach their potential. Laissez-faire leaders make themselves available but largely leave teams to self-direct. In contrast, servant leaders actively support each person's professional and personal growth through one-on-one teaching, encouragement, and mentoring, granting autonomy and nurturing potential.

Yet, certain aspects of laissez-faire leadership can be helpful when blended wisely with servant leadership. For instance, incorporating laissez-faire's increased autonomy enables servant leaders to unlock both independence and nurturing, and granting the right teams more ownership with servant leadership's supportive oversight sustains growth.

> **Democratic Leadership:** Like servant leadership, democratic leadership champions employee participation in decisions through consensus-building and majority rule, where leaders allow extensive discussion and input from the team before determining direction. However, democratic leadership prioritizes collective decision-making over individual growth. Democratics drive conversations to integrate diverse views into group decisions instead of nurturing individual talents through coaching or mentoring. In contrast, servant leaders focus first on supporting each person's growth through one-on-one teaching, encouragement, and development planning. While they incorporate team input, their central goal is nourishing each individual's potential.

Taken alone, endless deliberation in pure democratic leadership can breed analysis paralysis and inaction without balance from decisive leadership. Nevertheless, prudent integration with servant leadership offers benefits of both collaboration and ethical, people-focused service. For instance, incorporating consensus-building and employee voice from democratic leadership allows servant leaders to gain insights and engagement. Combining this with servant leadership's unwavering support for individual growth enables collective wisdom and progress through service.

CHAPTER 2   LEADERSHIP STYLES AND SITUATIONAL LEADERSHIP

Servant Leader: Revitalizing a Broken Culture

Working as a leader, you may inherit teams stuck in ruts from past management issues. However, committing to understanding individuals, repairing trust, and nurturing growth can revitalize even a disillusioned group. You can implement servant leadership to unlock potential with patience and moral courage.

Now, let's bring servant leadership principles to life through an example. This scenario illustrates how embracing service and empowerment can transform teams, even in difficult circumstances.

Anita is a seasoned engineering leader who embraced a new challenge at Acme Co. as their new Director of Engineering. It didn't take long to realize the fragile state of her new team. The previous leader's oppressive management style has beaten down her team members, eroding trust and breeding fear. Consequently, the engineering team was operating in rigid silos, rarely collaborating; any act of creativity could represent an opportunity for punishment instead of encouragement. The group delivered solutions robotically and strictly based on rigid requirements defined beforehand. They were too demoralized to go beyond and challenge the status quo.

Promptly acknowledging the situation, Anita started looking to understand the root cause of such behavior. She booked individual sessions with each team member and listened empathetically as engineers described feeling like interchangeable cogs, not valued innovators. They desperately wanted to create but were micromanaged into compliance. Over time, the group lost its passion, motivation, and vibrancy. During the sessions, Anita recognized past mistakes' weight and consequences and committed to a new servant leadership approach—first on an individual level and later on a group level. She knew a cultural change was necessary, and rebuilding trust through transparency, participation, and empowerment became her priority.

Anita connected with team members on a deeply individual level, allowing her to identify their strengths and weaknesses, creating opportunities for all to shine where they were good at, and learning based on current gaps. People became recognized as individuals with unique skills to impact business and the company's growth. Additionally, the new Director of Engineering has established an open-door policy and actively solicited ideas for improving processes; she reorganized rigid silos into flexible, collaborative pods. The autonomy and sense of impact weren't unknown feelings anymore.

While Anita promoted an environment of autonomy and collaboration, she kept herself close to guide and ensure the team was on the right track, applying any course correction quickly and adopting a directive style whenever needed. She removed obstacles along the way and provided mentoring and resources to equip the staff with the skills and resources to thrive. Soon, projects started breathing a new life, and the engineering team felt energized by creative freedom and Anita's trust in them, resulting in innovative solutions that exceeded expectations derived from blended diverse strengths and shared knowledge.

However, as autonomy spiked, some engineers struggled, and Anita had to discern when to coach patiently versus intervene to refocus efforts. Her approach to listening carefully before suggesting any correction allowed her to identify the origin of the issues wisely and strike the right balance, uplifting members individually and collectively.

Within months, the team culture transformed from disengaged compliance to energized innovation. Anita's servant leadership empowered them to rediscover their passion, and her integrity, compassion, and unwavering support of each person reignited their flame. The group, once paralyzed by fear, now dared to dream big. Their consistent breakthrough product launches wowed customers and positioned Acme Co. as a market leader.

Anita's journey reveals the power of servant leadership to repair broken cultures and unlock potential. With moral courage and commitment to service, you, too, can transform demoralized teams into inspired communities, achieving remarkable feats together.

In closing, embracing servant leadership represents a profoundly rewarding path for engineering leaders seeking to build empowered, values-driven teams. However, you can expect hardships and critics questioning if the juice is worth the squeeze. Yet, with consistent selfless service, you ignite pools of human potential and shape enduring legacies. So when fatigue looms, reflect on the growth you've kindled in colleagues, and when skeptics arise, remember your purpose—not to be served, but to serve.

Democratic Leadership: Fostering Collaboration and Inclusion

Embracing a leadership challenge requires you to guide your team toward success, and your decisions and the leadership approach can make or break your team's performance and morale. Of the many styles available, democratic leadership offers immense potential to build an empowered and collaborative team culture.

Democratic leadership has a rich history in Ancient Greece, where participatory democracy allowed citizens to contribute directly to governmental decisions and the nation's future. This philosophy of valuing diverse voices and inclusion has since taken root in management theory and practice. You, as a democratic leader, embrace facilitating team discussions to integrate varied perspectives and knowledge into decisions as your primary objective. Instead of consolidating authority, you distribute decision-making power across the team, and your role becomes less about commanding followers and more about orchestrating an ensemble of ideas to meet objectives, acknowledging that great solutions can originate from any team member, not just from the top.

Engineering teams handle complex challenges daily, requiring leveraging collective intelligence and collaboration between individuals with complementary technical strengths to build efficient solutions; this is where democratic leadership unlocks immense value. By adopting a participative style, you foster an environment with freedom for critical and analytical thinking where creativity and innovation flourish. In parallel, you build a culture where ego is not welcome but rather the recognition of the collective power as the main driver for success.

Beyond driving better decisions, democratic leadership promotes flat organizational structures, transparency, and employee empowerment. You mirror these values by promoting equality, dismantling rigid hierarchies, and ensuring you hear and consider empathetically all voices. You discern that people value autonomy, mastery, and purpose instead of being treated as robots or cogs in a machine.

The Democratic Leader's Toolbox: Core Characteristics

Guiding your team successfully as a democratic leader requires cultivating specific traits that empower group participation and foster collaboration. Let's explore some core characteristics that allow you to implement this leadership style effectively.

First and foremost, you must hone your emotional intelligence and empathy. Understanding team members' unspoken needs and motivations allow you to involve them meaningfully in decisions. Listening to their emotions and perspectives through compassion also promotes psychological safety and openness while you nurture a climate where diverse voices feel comfortable contributing.

Furthermore, listening actively is vital. Don't just pay lip service to input—be fully present and engaged when members speak up. Promote open dialogue by inviting fresh ideas and avoiding knee-jerk judgments. Apply discretion to prevent vocal individuals from dominating discussions. Your ability to listen profoundly keeps communication flowing.

In addition, embracing a collaborative mindset represents a key enabler—value building solutions together over competing as individuals. Recognize how blending complementary strengths and styles cultivates excellence and shapes an environment where every contribution has merit and mutual understanding is the priority. Unity of purpose propels achievement.

You must also adopt a facilitative approach when leading. Your role becomes empowering team members to think freely, speak openly, showcase their capabilities, and refrain from commandeering conversations. Instead, promote inclusive participation through artful facilitation to harmonize the team's talents.

Moreover, remain flexible and adaptable when collaborating. Adjust plans based on ideas that emerge from group discussions, accommodate new information, and be ready to change course. Democratic leadership demands agility to integrate diverse views.

Lastly, nurture transparency. Keep teammates informed about developments that affect them, explain the rationale behind choices to foster trust, seek candid feedback, and aim for openness, not opacity. With transparency, your team can align efforts confidently.

Principles for Practicing Democratic Leadership

Understanding the mindset and characteristics of democratic leadership is essential, but embracing the core principles to become an effective democratic leader will level up your journey and support you to live this supportive style through consistent actions. Let's explore some fundamental practices for implementing these principles day-to-day.

Promote a sense of shared responsibility among the group. Democratic leadership is a team sport, not a solo act—it leverages collective effort to achieve common goals. So, make it clear to all team members that everyone owns a piece of the outcomes, both successes and failures. Celebrate group accomplishments publicly, not just individually, and start using words like "we" and "us" when discussing team results once shared responsibility and interdependency breed more significant commitment to group objectives.

Furthermore, *encourage active participation* from all team members during crucial decisions and planning sessions and create an open forum environment where people's voices are regularly and directly invited, not discouraged. Draw out introverted teammates who may hold back. At the same time, you wisely manage dominant personalities to boost inclusion by routinely involving different individuals in decisions rather than defaulting to the most vocal. Consequently, you enrich collaboration through full participation and the diversity of viewpoints from all team members.

Inclusive communication is critical, so nurture open communication channels day-to-day and go beyond sharing generic information or need-to-know details; instead, you provide full context and reasoning to foster understanding. You make yourself accessible for candid feedback and debate about plans. Your top priority is establishing trust and psychological safety, so teammates feel comfortable surfacing concerns, suggesting improvements, and weighing options. Keeping communication free-flowing unlocks your team's full potential.

You must also pay close attention to *group dynamics and harmony* once these are the primary ingredients to excel as a democratic leader. You must actively promote cooperation over competition within the team, facilitate discussions tactfully to align varied perspectives, and avoid discord. Draw out disagreements into the open rather than letting tensions simmer, and ensure that diversity of thought is welcome while maintaining cohesion and congenial interactions.

In addition, *prioritize continuous development* of team capabilities by identifying growth areas for each member that align with and support business goals. Provide stretch assignments, training, and mentoring to help individuals level up, instilling intrinsic motivation for self-improvement and promoting learning as an ongoing habit, not a one-off event. A commitment to regular improvement sustains performance at the bleeding edge rather than allowing stagnation.

Embrace solid ethics and moral responsibility. Adhere to a moral compass when making choices, even if it means sacrificing potential short-term gains. Ensure through words and actions that doing the right thing matters here, and you'll infuse integrity as a shared value that bolsters the team's purpose and pride.

Finally, *make collaborative decision-making the norm, not the exception.* Engage the team constructively to leverage their diverse expertise and perspectives when evaluating options. Even though you facilitate the discussions, empower members to provide meaningful input to directly participate in decision-making, fostering an environment of collective accountability and shared purpose.

Putting these principles into consistent practice allows you to transform individual efforts into an empowered symphony that harmonizes team spirits, skills, and thinking, fully benefiting from democratic leadership and unleashing potential beyond what any member could achieve alone.

Avoiding the Pitfalls of Democratic Leadership

Decades of management experience have demonstrated that even the most well-intentioned democratic leadership approach can unravel or backfire without sufficient foresight and vigilance.

Embracing collaboration, different opinions, and collective decision-making carries massive potential advantages. However, you must thoughtfully navigate the inherent risks and pitfalls of the democratic style; without care and situational awareness, this type of leadership, once designed as a collaborative process, can devolve into frustration, gridlock, and diluted focus.

The good news is that forewarned is forearmed. By investing time upfront to understand the most common pitfalls and being ready to adapt your approach situationally, you can reap the fruits of democracy while nimbly dodging any bumps in the road. So, let's look deeper at several potential challenges you must keep on your radar screen and strategies for overcoming them. Avoiding these traps will allow your team to benefit from democratic leadership at most.

One prime challenge is prolonged decision-making processes. Seeking extensive team input understandably takes more time versus unilateral calls. But drawn-out discussions quickly breed frustration and decision paralysis, and you must safeguard against endless circular conversations. Keep meetings sharply focused, frame issues concisely to guide deliberations productively, and if talks circle endlessly, be willing to request a vote or use your executive judgment. Input is invaluable, but so is forward progress through closure.

Furthermore, disagreements and conflicts inevitably arise when blending diverse perspectives, and without proper facilitation, tensions can devolve into lingering discord that breeds resentment. However, to transform conflict into constructive progress, start by surfacing brewing issues early before they escalate, listen empathetically to understand all sides, identify common ground, reinforce shared goals, and reframe debates into collaborative problem-solving. Guiding your staff's conversations toward enlightened solutions that provide mutual gains is a powerful resource for avoiding ego and bias in a collective decision-making process.

Beware of over-collaboration bordering on design by committee. Excessive, wide-open input can muddy the waters and dilute creative focus, and recognizing that only some projects benefit from extensive consultation is paramount; sometimes, too many cooks spoil the broth.

Gauge when more collaboration will enrich versus bog down outcomes. Temper wide-open crowd-sourcing with mechanisms for ultimately driving decisions.

Moreover, achieving consensus sometimes becomes challenging, even with the best intentions. When opinions diverge widely, agreement stalls, and at some point, further consultation provides diminishing returns. If the consensus is ideal but remains elusive, don't hesitate and switch gracefully to majority rule or an executive decision as a backup plan. A collaborative environment sometimes also requires directiveness to flourish.

Avoid overemphasizing equality to the detriment of excellence. While collective effort matters, individuals still deserve rewards for outstanding contributions, lest you inadvertently create a race to the bottom. Seek the right balance between participative empowerment and pushing for standout results from top performers. Democracy works best alongside meritocracy, not replacing it.

Comparing Democratic Leadership to Other Styles

As an engineering leader, understanding how democratic leadership contrasts and blends with other approaches can expand your leadership toolkit. Let's explore how it stands apart from or integrates with prominent styles.

> **Autocratic Leadership:** Autocrats follow a commanding, top-down style that drives productivity through rigid control, consolidating decision-making power, and issuing unilateral directives to maximize efficiency. As a democratic leader, you take the opposite approach—distributing authority across the team and eliciting collective inputs instead of dictating unilaterally.

However, autocracy's decisiveness can be advantageous when quick choices are needed. In these cases, blend aspects of autocracy by setting clear boundaries around democratic inclusion to maintain momentum and your team's insights while retaining the ability to drive urgent decisions.

Transformational Leadership: Transformational leaders embrace a shared vision to lead through inspiration, high standards, and passionate motivation, focusing on propelling teams to exceed expectations when accomplishing ambitious goals toward the leader's vision. As a democratic leader, you similarly aim to motivate people but emphasize facilitating collaboration versus commanding compliance, and your focus is on integrating participants' perspectives. Yet, blending transformational leadership's inspiration and motivation with democracy's emphasis on participation enables you to inspire teamwork rather than just purpose.

Laissez-Faire Leadership: Laissez-faire leaders are known for their hands-off approach. They provide little oversight and grant team members extensive autonomy to determine their direction, risking poor cohesion and lack of vision. Conversely, you offer broader guidance and input as a democratic leader while encouraging independence in approaching work and balancing autonomy with alignment. By combining laissez-faire's increased autonomy with engagement from democratic guidance, you empower self-directed efforts aligned through participative coordination, promoting independence but retaining the benefits of your oversight and facilitation.

Servant Leadership: Servant leaders prioritize nurturing team members' growth through ethical, humanistic service. They focus heavily on understanding individuals' needs and supporting their well-being and development, whereas, as a democratic leader, you value employee empowerment but concentrate more on collective decision-making than only individual growth. However, blending servant leadership's humanistic support for people's needs with democracy's emphasis on collaboration creates an environment where all voices are valued, heard, and developed through shared growth, uplifting individual and collective efforts.

Democratic Leadership in Action

Now that we've explored democratic leadership's core traits and principles, let's bring this collaborative style to life through an immersive example, where an engineering leader embraces the democratic ideals to empower their teams, unlock their highest potential, and solve a complex dilemma through the power of collective intelligence and collaboration. Let's get down the business.

Jillian leads the engineering team at Acme Online Retail, an e-commerce startup aiming to disrupt online shopping through personalization. The group aims to introduce a robust machine-learning engine to capture customers' interests via historical purchases and keywords from the current search engine to generate tailored product recommendations to keep customers engaged. The executives and stakeholders see this new functionality as crucial for staying competitive.

At first glance, the team judged the feature as doable in a short period of time. However, as the business requirements became more precise, the unknowns increased proportionally, and the team started doubting their expertise and questioning their decision. During development, the immense complexity of architecting and building such a robust system soon overwhelmed Jillian's team. Engineers grappled with knotty problems across model training, scalable inference, low-latency data pipelines, infrastructure optimization—you name it.

Morale cratered as stress mounted and progress lagged. The unrealistic timeline felt crushing, and Jillian knew she needed to tame the team's frustration. During a frank all-hands meeting, she empathetically acknowledged the immense difficulty of their task and sincerely thanked the team for their efforts so far. While this stretched their skills, Jillian inspired confidence that they could find solutions by pooling knowledge and complementing strengths. Her heartfelt words re-energized the group.

Next, Jillian gathered with her team and brainstormed how to break down the complex feature into smaller chunks of work and embrace the "dividing to conquer" approach. This strategy allowed Jillian to create collaborative and cross-functional working groups, focusing on tackling sub-problems in parallel and facilitating active knowledge sharing across teams to enable holistic progress. Despite providing all the necessary information and resources, her objective wasn't to dictate how to build the solution but to guide and empower the team to deliberate on the best approach by themselves, removing any roadblocks blocking their discussions.

Due to the diverse nature of her team, she facilitated the research process by implementing written and anonymized brainstorming panels to ideate potential solutions without judgments, which would be discussed in the following design-thinking sessions. In whiteboard sessions, Jillian drew insights from introverts while tempering noise from vocal members. Inevitably, passionate debates emerged, and Jillian reframed arguments into joint problem-solving discussions. She encouraged trying bold technical experiments but supported measured risk-taking. Her constant guidance kept the team moving forward.

Jillian held participative reviews for constructive feedback on prototypes and synthesized varied technical inputs while soliciting the team's ideas to enrich decisions. After months of intense collaboration, Acme's disruptive recommendation engine launched successfully against the odds. Jillian praised the team for their remarkable synergy, emphasizing collective intelligence's power to achieve the finish line. No daunting challenge or pressure eroded Jillian's trust in her team's capabilities. Instead, she allowed all to collaborate, debate, and succeed as a unit.

Democratic leadership offers immense potential to empower teams by promoting inclusion, harvesting diverse insights through collaboration, and driving innovation. As important as cultivating the power of collective intelligence and cooperation is the ability to temper participation with decisive momentum, transform clashes into opportunities through emotional intelligence, and blend democratic ideals with compassionate boldness.

This leadership style exposes latent talents by giving everyone a voice. It unlocks human energy more potent than any technology alone when you lead ethically, stay true to principles of empowerment, and have the courage to embrace the power of "we," unlocking creativity and unleashing the full potential of your team. Ultimately, remember to balance your approach and blend the power of democracy with other leadership styles to avoid the misperception of a lack of leadership or endless discussions that may lead you to decision paralysis.

CHAPTER 2   LEADERSHIP STYLES AND SITUATIONAL LEADERSHIP

Laissez-Faire Leadership: Nurturing Autonomy and Ownership

By embracing laissez-faire, you recognize that cultivating autonomy and ownership within your team is instrumental in unlocking innovation and maximizing productivity. But it calls for a nuanced leadership approach centered on empowerment rather than control, and here is where laissez-faire leaders shine.

Laissez-faire leadership revolves around granting your team the freedom and authority to steer their work, where you provide high-level guidance and resources, then take a step back, resisting the temptation to micromanage. Your role transforms from an interventionist to an engaged observer, letting your team take charge while monitoring progress and providing strategic input where crucial.

This leadership style resonates with the innate human desire for independence and self-direction, and creating an atmosphere of empowerment catalyzes motivation, engagement, and responsibility within your team. Granting decision-making authority also unshackles creativity, allowing innovative solutions to blossom. When applied strategically, laissez-faire leadership can unlock your team's latent potential, ingenuity, and productivity.

Empowering Through Autonomy: The Guiding Principles of Laissez-Faire Leaders

While laissez-faire leadership centers on empowerment through autonomy, you shouldn't make it a synonym for complete abdication of guidance and accountability. To properly master this style, you must understand its central principles, which provide the missing link between granting independence and retaining alignment.

These principles offer crucial boundaries to empower your team while avoiding the pitfalls of misalignment that unchecked freedom can breed. They allow you to guide without commanding, granting wings while ensuring the team flies in formation.

Now, let's explore the core philosophies underlying effective laissez-faire leadership.

> **Empowerment over Control:** At its essence, laissez-faire leadership revolves around granting your team autonomy rather than exerting control. You provide the necessary tools, resources, and strategic guidance, then empower your team to steer the specifics of executing projects. Rather than micromanaging details, you trust their skills and allow them to exercise creative freedom in determining the "how" behind achieving goals, promoting engagement, accountability, and problem-solving skills within your team.
>
> **High-Level Guidance:** Even though you relinquish control over execution, you must still offer high-level guidance to your team, clearly communicating broader organizational goals, desired outcomes, and overarching timeframes or constraints. Still, you refrain from dictating detailed processes, instead letting your team innovate optimal solutions. Providing too little guidance risks misalignment, whereas too much slides into micromanagement, and as a laissez-faire leader, you must find the sweet spot—the clarity to inform direction while leaving room for individual discretion.

CHAPTER 2   LEADERSHIP STYLES AND SITUATIONAL LEADERSHIP

Accountability with Autonomy: Granting autonomy does not absolve accountability. Laissez-faire leaders empower teams with the freedom to steer projects independently yet maintain responsibility for the results. You make this duality clear from the outset—freedom is granted, not guaranteed, and your team must exercise sound judgment and deliver outcomes on schedule. Accountability gives weight to the autonomy you grant, ensuring it catalyzes, not hampers, productivity and innovation.

Engaged Detachment: The paradox of laissez-faire leadership is engaged detachment. You remain constantly engaged—monitoring team progress, facilitating resources, and providing high-level guidance. However, you intentionally detach from the close execution. Your engaged detachment allows you to grant creative freedom while ensuring alignment with organizational goals. Yet, tipping too far toward detachment risks disengagement, and too much engagement slides toward micromanagement. You must master balancing engaged observation with detached empowerment.

Selective Intervention: An adept laissez-faire leader recognizes when to intervene selectively and when to remain hands-off. If your team shows symptoms of misalignment or lack of direction, timely intervention realigns efforts. However, prescribed intervention risks undermining the creative latitude you seek to grant. Once you restore the group alignment, step back and observe progress with engaged detachment. Filtering when to intervene and when to let it go demonstrates you are invested while affirming your confidence in their autonomy.

The Shadow Side of Freedom: Accounting for the Risks

Although empowerment through autonomy can unlock immense potential, laissez-faire leadership poses risks that adept leaders must acknowledge and mitigate. At first sight, this is the perfect formula—empowerment drives engagement, which drives results. But this equation becomes incomplete once empowerment without accountability risks disengagement and discord, whereas autonomy devoid of purpose breeds wayward outcomes.

As an adept laissez-faire leader, you must acknowledge risks and navigate accordingly. Grant autonomy judiciously, align efforts to purpose, and match support to needs. Do this, and your team will steer confidently through the straits of independence into open waters of ownership and accountability. Let's explore some of the main risks associated with this leadership style.

> **Lack of Direction and Coherence:** Without proper guidance, teams may lose alignment on goals once competing priorities emerge, and productivity suffers from this lack of cohesive direction. Laissez-faire leaders must convey broader organizational goals while allowing autonomy in the details of execution. Periodic check-ins safeguard alignment as teams independently pursue objectives. Balance freedom with purpose—independence thrives within a shared framework.

Imbalanced Distribution of Workload: Laissez-faire leadership relies on intrinsic motivation, where proactive individuals may take on far greater workloads, while passive team members underperform without structured guidance. You must recognize imbalances early and redistribute duties to avoid burning out their stars while underutilizing others.

Lower Morale from Reduced Guidance: Less experienced team members often require closer support and feedback. Laissez-faire leaders, who minimize direct oversight, risk these individuals feeling directionless and morale declining without input. Mitigate by aligning teams appropriately—grant autonomy to skilled self-starters while pairing developing members with mentors for guidance, and adapt your approach to fit the needs of each individual.

Perceptions of Indifference and Indecisiveness: The hands-off approach may breed perceptions of indifference or indecision, especially if you avoid intervening in crucial situations. Laissez-faire does not imply abdication of leadership, and demonstrating situational awareness and willingness to assert authority when required is vital; lead quietly but decisively in critical moments to affirm your command capabilities.

Complacency from Reduced Oversight: Autonomy without accountability risks reduced standards and urgency; laissez-faire thrives only when freedom is granted, not guaranteed. You must uphold expectations through incentives and deadlines and curb complacency through clear objectives and routine check-ins on progress. Empowerment requires balance—a couple of latitude with accountability to avoid backsliding.

The Nuances of Laissez-Faire Leadership

Laissez-faire leadership holds an unusual space in the landscape of styles. Its hands-off approach stands apart from the control of autocracy, collaboration of democracy, nurturing of servant leadership, and motivation of transformational styles. Laissez-faire celebrates independence, for better or worse. This autonomy creates both vast potential and deep pitfalls. Without the vision of transformational leaders or the structure of autocrats, laissez-faire risks misalignment. But its freedom also unlocks creativity, ownership, and responsibility.

Let's explore how laissez-faire leadership uniquely compares to other prominent styles, highlighting when laissez-faire's autonomy uplifts and when it requires balance from more directive approaches.

> **Autocratic Leadership:** Autocrats dictate the action course without space for feedback, while laissez-faire grants autonomy. Autocracy provides alignment but stifling ingenuity, whereas laissez-faire enables innovation yet risks directionless. Still, both require vision and accountability, and you get a powerful framework by balancing the two—grant autonomy within a bold vision to nurture the creativity that ladders up to your north star.

Democratic Leadership: Democracy builds alignment through collaboration. Laissez-faire does so by granting freedom tied to a common purpose. Yet, consensus risks inertia, while autonomy empowers action. Blend laissez-faire's autonomy with democracy's deliberation when making major decisions to encourage self-direction within a framework of collective wisdom.

Servant Leadership: Servant leaders nurture by fulfilling individual needs, whereas laissez-faire leaders do so by granting independence aligned with growth. Excessive nurturing risks stagnation; too much independence breeds misalignment. Balance the two by granting autonomy yet providing developmental support tailored to individual needs.

Transformational Leadership: Transformational leadership inspires by tying work to a higher purpose. Laissez-faire does so by granting freedom to determine how to achieve that purpose. Transformational leaders risk over-structuring, whereas laissez-faire risks detachment. Combine them to enable autonomy in service of a motivational vision.

Unlocking Potential: A Case Study of Laissez-Faire Leadership

John led an AI engineering team at Acme Meds, a pioneering bioinformatics company. Their latest project, Anderson, aimed to develop an AI system for personalized medicine to synthesize patient data from diverse sources—genomic tests, EHRs, lab results—and use machine

CHAPTER 2   LEADERSHIP STYLES AND SITUATIONAL LEADERSHIP

learning to predict health risks and tailor treatment. However, during the development phase, the team hit roadblocks in training algorithms on the different massive and complex datasets. The unstructured data caused bottlenecks in preprocessing and information extraction, impairing the algorithm's accuracy due to the number of noisy inputs.

The team morale was low after months of grinding debugging efforts and little progress. John was feeling the pressure for a result from the Acme Meds leadership team. Still, despite the adverse scenario, he refused to command and adopt a directive style, trusting his team to self-motivate if given the opening. So he called a tense all-hands meeting, where frustration hung thick as summer haze. "Challenges will come," he began, "but our mission is unchanging – transform patient care through AI." He passionately restated Anderson project's primary objective and how his team would impact not only the company's future but also the market. He finished the meeting, stating, "I trust you all to get this back on track. Take ownership. Lead each other. You have the necessary incentive and skills to turn the ship around."

Right after the meeting, Ana, a veteran engineer, and the team's unofficial anchor, rose to the call. Her eyes blazed with John's speech as she volunteered to coordinate the recovery process. John smiled; relief was washing over him. She immediately tailored workflows to each member's strengths. Vijay, brilliant but unorthodox, got flexible assignments to refine the AI algorithms, freeing his innate creativity. Structure and rigor drove Jenny's talents, and Ana crafted structured two-week sprints to leverage her gift for meticulous system architecture and design; the team's effort was gaining momentum.

John hovered nearby during the recovery efforts, consciously providing support without intervening directly, facilitating resources, and fielding questions but letting Ana and the engineers determine the solutions.

When tensions inevitably sparked between Vijay and Jenny over contradicting approaches, John stepped in briefly to mediate. He met individually first with Vijay, validating concerns over Jenny disregarding his unconventional methods, and then he met privately with Jenny, empathizing with her need for rigor. Later on, in a joint session, John walked them through appreciating each other's distinct talents and gently but firmly reminded them that the symbiosis of their diverse perspectives was crucial to the project's success.

Vijay needed space for radical creativity and Jenny the discipline to implement effectively; John brokered a compromise among them—Vijay would get flexibility in refining the core algorithms while Jenny could design rigorous validation testing. This agreement would allow Vijay's innovations to flourish within Jenny's pragmatic frameworks, and both agreed this synergy could elevate the overall solution.

Soon, new energy infused the team's efforts. John had tapped into the group's intrinsic motivation by granting autonomy and providing a shared mission. In return, they rewarded his trust with sophisticated solutions that exceeded expectations, and the Anderson project was soon back on track. In later reflections, John validated Ana's leadership emergence and commended the team's ingenuity and ownership. Through freedom and purpose, he had awakened their potential.

The allure of laissez-faire leadership is undeniable—empowered teams driving themselves to unforeseen heights. Yet, as we've explored, granting autonomy requires wisdom; you must hover as an engaged observer, aligning efforts and providing selective guidance without over-intervening. But always remember—freedom bereft of purpose breeds wandering efforts. Latitudes without limits risk disengagement.

You must temper liberty with structure and autonomy with accountability—balance guidance with independence and oversight with empowerment. But carelessness imperils all potential. Tend this delicate balance wisely and purposefully, and laissez-faire leadership will unlock ingenuity and ownership, making your team blossom. They will become active partners on the path to audacious goals, requiring merely your guidance to stay the course. Lead through freedom, facilitate growth, and enable achievement—this is the calling of the laissez-faire leader.

CHAPTER 2   LEADERSHIP STYLES AND SITUATIONAL LEADERSHIP

Situational Leadership: Adapting to the Constant Changes

Throughout reading this chapter, you've explored various leadership systems—transformational leadership's inspiration, servant leadership's empathy, the firm direction of autocracy, democratic leadership's inclusion, and laissez-faire's autonomy—and recognized that each style offers valuable principles, mindsets, and tools to empower teams. However, you may have noticed limitations in applying any single methodology universally. Some methods thrive with experienced teams yet flounder with novices, whereas others unleash creativity but struggle with execution.

Transformational leaders uplift teams to surpass expectations, yet their elevated vision may overwhelm novices. Servant leaders develop people holistically but may struggle with execution. Autocrats achieve robust results yet risk disempowering teams. Democrats build consensus but can stall in times needing swift, decisive action. Laissez-faire leaders foster independence, yet their detachment can leave groups directionless.

Situational leadership provides the missing link—an adaptive framework to extract the essence from other styles and apply them appropriately based on your team's needs. This leadership model champions understanding each member deeply to pinpoint their strengths, motivations, and growth areas. With this insight, you can make discerning choices about when to direct, support, and empower based on their readiness levels. Rather than forcing a rigid style onto diverse teams, you meet them where they are and adjust your methods to move them forward.

Yet, to efficiently embrace this adaptative leadership approach, you must continuously improve your core abilities of observation, diagnosis, and communication. Seek to excel in your emotional intelligence and situational awareness so you can skillfully draw upon the full breadth of leadership styles. However, fear not if this approach sounds weird or nonsensical

CHAPTER 2   LEADERSHIP STYLES AND SITUATIONAL LEADERSHIP

initially; with experience, you will synthesize the best from established methodologies and implement them seamlessly based on your team's circumstances. The versatility and human-centeredness make situational leadership a highly effective approach in our fast-changing, complex world.

First Things First: Identifying the Readiness Level

As you adopt a situational approach, an essential first step is assessing your team's development levels across confidence and competence. These two attributes profoundly impact their readiness to perform tasks and roles.

Competence encompasses the skills, knowledge, and expertise to execute responsibilities efficiently. It often links to hands-on exposure and experience gained through practice in diverse scenarios over their career—engagement, and eagerness to learn also boost competence. Meanwhile, confidence represents faith in one's abilities fueled by overcoming challenges and achieving milestones.

Armed with this understanding, you can evaluate your team's readiness through four development levels:

> **Level 1:** Members are bright-eyed newcomers brimming with eagerness despite their lack of experience. Like intrepid explorers, they plunge enthusiastically into unfamiliar territory. However, their skills remain nascent, requiring substantial guidance to grasp role expectations and execute responsibly. Their exuberance may even need tempering to avoid rushing ahead recklessly. Still, their sponge-like absorption of knowledge and guidance is impressive. With careful direction, these novices will swiftly gain competence. It is an exhilarating start to their journey.

Level 2: Members transition from passive learners to active contributors as their know-how improves. However, self-doubt often outpaces their burgeoning competence. Although they understand expectations, they hesitate to take the initiative or work independently. Your coaching must boost their confidence and technical abilities in tandem, so give them room to spread their wings with support until they gain flight. The momentum is building along their journey, and their impact amplifies.

Level 3: Members have grown into competent yet cautious solo contributors. They possess the expertise to deliver quality work independently yet may balk at ownership or decision autonomy. While technically able to fly solo, they seek reassurance before taking flight into more complex tasks or projects. They need encouragement framing their knowledge as strengths rather than areas for self-critique. Progress may seem slow, but the upside is immense once their mindset shifts. At this point, the journey has taken off, but some turbulence remains.

Level 4: Members are veterans brimming with competence, confidence, and initiative. Give them a goal, and they will independently devise and execute strategies with flair. Their adaptability and breadth of skills make them invaluable assets. They thirst for challenges and relish mentoring others. Smooth sailing does not stimulate them; rather, they chart the team's course through unexplored territory. These experts and leaders have reached cruising altitude and help lift others.

CHAPTER 2   LEADERSHIP STYLES AND SITUATIONAL LEADERSHIP

The Compass Within: Navigating Situational Leadership Styles

As your team members progress through distinct stages of development, your leadership approach must also evolve to guide them adeptly. Situational leadership demands adapting your style to each individual's level of competence and confidence, and finding the right blend of directing and delegating, coaching, and supporting is paramount to unlocking their potential.

Let's navigate the leadership styles to steer your team forward:

Directing (S1—for Level 1): In this style, you become the team's guiding light, clearly laying out the path ahead, defining each step and expectation, and providing continuous guidance. Your communication flows one-way as you convey the knowledge and experience to illuminate the way forward and monitor their progress closely, promptly correcting any missteps or errors along their journey. Your team relies heavily on your direction and feedback to advance, like following a compass through unfamiliar terrain. This hands-on and directive approach provides the structure for novices to learn the ropes in a focused and accelerated manner.

Coaching (S2—for Level 2): Here, you add a second layer as a coach to your directing role. While still guiding the way, you now foster two-way dialogue through listening, advising, and motivational feedback. You empower your team to take on more responsibilities, encouraging calculated risks and collaboration. Your guidance helps build their confidence to take the lead occasionally while you provide a safety net as needed. Your team starts owning their development, buoyed by your patient coaching. You advise but also validate their ideas and progress, catalyzing their growth.

Supporting (S3—for Level 3): Your focus morphs from instructor to facilitator as competence increases. You support and reinforce, guiding when asked but empowering your team to direct their progress, boosting their confidence to tackle tasks independently while offering assistance as a supportive sounding board. Your listening and encouragement provide reassurance when they occasionally second-guess themselves. You allow freedom to build ownership but remain present to clarify doubts. This autonomy accelerates their self-sufficiency and decision-making skills.

Delegating (S4—for Level 4): You step back into a monitoring role, fully entrusting your team with responsibility. You provide overall objectives but empower them to devise plans and make decisions. Your involvement is limited to consultations when requested and monitoring for major roadblocks. Otherwise, you believe in their competence to direct their journey. This autonomy helps cement their self-reliance, resourcefulness, and confidence, driving your team members to leverage strategic capabilities at an organizational level.

These four styles form a flexible continuum representing your evolution as a leader. At first, you may rely heavily on directing, incorporating the clear vision and command of autocratic leadership to provide structure and guidance to novices.

As your team develops basic competence through your coaching and support, utilize the inspirational motivation of transformational leadership to encourage team members to reach new heights. Apply servant leadership's deep empathy and ethics to understand members' needs and reassure those needing confidence. Once your team gains more experience, progressively empower them with greater autonomy, channeling the participative decision-making and teamwork of democratic leadership. Give your most seasoned members independence to showcase their skills, embracing the autonomy promoted by laissez-faire leadership. Remember, you must navigate the different types of leadership styles based on the readiness level of your team members.

Situational leadership provides a toolkit to dynamically blend the most useful elements of other styles to lead your unique team most effectively. Recognize when clear directives, inspirational motivation, empathetic support, participative decision-making, or total autonomy are required and shift your approach accordingly.

Situational Leadership and Its Intrinsic Challenges

As you embrace the adaptability of situational leadership, anticipate three prevalent hurdles. First, the relentless evaluation and adaptation required can become mentally exhausting. You must dedicate substantial time to understanding each individual's abilities, motivations, weaknesses, preferred workstyles, and interpersonal dynamics, and this level of personalized engagement across all team members demands immense energy; without proper self-care, burnout looms. Also, solicit insights from others, like technical leads who interact regularly with specific members and avoid trying to diagnose every situation alone.

Secondly, selecting the optimal leadership style for diverse situations can be a tall task, especially in complex engineering projects. Carefully weigh members' proficiency, willingness, task complexity, deadline pressure, and team dynamics before choosing the appropriate leadership style. For example, an experienced engineer may need little oversight on technical work but require encouragement to mentor jittery junior members or tight deadlines may necessitate more directing to keep members focused. You must take a holistic, nuanced view when diagnosing the best approach. Although situational leadership provides a valuable framework, real-world intricacies mean judgment calls are inevitable, so accept that missteps will happen as you hone your diagnostics and routinely seek input from mentors on gray areas.

Finally, inaccurate assessments of your team's readiness lead to ineffective leadership actions. Providing too much support to those needing autonomy or too little guidance when members lack proficiency hinders performance and causes frustration. To mitigate this risk, regularly sample team members across levels for feedback to validate your situational understanding, and if you misjudged someone's needs, embrace it as a growth opportunity, not a personal failure. Use misfires to continually refine your situational awareness, realign your approach, and be willing to apologize sincerely and correct course if your style proves mismatched. Use mistakes to sharpen your leadership.

The Making of an Engineer: A Situational Leadership Case Study

The journey from novice to expert is a tale as old as time. We've all been the wide-eyed rookie, unsure if we could ever attain the effortless mastery of seasoned veterans. For engineers, the path from student to accomplished professional is winding and steep. It takes patience, perseverance, and the guidance of leaders who can adapt to nurture growth at each stage.

CHAPTER 2 LEADERSHIP STYLES AND SITUATIONAL LEADERSHIP

The story of Eli and his manager, Sarah, illustrates the beauty and rewards of situational leadership in action. Let's step into their journey and see how Sarah's ability to diagnose Eli's needs and adjust her leadership style empowered him to transform from an uncertain graduate to a self-assured engineering leader. Their experience offers insights for leaders seeking to unleash others' potential.

On his first day, Eli stepped into the sleek offices of Acme Co., brimming with enthusiasm, ready to soak up all the skills needed to become an expert software engineer. But his eagerness was tempered by self-doubt—could he handle the complexity of real-world projects?

Sarah, his engineering manager, recognized the hunger in Eli's eyes along with the uncertainty in his hesitant posture. She knew she needed to provide meticulous guidance to this promising yet inexperienced newcomer. In the early days, Sarah outlined each task step-by-step, checking frequently on progress and patiently correcting any missteps. She made herself readily available for Eli's endless stream of questions, no matter how basic. Her detailed directives and frank yet compassionate feedback gave Eli a safety net as he navigated many new tools, frameworks, and processes. Over time, comprehension began to replace confusion as Eli grasped the essentials. But he still clung tightly to Sarah's detailed instructions, afraid to veer off-script.

Sensing Eli's growing but fragile understanding, Sarah gradually transitioned to a coaching style. She assigned more ambiguous problems that required Eli to strategize solutions himself, stepping in to ask thoughtful questions that led him to answers rather than giving direct advice. In team meetings, she acknowledged Eli's contributions and validated his ideas, noting areas of improvement using encouraging language.

Under Sarah's wing, Eli slowly unfolded from an uncertain novice into a capable practitioner. He began to speak up more in brainstorming sessions, unafraid to voice half-formed opinions and questions. His valuable insights earned appreciative nods from colleagues.

CHAPTER 2   LEADERSHIP STYLES AND SITUATIONAL LEADERSHIP

As months passed, Sarah noticed Eli completing tasks independently with precision. But he still sought her reassurance before executing anything novel or complex. To nurture confidence, Sarah gave Eli autonomy over an entire module. She made herself available but provided support only when asked. When he inevitably made mistakes, she framed them as learning opportunities, reminding Eli of how far he had come. Her belief in him was unwavering. Soon, Eli shed the last vestiges of self-doubt, tackling challenges with poise and skill. Sarah handed off leadership of critical projects, knowing Eli could direct teams adeptly. His knowledge and unshakable confidence made him the perfect mentor for the next generation of novices.

Sarah reflected fondly on the journey from doubting novice to self-assured expert. Her ability to meet Eli where he was at and guide him to the next level was the key. Now, whenever she saw him mentoring new hires, she knew the seeds she had planted had blossomed into mastery.

Situational leadership demands reading each individual's needs and adopting the appropriate style to unleash their potential. Recognize when to push with clear directives, reassure with compassionate support, and empower with full delegation. This discernment allows you to blend the most valuable elements of other styles and help each person excel.

Keep assessing your team's growth and adjust your leadership style accordingly. The beauty of this approach is its acknowledgment that it needs to evolve. You must remain agile and responsive, dynamically integrating the principles that best serve your team in each moment. With dedication and persistence, your situational leadership will unlock unlimited potential in your team.

CHAPTER 2   LEADERSHIP STYLES AND SITUATIONAL LEADERSHIP

Choosing the Right Leadership Style for Your Team

Determining the optimal leadership approach for your team is a complex endeavor requiring remarkable perceptiveness and adaptability once there is no one-size-fits-all solution. Leadership styles like transformational, servant, democratic, and laissez-faire offer valuable principles and mindsets. However, their efficacy depends significantly on the specific situation, team composition, organizational culture, and individuals involved.

Transformational leadership can generate momentum by inspiring teams toward bold, shared visions. Its emphasis on framing work as pursuing higher ideals and purposes can compel team members to exceed expectations. However, taken too far, transformational leadership risks overwhelming teams with impossibly high expectations and over-structuring their efforts.

Servant leadership builds trust and engagement by prioritizing ethical service to teammates' growth and well-being. It focuses on understanding individuals empathetically and holistically supporting their needs to foster solid communal bonds. However, servant leadership's heavy emphasis on nurturing risks complacency and aimlessness without complementary approaches to drive execution and accountability.

Democratic leadership unlocks innovation, commitment, and inclusive thinking by engaging team members actively in decisions through consensus-building and majority rules. Its participatory approach gives everyone a voice. However, democracy's extensive deliberation and collaboration can stall progress and decisive action without counterbalancing elements of executive decision-making.

Laissez-faire leadership can empower experienced, self-driven teams through extensive autonomy and freedom. However, taken to an extreme, its hands-off approach can foster a lack of alignment, inadequate support for struggling team members, and diffusion of focus and urgency.

CHAPTER 2   LEADERSHIP STYLES AND SITUATIONAL LEADERSHIP

Situational leadership provides a helpful model for matching leadership approaches to team members' specific developmental levels across competence and confidence. By accurately diagnosing individuals' needs, situational leadership allows adapting, directing, coaching, supporting, and delegating styles to catalyze growth. However, rigid adherence to any one framework often backfires in complex contexts.

The hallmark of successful leaders is accurately diagnosing their team's evolving needs and motivations and then adapting their style accordingly. This blend of perceptiveness and adaptability enables applying the most relevant strengths of various approaches situationally to guide teams forward effectively. That said, the "right" style aligns with your team's unique needs, motivations, and circumstances; avoid rigid adherence to any one style or theory. Instead, stay receptive, constantly learning, assessing, and thoughtfully evolving your approach.

Leadership demands courage, empathy, and dedication to support your team holistically. By embracing nuance over formulas, you unlock your leadership potential and become a better professional and person. Reflect on experiences, listen to feedback, and keep developing your situational awareness. Your perception, adaptability, and growth mindset will compound, making you an increasingly influential leader.

Takeaways

1. Autocratic leadership provides clear direction through centralized control but risks disempowering teams.
2. Autocracy streamlines decision-making but can stifle innovation, development, and timely awareness of issues.

CHAPTER 2   LEADERSHIP STYLES AND SITUATIONAL LEADERSHIP

3. Blending autocracy with some servant leadership empathy and transformational motivation retains benefits while mitigating burdens.

4. Transformational leadership inspires teams by connecting work to a higher purpose and intellectually stimulating followers.

5. The four I's—Inspirational Motivation, Intellectual Stimulation, Individualized Consideration, and Idealized Influence—form transformational leadership's core.

6. Transformational leadership risks impossibly high expectations, loss of momentum, organizational fragmentation, and complacency without vigilance.

7. Servant leadership focuses on ethical service to teammates' growth and well-being through empathy, humility, deep listening, and foresight.

8. Servant leadership risks perceived inefficiency, eroding authority, and aimlessness without balancing empowerment with accountability.

9. Servant leadership complements autocratic decisiveness and transformational motivation when blended prudently.

10. Democratic leadership fosters inclusion and innovation by promoting participation, collaboration, and consensus-building.

11. Democracy risks prolonged decision-making, conflicts, design by committee, and inertia without decisive leadership balance.

12. Laissez-faire leadership grants experienced teams autonomy to unlock ingenuity but risks a lack of alignment and direction without oversight.

13. Laissez-faire autonomy complements transformational vision, servant leadership support, and democratic participation when applied judiciously.

14. Situational leadership adapts directing, coaching, supporting, and delegating styles to team members' specific competence and confidence levels.

15. Situational leadership provides a flexible framework to appropriately apply the most useful elements of other styles.

16. Situational leadership demands relentless evaluation of team needs and motivations to pinpoint optimal leadership approaches.

17. The right leadership style aligns with the team's unique needs, motivations, and circumstances rather than rigidly adhering to one system.

Time to Practice

1. Reflect deeply on an experience as a leader where you needed to make an important decision that would significantly impact your team or organization. Carefully analyze your approach in that scenario—did you choose autonomously using your judgment or involve your team democratically by gathering diverse inputs and building consensus?

CHAPTER 2   LEADERSHIP STYLES AND SITUATIONAL LEADERSHIP

2. Recall a specific scenario when you needed to motivate your team to higher performance or re-engage them during a challenging period. Did you attempt to inspire them through bold, ambitious vision-setting and passionate encouragement to exceed their limits? Or did you focus more on deeply empathizing with their needs and emotionally supporting them?

3. Consider a scenario where you noticed a team member struggling with a task. How did you diagnose the reasons behind their challenges? Did you pinpoint gaps in their competence or confidence levels? Once identified, how did you adapt your leadership approach to provide more direction or support based on their needs? For instance, if they lacked skills, did you switch to a more directive style with detailed coaching? Or if they needed confidence, did you motivate them more inspirationally? How can you become even more discerning in assessing individuals' competence and confidence gaps to continue adapting your style situationally?

4. What patterns emerge about your innate preferences toward certain leadership styles based on reflecting on your past experiences? For example, do you lean more toward participative or directive approaches? What insights does this provide into your strengths and areas for growth as a leader?

5. Considering your natural leadership style preferences and development areas, what 1-2 leadership principles from this chapter will you focus on first to expand your approach? For instance, how can you integrate more empathy if you tend to be more directive?

6. Reflecting on your journey, what 2-3 leadership styles feel most intuitive to you so far? For example, do you lean more autocratic or democratic? How might you push yourself to blend in elements of other, less comfortable styles to become more well-rounded?

CHAPTER 3

Collaboration and Team Dynamics

The leadership styles we explored serve only as tools—they alone can't stimulate human potential. However, mastering leadership requires looking beyond strategies to nurture your team's passion and capabilities. While these leadership models serve as relevant pieces to complete the puzzle, your team's cohesion and complementary skills are critical to exponentially accelerating the organization's overall success. From the moment you dedicate yourself to creating individual bonds and adapting your leadership style to meet the current needs of the group and individuals, your team becomes an unstoppable collective force, united in purpose and multiplied in talent. On the other hand, a fragmented and disengaged group struggles to succeed despite your best efforts as a leader. The difference is in emotional intelligence and situational awareness to foster trust, resolve conflicts, align values, and reveal interdependence.

This chapter covers techniques for strengthening bonds and extracting synergies through diversity, and you'll learn ways to navigate personal relationships and discover motivations to resonate with your team's aspirations. You will also learn to reshape perspectives through storytelling and overcome divisions by revealing shared humanity. Master interpersonal leadership, and your team will excel technically. Lead with compassion, communicate with courage, and resolve tensions wisely—here is the key to community and fulfillment.

CHAPTER 3   COLLABORATION AND TEAM DYNAMICS

No matter how good your situational awareness and leadership style is, maintaining synergy in your team dynamics and collaboration is an arduous and often scary path. In the meantime, remember your journey so far and your abilities. Regardless of the situation, you must lead with your heart, reasoning, and hope. Human potential often remains dormant, and only a good leader can awaken a person's most hidden abilities. Still, it is necessary to recognize that there are no shortcuts to creating a solid team where collaboration is a premise. This requires dedication, effort, and genuine interest in getting to know the people around you beyond the professional environment; you must look at the human core and unlock potential through connection and collaboration.

To begin this journey, we will explore techniques for discovering the individuality of each team member. Understanding their unique strengths, motivations, and aspirations is the first step to nurturing your potential and aligning your skills to multiply the team's success.

Uncovering the Individuality Within Your Team

As a leader, understanding your team at an individual level is as imperative as understanding the business needs to optimize results and unlock your organization's full potential. You must avoid focusing solely on project management, velocity, and output. You lead people; thus, it requires recognizing that you can only ignite excellence within your team by first comprehending the unique attributes of each member. Although collaboration relies on aligning professional goals, lasting loyalty stems from personal connections. By digging beneath the surface to reveal the individuality within your team, you transform your rapport from transactional to transformational.

Connecting with individuals' strengths, weaknesses, values, and principles requires dedicating time to deeper one-on-one conversations. This investment offers exponential returns by shedding light on motivations, work styles, and development needs you may have otherwise overlooked. Equipped with richer context, you can play to each person's strengths, tailor coaching, and stretch opportunities, fostering environments where they can excel. Rather than leading through top-down assignments, you tap into the wellspring of potential within your team.

Moreover, uncovering individuality enables adjusting your leadership style to resonate with each team member. Adapting how you communicate, delegate, motivate, and develop based on personal preferences improves engagement and outcomes. You build higher levels of mutual understanding and trust by showing engineers you see them for their unique abilities and perspectives, not just as fungible resources. Although time-intensive upfront, this foundation gives your team resilience to weather future challenges united, not divided.

Forging Authentic Leadership Connections: A 4-Session Framework

As observed in the previous sections of this book, developing open and trusting relationships with your team is the foundation for empowering their growth and maximizing their potential. However, you can't force or rush to build authentic connections; you must build them over time with persistence, diligence, and passion. What follows next is a helpful framework to support you in nurturing meaningful relationships with your reports and peers. The framework is suitable for whatever situation, but it holds a special significance whenever joining a new team or onboarding a new member, once the relationship starts from scratch and unknowns.

This 4-session framework guides you through crucial conversations that enable candid partnerships grounded in mutual growth and focus on setting ground rules, understanding personal stories and dreams, and

CHAPTER 3   COLLABORATION AND TEAM DYNAMICS

setting expectations for leaders and reports. By courageously approaching more personal topics in a professional setting, you demonstrate your sincere commitment to seeing the whole person, not just their output.

While initially uncomfortable, resisting transactional tendencies leads to transformational bonds rooted in common purpose and care for the individual. When you dedicate yourself to unveiling the authentic human behind the professional persona, you gain priceless context to nurture their development in alignment with their inner drivers and values. This holistic understanding accelerates team success by unlocking discretionary effort and longevity.

Session 1: Preparing the Ground

Set aside at least 45 minutes for this introductory session focused on laying the foundation for your partnership as a leader. Begin with introductions and relationship-building—background, hobbies, and professional trajectory. Then, seek to understand how the engineer prefers receiving feedback and communicating. Do they choose direct and candid input or oblique suggestions cloaked constructively? Do they process better in written form or verbally? Next, outline ground rules and expectations for your one-on-one meetings. How frequently should you meet? Will there be standing agenda items or free discussion? Are there boundaries around vulnerable sharing? Do they prefer a formal or informal tone? Aligning these topics beforehand breaks the ice, fosters psychological safety, removes uncertainties, and establishes the tone to build trust.

Additionally, discuss preferred communication mediums and styles outside formal meetings. Does async messages, email, or calls work best? Can you mention them publicly, or do they like privacy? How do they like to treat themselves? What are their preferred working hours, and how can you adapt the team demands with their personal preferences to create a win-win situation?

Finally, explain your intention to invest in their development and enhance their success through collaboration. Share that you base your leadership approach on mutual understanding and partnership, and explain your working methods and leadership style. Briefly describe the objectives of the following three sessions and emphasize that these discussions aim to discover motivations, dreams, and expectations so that you can understand the best way to contribute to their growth in a personalized way. Once the expectations around your development investment in them are clear, you're ready for subsequent conversations.

Session 2: Life Story

The life story conversation represents the first critical step to understanding what truly motivates each person in your team. Set aside at least one hour of uninterrupted time for this one-on-one discussion, and in advance, explain that the objective is to hear their life experiences from childhood through the present; this conversation requires deep reflection and preparation. Ask them to vividly share memories of growing up, recall impactful events throughout their infancy, and chronologically recount major professional and personal milestones and transitions.

As they narrate pivotal moments, listen intently for insights into their enduring passions and evolving aspirations. Still, resist the natural impulse to turn this dialogue into a standard performance discussion focused on skills, projects, or responsibilities. This conversation is not about their output but about their underlying drivers. Allow them to open up at their own pace, and make it clear through your body language and engaged listening that you are prioritizing their story.

Pay close attention when they describe inflection points of change in their life's trajectory. Ask thoughtful follow-up questions to unpack the motivations and priorities behind those pivotal choices. For example, if they made a bold career switch, delve into the reasons that compelled them to take such an impactful risk. Or, if they turned down a lucrative promotion, probe to understand why prestige and advancement were not their top considerations.

Capture the key motivational themes that emerge from the arc of their life story. Feelings of financial insecurity, desire for personal growth, work-life balance, and leaving a legacy for the future—these deeper motivators often emerge in the timeline of their experiences. Notice where their priorities have changed over the years as new responsibilities and perspectives have shaped their view of the world. Listen carefully to the elements that give meaning and purpose to their life and let go of any preconceived assumptions you may have formed; avoid making judgments based on superficial stereotypes. Let their authentic story expand your understanding of the unique motivations forged along their journey.

However, be alert for signs of discomfort if you surface some specific topics they may not wish to discuss now; this conversation requires trust, so be patient and believe in the process. While aiming for openness, respect their boundaries if they refuse or show resistance to elaborate on sensitive aspects of their upbringing or personal lives. In those cases, gently change the subject and refocus the dialogue on less private recollections to avoid shutting down the sharing of their story. Rebuilding that openness and trust can take time.

Session 3: Dreams

To start, set aside at least one hour for the Dreams conversation to create space for deep reflection. Explain to the individual that the objective is to openly share both professional aspirations and personal dreams beyond their career. You must intentionally use the term *"dreams"* rather than more professional phrases like "goals" or "ambitions" to send signals that you want to uncover their most profound visions for a life well-lived, not just professional advancement.

Encourage introspection into three or four pivotal dreams representing their highest ideals and a sense of purpose across all life domains. With only a short list of dreams to focus on, they will feel comfortable tapping into sources of meaning beyond their daily job. For example, they may share dreams of raising a family, writing a book, or starting a nonprofit side hustle. Raising a family stems from the motivation of nurturing lifelong connections through parenthood; writing a book can be driven by desires for self-expression, leaving a legacy, or sharing knowledge; founding a nonprofit organization often comes from deep passions around a cause like society, education, or the environment. Personal dreams like these can reveal motivations for fulfillment, creativity, and purpose that climbing the corporate career ladder alone can't provide.

Next, as the individual describes future visions of achievement or legacy, listen with genuine curiosity, no matter how unconventional the dream is, and expect thoughtful pauses as they search internally to articulate buried passions. Embrace moments of silence rather than rushing to fill gaps. Silence creates space for authentic revelations, not just predictable responses tailored to an audience, allowing them time to find the courage to share intimate aspirations they rarely vocalize aloud.

Then, explore collaboratively how current work responsibilities could expand to incorporate skills, knowledge, or experiences that may enable specific dreams. For instance, an engineer hoping to launch a creative side business could build relevant expertise by leading brainstorming workshops, design sprints, or planning team initiatives. You may discover unexpected connections between professional development and personal growth with an open mindset.

Conclude the conversation by mutually defining one or two tangible next steps for each dream that could involve introducing them to helpful resources or contacts or tailoring their work to build relevant skills. Outlining actionable progress indicators demonstrates your support for breeding their ambitions over time. Show you are keen to invest in their growth beyond career advancement by helping them thoughtfully weave dreams into their professional development.

CHAPTER 3   COLLABORATION AND TEAM DYNAMICS

Session 4: Setting Expectations

Set aside at least 45 minutes for the Expectations conversation to openly discuss responsibilities and needs. Begin by asking probing questions to grasp how the engineer perceives their role and priorities fully. Get them to explain their typical duties, objectives, and challenges in their own words. Listen closely for any misalignments between their view of the role and the actual expectations you or the company have set, and gently surface ambiguities or gaps in awareness that could benefit from clarity.

Next, transparently outline your standards, priorities, and stretch goals for their performance and development in this role. While covering core responsibilities, you may deliberately push boundaries to accelerate their growth. For example, if cross-team mentoring could build leadership skills, consider enhancing expectations to include that stretching opportunity even if not formally required. Or make it clear that you expect every engineer to take the initiative to grasp the root causes behind issues, not just follow prescribed solutions. Set the expectation to constantly question *"why"* something is happening, even if they lack seniority.

Finally, invite the engineer to share what they expect and need from you as their manager to excel and feel empowered. People may feel surprised by this question and automatically deliver a generic answer. If that's the case, persist and ask the same question again. Listen to expectations around hands-on training versus autonomy, resources versus interference, honest feedback versus praise, and many others. Some expectations may look simple, but they are significant for the person. This two-way dialogue builds trust and empathy by demonstrating that you care about their perspective. Through this candid exchange, both parties gain alignment on the role while respecting needs and boundaries, and you empower your team member to maximize their contributions and pursue growth opportunities.

Illuminating Inner Motivations: Unearthing Hidden Values and Evolving Principles

To influence lasting change in an individual, you must understand the roots that nurture their growth and development. Consider your external behaviors, like the visible leaves of a tree swaying flexibly in the wind. Although these behaviors constantly change based on circumstances, they are supported and influenced by the attitudes of the individuals representing the branches. Attitudes can bend and adapt, remaining solidly linked to the metaphorical trunk. This firm trunk symbolizes the individual's deeply held beliefs, cultivated firmly from the fundamental values and principles buried beneath the surface, like the extensive root system of a tree hidden from view, providing stability, nutrients, and life. These roots of values and principles remain invisible, stored deep in the unconscious mind. But they inform every decision, opinion, and action the individual takes, shaping the trunk of beliefs, the branches of attitudes, and the leaves of observable behaviors.

Although principles remain steady over time, values can shift as people experience major life events, new responsibilities, and changing priorities. For example, consider an engineer who arrives at your company cherishing prestige, competition, and individual accomplishments cultivated from an intense work culture in their previous role, driven to stand out and win at all costs. However, after several months of immersion in your team's collaborative, supportive environment, they start reshaping their values. Contributing to group success emerges as an essential driver that was dormant before rather than succeeding as a solo player.

You notice this shift reflected in their attitudes and behaviors. They voluntarily spend most of their time helping teammates meet deadlines and grow, even if it means sacrificing individual goals. In meetings, they highlight group accomplishments before their wins and eagerly mentor juniors rather than hoarding knowledge to stay ahead.

This example illuminates why regularly uncovering both established and emerging values is critical for a leader. When you recognize that a person's values have evolved from individual achievement to team success, you gain context to nurture opportunities aligned with their reshaped motivations. In this case, you could emphasize cross-functional collaboration rather than solo projects, encourage leading team initiatives rather than individual tasks, and expand mentoring of junior engineers to tap into their renewed purpose. Unless you grasp this evolution, you may keep assigning standalone work that now demotivates them by mismatching their shifting values.

Beyond specific opportunities, leaders aware of value changes can coach their team members to recognize the shifts. Raise self-awareness by asking targeted questions focused on what is important to them about their work, interests, and aspirations now versus when they started. Ask follow-ups like "What else is important to you about how you spend your time now?" to uncover their evolving drivers.

Very quickly, let's picture how this conversation could happen:

> **You:** What was important to you about your work when you started here?
>
> **Engineer:** I really enjoyed the intellectual challenge and sense of personal accomplishment from independently solving complex engineering problems.
>
> **You:** Nice, so you like solving complex problems. What is important to you about solving complex problems?
>
> **Engineer:** I've come to appreciate the reward of helping and teaching teammates to tackle tricky issues together.

CHAPTER 3   COLLABORATION AND TEAM DYNAMICS

You: When you tackle those problems collaboratively, they sound funnier to solve, right? But what else is important to you about solving complex problems?

Engineer: That's true. Time flies when we are solving them together. I now care more about deeply understanding the business impact and user value beyond technical elegance.

You: It sounds like you originally valued the self-affirmation and pleasure from solving hard problems yourself. But over time, collaboration with others and delivering broader business value have emerged as more important drivers. Does that resonate?

Engineer: Yes, you're right—I've shifted to valuing teamwork and customer impact more than just exercising my skills independently. I love to understand how the solutions we build impact business and customers. Interesting insight!

Make uncovering established and emerging values a consistent habit through curiosity and focused questions. An individual's values provide glimpses into their deepest motivations and shape the opportunities and guidance you offer as their leader. However, avoid acting on assumptions—always get confirmation that your conclusions about their values resonate with their lived experience—notice the *"Does that resonate?"* part in the example. You are helping surface unconscious values, not making decrees.

As a leader, tend carefully to the shifting motivational roots of your team members with patience and understanding, and recognize that an individual's values may evolve and grow in new directions, just as a tree's branches can, as life changes shape them over time. While values may shift, trust that the essence of who a person is remains steady. Adapt your support as their new priorities emerge while respecting their inner integrity. Yet, remember, your role is not to control their growth but to nurture conditions that empower their development. Promote their increasing self-awareness, and let that illuminate their path forward.

The journey to know your people's authentic selves requires perseverance, but reaching the destination fuels their rise and your organization's success. While you may feel pressed for time or tempted to focus solely on output, resisting cutting corners and investing in understanding motivations and dreams in one-on-one conversations pay exponential dividends over the long term, even if initially arduous. Moreover, when you comprehend an engineer's origin story, you gain precious context to nurture their growth in alignment with inner drivers, allowing you to create opportunities personalized to their values and passions to satisfy soul-deep needs.

Finally, candidly aligning expectations creates clarity while respecting both parties' needs and establishes the foundations of trust and mutual understanding through consistent commitment, allowing a sacred partnership to emerge and drive individual and shared success.

While long, the journey you embark on together traverses meaningful terrain: from young dreams to maturing values, from past experiences to future ambitions, from misalignment to aligned purpose. At the journey's end, human potential realizes itself fully. But most rewarding of all, you traverse it together.

Cultivating Trust Through Accountability, Integrity, and Restorative Leadership

Trust is one of the most critical elements to building a solid leadership character and becoming an effective and efficient engineering leader. If people don't trust you, you will struggle in vain to inspire, motivate, and guide your team thrive. Reliability entails more than just competence in technical skills and expertise; it requires honesty, transparency, vulnerability, and emotional trustworthiness in your actions and communications.

When your team members trust you, they believe you have their best interests in mind, and they trust that you will stand up for them, protect their needs, and support their growth, even if it means pushing back against pressure from above. With trust, your staff knows you will be consistent, fair, and follow through on commitments, not just pay lip service. Your openness, integrity, and care for their well-being are fundamental to setting the tone for how the group collaborates and works together.

This profound faith liberates team members from being authentic without fear of judgment or retaliation. Psychological safety flourishes, fueling creative dissent, innovation, and a solutions-focused mindset during disagreements. Your team knows you have their back during challenging times, and they understand setbacks won't jeopardize their reputation or position. This safety net encourages them to focus on navigating obstacles, not worrying about potential blame or job security.

In the absence of trust, however, none of this is possible. Your team hesitates to share vulnerabilities, disagree openly, or admit mistakes if they doubt your intentions, masking their true feelings and needs, defaulting to self-protection, and avoiding risks that may expose weaknesses. Vital information gets buried; you lose visibility into problems until they fester into crises—misalignment and cynicism toward leadership creep in, and progress stalls. That's why nurturing trust must remain an unwavering priority for every leader. Consistently demonstrate your compassion through actions, admit your limitations humbly, allow yourself to be vulnerable and receptive to feedback, and explain the rationale behind decisions transparently. Make it safe for people to come to you with concerns early.

CHAPTER 3   COLLABORATION AND TEAM DYNAMICS

Leading By Example: The Catalyst of Trust

As we dig deeper into trust, we see that it fundamentally depends on leaders demonstrating reliability and integrity daily. Leading by example moves from an abstract principle to a concrete requirement. Yet, it's easy for leaders to proudly advocate for these values in speeches or written policies. But words on paper mean little if a leader's behaviors contradict stated principles. This *"do as I say, not as I do"* style severely corrodes team trust and morale.

Your teams watch you closely—they notice your actions deviate from advertised values every time, even if you hope no one is looking. When you demand extraordinary diligence from people but then consistently miss deadlines yourself, it breeds cynicism. People see through the hypocrisy of preaching accountability yet deflecting blame for failures we spearheaded, and double standards signal that the rules binding workers don't apply equally to leadership. Over time, this perception destroys motivation and sparks resentment once people feel leaders place burdensome expectations on others that they won't carry themselves. Soon, your teams start mirroring your own indifference rather than the stated principles.

Extensive research in leadership psychology demonstrates this link between modeled consistency and heightened trust. Seminal work by experts like James Kouzes and Barry Posner reveals that when leaders model consistency between their words and deeds, their team members feel far more confident embracing their vision; they see the leader's past actions as an accurate forecast of future reliability. This stability liberates team members to take risks and make themselves vulnerable, knowing their leader has proven their relentless support.

Still, leading by example amid immense stress requires emotional discipline and perseverance. Under pressure, it's tempting to abandon ideals and take convenient shortcuts. But your teams ultimately judge you by your worst behaviors during those pivotal crucible moments, not your best intentions. Exhaustion from long hours or urgency from approaching deadlines may obscure your vision, causing you to make rushed decisions that contradict your values. In these times, pausing for deep reflection rather than reaction becomes vital. You must recognize your limitations—gather your thoughts, and act for the right.

Cultivating Accountability, Earning Trust

Trust lies at the heart of effective leadership, and accountability is a vital mechanism for building trust within your teams. However, you can't envision accountability as a top-down mandate. Instead, it must become ingrained as a cultural norm across your team through persistent nurturing of shared ownership.

As a leader, you can spearhead this culture shift by implementing organizational structures that promote clarity and responsibility. Start by clearly defining individual roles and responsibilities so no ambiguity exists about who owns which initiatives. Institute collaborative and measurable goals to benchmark progress transparently, not assumed opaquely. Maintain routine touchpoints for status reviews to surface roadblocks before they escalate, and ensure the team understands they are also responsible for mapping and mitigating any potential risks that damage the team dynamics over time.

Additionally, you must facilitate constructive handling of inevitable missteps through collective learning rather than finger-pointing; creating a blameless culture must be your priority when building trust. Refrain from targeting individuals during retrospectives to facilitate psychological safety and encourage openness among the team; guide teams to strengthen skills and safeguards in unison and frame accountability as enabling excellence, not penalizing failure.

Furthermore, genuine peer accountability requires establishing norms of caring personally yet challenging directly with candid feedback and mutual trust. You empower it by modeling and giving empathetic feedback focused on improvement rather than criticism. For example, praise your junior engineer's efficient algorithms and logical flow during a code review before constructively challenging them to strengthen error handling by incorporating more informative logging and exception-catching. The care shown in noticing their strengths builds rapport, laying the groundwork for receptive growth from your candid feedback on areas needing improvement. Highlight growth through team members holding each other accountable and rotate facilitators of retrospectives to broaden ownership. Make responsibility a habit for your team, especially those in early-stage careers.

Moreover, consider forming cross-functional "responsibility groups" with autonomy while maintaining overall alignment through experienced oversight. Allow both senior and junior staff to undertake meaningful leadership roles, as accountability should never be limited to the upper echelons alone. For junior engineers, responsibility groups empower taking ownership of substantial components rather than isolated tasks, gaining experience in making architectural decisions and interfacing with stakeholders. In contrast, seniors provide guidance, accelerating their ability to design, execute, and lead projects autonomously. These groups enable you to coach senior members to become more influential through firsthand collaboration, proving wisdom and oversight but avoiding micromanaging. You let them gain insight into their rising talent and gradually help them transfer relevant knowledge to junior members. This strategy is the magical formula to facilitate professional development on both sides.

Transforming team culture requires persistence, as it is difficult to break old habits. However, the immense benefits of trust, engagement, and excellence make it worth persevering through setbacks. Progressively, your team internalizes accountability, viewing it as liberating rather than confining. This entrenched accountability strengthens trust, enabling teams to reach new heights.

CHAPTER 3   COLLABORATION AND TEAM DYNAMICS

Restoring Trust After It's Broken

While cultivating trust across your team remains essential, reality inevitably arises where trust gets compromised through errors or lapses in judgment. Trust is fragile—once compromised, it requires relentless effort, persistence, and hard work to get it back, and as a leader, how you respond to these fractures within your team can make or break the team dynamics and collaboration among team members ultimately.

First, acknowledge the breach openly and authentically rather than sugarcoating the problem or avoiding difficult conversations. When trust breaches, your team looks to you to respond with courage, compassion, and sincerity, and the attempt to gloss over issues or restore normalcy too quickly will backfire by deepening doubts. Instead, confront problems head-on confidently and demonstrate a willingness to lean into the discomfort to restore the team. This behavior signals remorse for lost trust, reaffirms shared values, and kick-starts the healing process, demonstrating you want to address the problem with humility and integrity.

Next, dedicate time to investigate root causes thoroughly yet objectively before drawing conclusions; it's vital not to jump the gun or let emotions cloud judgment. Facilitate retrospectives for open dialogue and distribute anonymous surveys to understand different perspectives. Have one-on-one conversations with involved parties to grasp their vantage points fully. Dig into records and data for insights on where communication or system breakdowns occurred. Remember, you must navigate these discussions with empathy, wisdom, and emotional intelligence, resisting confirmation bias. Explore conflicting accounts and inconsistencies without defensiveness and gather comprehensive context from all sides before defining the core issues. The goal is to map root causes, not reactively ascribe blame accurately.

Then, facilitate open and honest team dialogue through a faultless meeting framework. Establish ground rules upfront, like "assume positive intent" and "explore ideas without judging" to foster psychological

CHAPTER 3   COLLABORATION AND TEAM DYNAMICS

safety, and structure the discussion to allow all affected parties space to voice their perspective, concerns, and feelings about the trust breach. Listen attentively without interruption and probe gently to understand underlying issues. Equally important is to set time expectations upfront so everyone feels heard but understands that a conclusion is needed. Even though a breach of trust requires urgency to get restored, you must offer space for people to process events and air unresolved issues safely. Suppressing tensions will only worsen them.

After providing a forum for addressing the team's concerns, outline actionable steps to rebuild trust through revised incentives, new communication workflows, leader/team training, or other structural improvements. Set clear expectations, follow through consistently, and continuously monitor team interactions through one-on-one sessions, surveys, and tracking interaction metrics.

Understand that rebuilding broken trust requires persistence, compassion, and leadership resolve. So, don't get frustrated if you don't see an immediate change in the team's posture. With dedication, resilience, and empathy, you can transform trust breaches into growth opportunities that ultimately strengthen team bonds for the long term, fostering renewed cohesion and generative culture. But this first requires confronting hard truths openly, listening with care, and learning together.

Navigating the Minefield: Mastering Conflict Management

Conflict is an inevitable reality within engineering teams. As you lead a group composed of seasoned veterans, rising stars, and ambitious newcomers, disagreements and tensions will undoubtedly emerge. Managing conflict represents one of the most vital yet tricky balancing acts for any leader. Although some conflict proves harmful and corrosive, the right kinds of creative friction can spark innovation, sharpen critical thinking, and yield improved solutions. That said, you must not label every conflict as detrimental, but instead, you must reflect to distinguish productive conflicts that add value from destructive disputes that fracture team cohesion.

Spotting these team disruptions early and intervening promptly are critical to avoid escalation. As a leader, remain alert to shifts in team dynamics that signal simmering conflicts under the surface. Watch for increased tension during meetings, terse message exchanges, avoidance behaviors, or sudden drop-offs in collaboration between certain members. Also, look for signs like lack of enthusiasm or engagement during collaborative work, which may indicate team members are preoccupied with interpersonal issues rather than focused on the task. Increased unconstructive criticism during feedback suggests personal frustrations are bleeding into emotional debates. Furthermore, avoiding responsibility and blaming behaviors when issues crop up, rather than taking ownership, signals a lack of psychological safety, preventing honest discussion. You must probe these cues gently through one-on-one conversations to understand root causes before they catch fire.

The Most Common Shades of Conflict

You will encounter various forms of conflict as you progress in your journey as a leader. Technical disagreements frequently arise as engineers debate architectural decisions, analyze trade-offs, and reconcile diverse perspectives. For instance, your team may lock horns on whether to build a feature natively or integrate a third-party service. Resource allocation conflicts also flare up as teams juggle priorities and make tough choices on budget, staffing, and time investments. Politics and power struggles occasionally rear their head, especially during reorgs.

Most challenging, however, are interpersonal conflicts rooted in clashing work styles, values, or personalities. Unlike technical debates, these conflicts often turn personal and emotional, and when left unchecked, they can poison team chemistry and output. As frustrations with colleagues mount, people disengage during meetings, dread collaborating across subgroups, and withdraw from team activities. Negative gossip spreads, and overall motivation plummets amid the tension, making the team focus more on navigating personal landmines than solving technical problems. You must see interpersonal conflicts as snowballs: If not managed promptly, once started, it will breed anxiety, erode trust, harm output, and cause talent bleed, and your team's performance will decline. The finish line is one: your team members will start quitting to escape the toxic environment.

Fostering Open Dialogue to Resolve Conflicts

Transparent, open communication represents the lifeblood of managing conflict skillfully, and you must cultivate an environment where people feel psychologically safe candidly discussing issues without fear of reprisal or judgment. Establishing norms for respectful, compassionate dialogue makes bringing up concerns feel constructive rather than risky.

Start with promoting openness through leading by example—be receptive to feedback, admit your own mistakes, and demonstrate that you welcome transparency. Make yourself approachable by keeping an open door, managing by walking around, and looking to people as people, not resources. Spend time reflecting on what you can set to facilitate the communication of emerging conflicts, such as creating forums for airing issues, periodic touchpoints, anonymous surveys, staff meetings with open agendas, and one-on-one focused on listening. Then, set the expectation that speaking up about disagreements early prevents more significant problems later; discourage stewing in silence or backchannel gossip. When conflict arises, resist the urge to minimize concerns or force quick solutions. Instead, listen earnestly, probe to understand all perspectives, and let people feel heard. Even if you disagree with the complaint, acknowledge people's right to voice it.

CHAPTER 3   COLLABORATION AND TEAM DYNAMICS

Mediating Disputes and Facilitating Constructive Dialogue

As a leader, you must often step into roles mediating disagreements or facilitating team discussions to navigate conflict productively.

Mediation involves a neutral third party guiding conflicting groups toward mutually acceptable solutions and excels at resolving complex or emotional conflicts where an outside perspective is required. As a mediator, refrain from imposing outcomes. Instead, you must enable open communication and exploration of options. For example, you may mediate a tense conflict between two engineers on your team who have had an interpersonal falling out due to clashing work styles. After understanding perspectives privately, you bring them together to openly air grievances under the ground rules you set, helping to humanize each side to the other, prompting reflections on unintended harms. With time, they agree to specific behavioral changes and communication norms to work together professionally.

Facilitation encompasses broader skills for guiding collaborative discussions, not just disputes. As a facilitator, you optimize information flow, ensure all voices get heard, and keep conversations productive. You promote regular team conversations by drawing insights from quieter members, steering off-topic tangents back on track, and managing time constraints. During the conflict, facilitation transforms heated debates into constructive dialogue through active listening, guiding awareness of other perspectives, and identifying shared interests. For instance, during a heated retrospective analyzing recent project failures, you facilitate by encouraging empathy, discouraging finger-pointing, and steering the tone toward mutual learning. You draw insights from quiet members, probe for root causes, and focus the discussion on process improvements.

As a leader, you must gauge when stepping into mediator and facilitator roles becomes necessary, such as when conflicts disrupt team cohesion or output. Tread carefully, as involvement risks escalating tensions. First, have private conversations to gauge whether your intervention would further help or strain relationships. When you engage, take an impartial, objective stance and avoid power struggles or displays of authority. Your influence flows from trust and empathy, not formal power. Success means resolving issues to mutual benefit, not proclaiming winners or losers. With skill and compassion, mediation and facilitation represent potent tools for transmuting conflict into growth.

Mastering the Art of Mediation and Facilitation

When stepping into the role of mediator or facilitator during team conflicts, adhere to certain fundamental principles and skills to steer the discourse toward constructive resolution. Mediating heated debates and facilitating thoughtful dialogue amid tension represent nuanced arts requiring wisdom, impartiality, and emotional intelligence.

Though each situation differs, the following guidelines form a framework for effectively catalyzing communication, mutual understanding, and creative problem-solving. Internalize these principles through repeated application, self-reflection after conflicts, and soliciting candid feedback on areas needing growth. Over time, your ability to mediate disagreements and draw out the best collective thinking will compound and become a cornerstone of your leadership.

Maintaining impartiality remains paramount when mediating heated debates. Refrain from favoring specific solutions or taking sides, even if you have personal biases. Never let your tone or body language reveal favoritism, as people will notice subtle cues. Demonstrate that you hear each perspective fairly by accurately restating the core arguments from all sides, and balance airtime distribution and how you respond to feuding groups. If you lose neutrality, your mediation ability erodes, so continually self-reflect on your inner reactions.

CHAPTER 3   COLLABORATION AND TEAM DYNAMICS

Actively listen without interrupting as people voice concerns. Don't just wait for your turn to talk—give your full attention. Reflect on key points to confirm understanding. Ask clarifying and open-ended questions to fully grasp issues and probe for underlying needs versus stated positions, and ensure all parties feel heard by giving them adequate time and space to express themselves rather than rushing to respond. Remember to take notes to keep track of complex dynamics, enabling the discussion of potential action points and further commitments. This approach builds trust and transparency in the process.

Help the team uncover the underlying root causes of disagreements, which often differ from initial surface-level triggers or positions. What may appear as a conflict on the surface over architecture choices may stem from differing prioritization frameworks or poor communication habits. Take time to dig beneath stated positions, pinpoint areas of philosophical misalignment in perspectives that may fuel tensions, and correct inaccurate assumptions team members make about each other's motives that may be exacerbating things. Look for gaps between the argument and the actual fundamental problem, and boil the core issue down to a clear, concise problem statement to prevent scattering focus. Identifying the true north of the conflict is essential to mapping solutions that satisfy all parties' core requirements.

Establish simple ground rules upfront to create a framework for productive dialogue. For example, ask the team to agree that only one person will speak at a time to prevent uncontrolled outbursts. You must guide the team to maintain constructive and professional language to avoid letting emotions escalate discussions into personal attacks or unhealthy arguments. Refraining from direct insults, passive-aggressive remarks, sarcasm, or dismissive body language keeps things focused on progress. If conversations still spiral into unconstructive hostility despite the rules, intervene swiftly but compassionately—pause the discussion, remind them of the goals, and give empathy while resetting the tone. Also, set reasonable timeboxes for each debate phase, clarifying how much time will be devoted to the initial airing of issues versus exploring solutions to prevent endless venting or arguing in circles. Simple rules provide clear expectations, instill a sense of order, especially amid the chaos, and foster the psychological safety required for open and authentic dialogue.

Promote collaborative, integrative problem-solving over zero-sum competition; saying "us versus the issue" rather than "us versus you" reminds people that they ultimately share common goals. Have each side reflect on how they may have unintentionally contributed to the dispute; this builds empathy and mutual understanding. Identify mutually beneficial solutions that satisfy the core needs of all sides rather than just splitting the difference and seek creative ways for both parties to help fulfill each other's goals. Collaboration focused on collective benefit unlocks integrative solutions superior to compromise, enabling one to move past surface-level statements to discover the win-win potential underlying most conflicts.

Finally, *diligently document all mediation and facilitation outcomes, action items, and agreements reached in a shared location accessible to the team.* Schedule timely follow-ups to review progress and proactively address any renewal of tensions. Verify that both sides adhere to the agreed-upon behavioral or process changes and look for opportunities to celebrate successful conflict resolution and reaffirm team cohesion. Providing closure through documentation and sustained engagement demonstrates your commitment to restoring harmony for the long haul. It enables institutional learning to swiftly diffuse similar disputes in the future by applying proven strategies. Rest assured that embracing even the most bitter conflicts can transform into growth catalysts that renew team spirit.

CHAPTER 3   COLLABORATION AND TEAM DYNAMICS

Embracing Customer-Centricity Within Engineering Teams

Before moving forward in this section, it's essential to understand that customer-centricity refers to making customer needs and perspectives the guiding priority in all aspects of product development, involving profoundly understanding target users and designing solutions focused on delivering the most value to them. Adopting this mindset is crucial because engineers often prioritize technology over end-user value, leading to products that fail to resonate with customers. A product built with the latest and top-notch technologies that fail to deliver tangible value to customers is nothing more than a fancy paperweight.

As an engineering leader, you must champion customer-centricity to guide your team toward developing solutions that solve real customer problems versus engineering for engineering's sake. This mindset change starts with you embracing customer focus as a personal mission and modeling it daily. When your team sees you prioritizing user needs, you inspire them to realign their efforts toward maximum customer value.

Instilling a customer-centric culture within engineering teams requires overcoming the traditionally inward-looking perspective many engineers adopt. It's common to focus narrowly on technical tasks like coding features and optimizing system architecture, diligently applying their specialized skills without always considering the broader context of how their work impacts end-users or the business. Even though their technical expertise is crucial, engineers must broaden their perspective beyond technology to customers; you want to avoid ending up with a fancy but useless product. Customer perspective needs to be the north star guiding all product development initiatives. Engineers must seek the whys to understand how they help direct customers to success and the company growth overall, not only the state-of-art in engineering.

CHAPTER 3   COLLABORATION AND TEAM DYNAMICS

Strategies to Foster a Customer-Centric Culture

Becoming a truly customer-centric engineering organization demands comprehensive changes across people, processes, and technology. While challenging, the long-term benefits make this culture shift invaluable. When engineering teams focus on solving real-world user problems, they produce solutions that delight customers and drive sustainable business growth.

By facilitating immersive collaboration with customer-facing roles, aligning objectives to user needs, gathering continuous feedback, and bridging stakeholder gaps, you will transform teams skilled at developing elegant technology into partners devoted to a value-driven culture. Yet, you must approach these strategies persistently once reshaping culture takes time.

Promote Cross-functional Collaboration

Don't just encourage collaboration between engineering and customer-facing roles—actively facilitate it through immersive touchpoints. Include engineers in customer advisory board meetings to get direct exposure to user needs and pain points. Make support ticket analysis a weekly ritual where engineers can gain visceral insight into common challenges customers face. Conduct quarterly user interviews with engineering, sales, and design participation so cross-functional debriefs can build empathy across teams. Send bi-weekly customer newsletter updates to engineering highlighting trends and opportunities uncovered by customer-facing roles. Host co-design workshops where engineers can brainstorm solutions alongside customer-facing team members, merging technical feasibility with user desires. Embed engineering representatives in customer site visits or calls to witness real-world usage environments and workflows.

These touchpoints aim for engineers to absorb the customer perspective as their own. When they hear firsthand accounts of suboptimal experiences and product limitations, it sticks with them, and they begin seeing product decisions through the customer's eyes, not just their technical view. This mentality shift is catalytic for instilling customer-centricity because, suddenly, every engineering choice has a human face behind it. Cross-functional collaboration helps break engineering free from the echo chamber of technical KPIs by connecting their work directly to customer value.

Set Objectives Aligned to Customer Needs

Rather than just set technical metrics like uptime or performance benchmarks, define targets aligned to the customer experience. This change in strategy includes tracking adoption rates of new features that solve key user needs. Hence, engineers know they built something users genuinely need to drive their businesses to success. Conduct periodic customer surveys to quantify improvements in satisfaction across areas like usability, complexity, and utility. Monitor support ticket volume in sections related to churn risk—a decrease signals engineering solutions improved sticky product elements. Establish resolution time goals for common user problems so improvements directly correlate with customer pain points. Watch for upticks in CSAT scores related to ease of use to indicate that engineering teams simplified workflows. Similarly, you must aim to reduce complaints around frustrating or confusing processes as proof that engineers addressed real complexity issues.

Goals rooted in customer experience versus theoretical or technical metrics serve as forcing functions for teams to maintain focus on real user needs. When engineering knows their success is measured by moving the needle on customer-centric KPIs, they make different product decisions. Consequently, optimizing conversion funnel drop-off rates feels just as important as refactoring infrastructure for marginal latency gains. Resources get allocated to problems that may seem minor technically but severely hurt customer experience. In summary, linking engineering goals to customer needs reinforces that the "why" behind their work is solving real human problems—the foundation of customer-centricity.

Gather Continuous Customer Feedback

Continuously gathering customer insights is indispensable for seeding customer-centricity within engineering teams. Various feedback channels provide ongoing signals into user pain points, product limitations, and improvement opportunities. Analyzing these inputs should directly inform prioritization and planning. The tighter the feedback loop, the better engineering can address the most substantial pain points through continuous improvements.

Support Tickets: Reviewing support tickets highlights common user problems and sources of confusion, and rotating support ticket duty gives engineers firsthand exposure to these issues. Understanding customers' challenges when contacting support brings product limitations to life, providing visceral, recurring signals into pain points that engineering should aim to alleviate. Analyze support tickets to identify pervasive issues rather than treating them as isolated cases. *What issues keep arising that point to flawed product flows or ambiguous interfaces?* Support insights spotlight areas where engineering can make a high-impact difference in customer experience.

CRM Notes: CRM notes capturing customer complaints reveal frustrating workflows and areas of ambiguity within the product, and regularly reviewing these documented interactions identifies recurring issues that annoy users. Engineering teams can analyze CRM insights to pinpoint unnecessary complexity and confusion in key processes once these notes provide qualitative data on obstacles customers encounter trying to use the product successfully. By studying them, engineering gains insight to simplify the product functioning and address pitfalls that hinder adoption and satisfaction.

Exit Interviews: Exit interviews gathering churn drivers put faces to defections, with customers often citing fixable experience gaps as reasons for leaving; spotting these patterns through churn analysis prevents further attrition. When engineering learns which product limitations directly correlate to cancelations, they can preempt more defections by addressing those weaknesses. Exit interview insights might point to arcane interfaces, missing features competitors offer, integration difficulties, or performance roadblocks. Although product deficiencies might seem minor internally, they could be significant adoption blockers externally. Shedding light on churn drivers fuels customer-focused product remediation.

Customer Reviews and Comments: Customers often provide direct feedback on the product and specific features through channels like app store reviews, social media, community forums, and customer support conversations. Monitoring these channels gives ongoing visibility into which aspects of the product resonate with users and which need improvement. Also, it enables the team to identify strengths to double down on and weaknesses to address. For example, overflowing praise for a new feature confirms it solves a major user need, whereas complaints about confusing interfaces or missing capabilities highlight areas for refinement. Incorporating product/feature feedback helps engineering focus on improving elements core to the customer experience versus those sitting on the peripheral. Listen to what users say about your product experience and let this direct feature priorities.

Balance Customer Needs with Business and Technical Priorities

Creating a genuinely customer-centric culture requires carefully balancing user needs with other essential priorities like business goals and technical excellence. Overly catering to every customer demand can result in short-sighted decisions that generate technical debt, hurt operational efficiency, and stifle innovation. For example, allowing extensive customization may please some vocal users but slow development velocity long-term, making the product relevant for a specific group or user but not that attractive to others. On the flip side, rigidly prioritizing business metrics or technical purity over user experience risks alienating customers, manifesting as refusing to build a highly requested feature because it doesn't directly drive revenue. Or insisting on a technically complex infrastructure overhaul despite no discernible user benefit.

Instead, leverage data and research to identify high-impact initiatives that meet customer needs while driving the business forward. For example, qualitative user interviews can reveal that streamlining a conversion workflow improves understanding and increases conversion rates—a win-win for user experience and revenue. Continuously

CHAPTER 3   COLLABORATION AND TEAM DYNAMICS

reevaluate priorities as the landscape changes, as evolving customer expectations may require realigning technology investments to address new pain points. Business objectives may shift from aggressive acquisition to retention, requiring a review of persistent product elements with a customer-centric lens.

There is no perfect formula, but often, the right balance comes from a long-term customer perspective. Studies like the PwC Future of Customer Experience survey from 2017[1] show that 80% of customers say experience is as important as products and services. Additionally, Gartner's 2019 Customer Experience Management Study[2] found that organizations with more mature CX management practices enjoy 36% higher customer retention rates. Investing in user experience drives increased loyalty, lower churn, and reduced acquisition costs—enabling sustainable growth. Even small frustrations accumulate, while satisfied customers become a company's biggest advocates.

Aim to strike the ideal balance but let customer-centricity be the tiebreaker when trade-offs emerge. This path may have short-term costs but catalyzes lasting success by delivering extreme value to the people who matter most—your users.

Overcoming Roadblocks to Customer-Centricity

The strategies for gathering customer insights may seem outside the traditional scope of engineering leaders. You may think interfacing directly with users should be handled solely by product teams or customer-facing roles. However, adopting the *"we are all product"* mindset is essential in a

---

[1] www.pwc.com/us/en/advisory-services/publications/consumer-intelligence-series/pwc-consumer-intelligence-series-customer-experience.pdf

[2] www.gartner.com/en/marketing/research/2019-customer-experience-management-study

genuinely collaborative product company, demanding recognizing that we share the unified goal of delivering value to users regardless of department.

While cross-functional collaboration presents inevitable roadblocks, persevering through the challenges is paramount. As a leader, you are crucial in navigating your team through obstacles to become customer champions. This next section will explore common difficulties when evangelizing customer focus and strategies to overcome them. Remember, establishing an engineering culture fixated on customer needs has no shortcuts.

Resistance to Cultural and Mindset Shifting

A thriving customer-centric engineering culture starts with the cultural and mindset shift to prioritize user needs. Adopting this "customer first" mentality allows engineers to deeply understand user problems, develop targeted solutions, and deliver superior experiences. Yet, changing ingrained perspectives and habits can be difficult once long-time engineers may be skeptical about incorporating customer feedback, believing their technical expertise replaces user input. In contrast, some may fear that slowing down to gather customer insights will hamper speed and productivity. Additionally, engineers pride themselves on elegant technical solutions, making it tough to prioritize utility over optimal architecture.

As a leader, expect and understand resistance, but remain focused on reshaping mindset by highlighting the benefits of customer-centricity. Provide concrete examples of how user-informed decisions lead to improved product-market fit, increased retention, reduced churn, and ultimately greater business success. Relate these benefits directly to engineers' work so they grasp the tangible upsides of aligning engineering efforts with customer needs.

Involve them in defining customer-centricity for your specific organizational context and make it tangible with clear principles reinforced through training and guidance. Adapt your definition over time as needs change, but maintain alignment with core company values. The transformation requires internalizing "customer first" as integral to their identities, not just as a directive from management.

Facilitate this self-realization by encouraging engineers to participate directly in customer research through shadowing support agents, observing user testing, and analyzing feedback; nothing cements customer focus like hearing practical stories of users struggling with their designs. Lastly, publicly celebrate customer-centric behaviors and outcomes, sharing success stories, customer quotes, and business impact metrics, and reinforce that excelling at customer focus leads to professional growth and peer admiration.

Break Down Silos Through Collaboration

Siloed departments can severely impede customer-centricity by creating disjointed, inconsistent experiences. When teams operate in isolation, they focus narrowly on internal metrics versus the end-to-end customer journey. This fragmented approach breeds duplication of work, inefficient processes, and conflicts across teams, becoming customer-centricity's worst enemy.

Engineers may hesitate to collaborate with customer-facing roles like support or sales because they fear overstepping boundaries or wasting other teams' time. For example, engineering teams might refrain from sitting in on customer calls to gather feedback directly, assuming that this duty falls under the responsibility of account managers. In contrast, roles like customer success may feel uneasy directly suggesting specific product changes or improvements to engineering, assuming engineers know the technical constraints and trade-offs best.

This reluctance from both sides to actively collaborate results in missed opportunities, generating a lose-lose situation, where engineers lose out on deep qualitative insights to inform development, and customer-facing roles miss the chance to contribute ideas that could significantly improve user experience directly.

The root causes often come down to rooted assumptions about responsibilities. Engineers think product decisions belong solely to product managers. Support agents believe they should file tickets, not strategize improvements. Salespersons want to sell the product and increase revenue. Engineers want to build high-performing solutions. But in a customer-centric culture, these barriers disappear, replaced by proactive collaboration focused on delivering exceptional user experiences, no matter what.

The path to a truly customer-centric engineering culture is difficult, but persevering through the obstacles is an immensely worthy investment. By championing customer-centricity and relentlessly focusing your team on user needs through cross-functional collaboration, aligned objectives, tight feedback loops, and overcoming roadblocks, you lay the foundation for customer-focused engineering that catalyzes innovation, loyalty, and growth. Despite the challenges associated with embracing this philosophy, your empowered, customer-obsessed engineering teams will propel your products and business to new heights over time.

Collaborating with Product Teams

As an engineering leader, building a seamless partnership with your product management counterparts is the bedrock for consistently delivering customer-centric products that fuel business growth. When engineering and product operate in silos rather than collaborating, the risk of building products disconnected from the customer needs becomes too tangible, sabotaging your team's delivery and morale, stickiness to your product, and consequently, the company's growth.

CHAPTER 3   COLLABORATION AND TEAM DYNAMICS

Despite the differences in responsibilities of both sides, one can only exist with the other. A product team that shapes the product vision without considering the technical constraints risks creating unrealistic roadmaps that are impossible for you to execute. In contrast, an engineering team that builds solutions relying solely on their technical prowess fixates on technically novel but ends up with useless features rather than solving real customer needs. Ignoring the natural interdependency between product and engineering breeds misunderstandings that reduce output quality and slow delivery velocity. The absence of a collaborative spirit stunts innovation and results in solutions that are likely to fail in the market.

Yet, you and the product folks can surpass individual limitations to achieve shared success through close coordination, mutual respect, and shared vision. Engineering gains vital customer context to build pragmatic solutions balancing realism and idealism, whereas product benefits from your technical expertise to formulate practical roadmaps grounded in reality.

Defining the Product and Engineering Roles

Before exploring how to foster this necessary collaboration, let's outline the roles of product managers and engineering leaders.

The product manager guides the product strategy and roadmap as the user and market expert, and their core responsibilities start with deeply understanding target users. They research, develop personas, and interview customers to determine pain points and unmet needs. Next, they perform competitive analysis to benchmark capabilities and spot differentiation opportunities. Driving the product vision also falls under their domain, where they define positioning and messaging. With the vision in place, they manage the entire product lifecycle based on Agile Principles,[3] from ideation to launch to iteration.

---

[3] https://agilemanifesto.org/principles.html

Furthermore, they translate user needs into actionable user stories and requirements, ensuring the team builds the right solutions, whereas prioritizing the roadmap and backlog focuses development on the capabilities that will drive maximum business value. Finally, gathering direct user feedback through surveys, beta testing, and app reviews enables continuous improvement of the products based on accurate data.

On the other hand, engineering managers' responsibility starts with feasibility, and they lead the team to transform the product vision into high-quality and scalable solutions. They assess technical complexity, map inter and direct dependencies across resources, provide estimates, evaluate engineering trade-offs, and tackle performance constraints. With feasibility confirmed, they break down large user stories into bite-sized engineering tasks and create delivery plans for organized execution. You must not shy away from code and design reviews but rather make them another key responsibility, upholding robust architecture, best practices, and product goals. Remember, you must understand business intricacies, but you are also responsible for the technical quality of the deliveries derived from your team.

Building skilled and productive teams comes next. Engineering leaders mentor and advance engineers through coaching, candid feedback, and supporting career growth. Owning the recruitment process and the team's growth is vital to expanding the team's capabilities. Supporting agile processes is another focus area; they facilitate planning, standups, retrospectives, and demos to enable iterative development. Lastly, engineering leaders remove impediments to improve team productivity, efficiency, and output.

Dispelling Ownership Misconceptions

Now that we've outlined the core responsibilities of product managers and engineering leaders, let's explore some common misconceptions that can emerge around ownership and collaboration between these roles.

CHAPTER 3   COLLABORATION AND TEAM DYNAMICS

Dispelling outdated myths lays the groundwork for building a shared mindset and complementary partnership.

Product Dictatorship Myth: This myth refers to product managers simply handing down requirements and solutions to engineering without collaboration. This approach leads to friction, misalignment, and suboptimal outcomes, impeding the engineering organization's ability to operate efficiently and deliver excellently. For example, PMs may define intricate features and set unrealistic timelines without consulting engineering before making commitments. Treating development teams as order-takers and ignoring technical constraints result in sloppy scopes, compressed schedules, and technically flawed solutions built to sugarcoat products instead of solving relevant user issues.

Engineering Autocracy Myth: Conversely, engineering autocracy refers to development teams charging ahead on building features without properly aligning to product strategy and customer needs, falling under the assumption that due to their technical expertise, they know best what users want. This strategy leads to well-executed but pointless products that fail in the market. For example, engineers may fixate on infrastructure and architectural redesigns without contributing to product value, demanding them to step back and review broader objectives and customer needs to reconnect to user value. The consequences are wasted time and effort and a team with eroded morale.

CHAPTER 3   COLLABORATION AND TEAM DYNAMICS

Planning in Silos: It's the dangerous line where both myths come together. It refers to product and engineering teams elaborating distinct roadmaps and development planning independently without cross-functional collaboration, naturally leading to disconnects such as excessive technical debt, duplicated efforts, and products mismatched to market needs. The product folks keep promising unrealistic features with unachievable deadlines, whereas engineering teams disregard strategic product priorities guided by customer insights. It's a total disaster, and you only find disappointment at the finish line.

You must question yourself, *"How can product and engineering leaders cultivate healthy shared ownership instead of operating in silos driven by misconceptions?"*

The first step involves identifying areas of overlap between the roles to increase collaboration. Seek opportunities for joint decision-making instead of throwing solutions over the wall. For example, product and engineering can merge during the feature discovery phase to shape initial requirements, define together scopes for minimum viable products[4] to validate ideas and concepts as a unit.

Furthermore, develop processes for providing open and early feedback on proposed ideas across teams. Empower product managers to highlight potential technical risks early and enable your team to pinpoint where certain features may not fully align with customer needs; remember, it's a two-way street. Then, promote activities that unite the teams and increase mutual understanding of the what, why, how, and when. Build cross-functional rituals into the development cycle to facilitate shared planning

---

[4] https://en.wikipedia.org/wiki/Minimum_viable_product

sessions such as story mapping, design thinking, and brainstorming. Conduct collaborative release, sprint, project milestone planning, solution demos, and architecture reviews to unify both perspectives and define shared priorities and goals.

Finally, cultivate a culture of transparency through ongoing communication to create opportunities for informal chats between team members to discuss insights from customer research collaboratively and explore how engineering innovations could open new product opportunities.

Aligning on What Comes Next: Product and Engineering Partnering on the Roadmap

As a shared understanding of responsibilities dispels outdated myths, the stage is set for product managers and engineering leaders to align on what comes next in the product roadmap. Rather than operating in silos and making unilateral decisions, this close partnership enables you to prioritize features and capabilities that will drive maximum customer and business value.

Even though product managers drive the ideation and definition of new capabilities that align with strategic goals, you, as an engineering leader, play a critical role in shaping the scope and sequencing of features through constructive feedback and technical expertise. By highlighting feasibility concerns, complexity trade-offs, and feature dependencies early in the process, you guide breaking epics into well-scoped stories with clear acceptance criteria and well-defined scopes, facilitating the understanding of the whys to enable the team to define the hows. Additionally, you ensure the business impact is clear, leveling up your solutions to maximize customer value while minimizing technical debt.

CHAPTER 3   COLLABORATION AND TEAM DYNAMICS

Beyond shaping individual features, both leaders must partner closely on the broader delivery cadence and balance short and long-term investments. With shared context on business objectives and technical landscape, product and engineering can align on iteration velocity, technical limitations, intrinsic dependencies across features from different contexts, technology evolvement, business needs changes, and large cross-functional initiatives. This big-picture perspective ensures the roadmap strikes the right balance between releasing quickly and thoughtfully evolving the product and your technology foundation.

But how exactly you and your product counterpart can collaborate to focus on what's most important? Establishing a shared vision is the secret sauce enabling teams to deliver value quickly.

The first step is to ensure both teams speak the same language, and using structured processes gives equal voice to business context and technical constraints to arrive at high-impact solutions. There are many prioritization frameworks in the market with a proven track of success on which product and engineering leaders can rely to foster a shared language to discuss urgency, importance, and effort, such as the Kano Model, MoSCoW Method, RICE Scoring, and Weighted Shortest Job First; they all focus on customer needs to drive informed prioritizations.

Next, establish regular ceremonies to create space for open dialogue, surface insights early, and nurture the partnership. For example, consider making a bi-weekly product development alignment meeting between all product managers, designers, engineering leaders, and architects to shape the upcoming product evolution across both teams jointly. Kick these sessions off by celebrating recent wins to foster shared pride. Using structured models such as the IDS—Identify, Discuss, Solve helps to enable transparent conversations on the feasibility of upcoming capabilities, release planning, customer feedback analysis, and balancing the short and long-term technology investments required to bring the roadmap to life. Keep the agenda open for every team member, and discuss the topics with an open mind and ego aside. These meetings are

CHAPTER 3   COLLABORATION AND TEAM DYNAMICS

not about you but the product, so be ready to push for the engineering side but be flexible to optimize the product impact. If any action points are needed, write them down, assign the owner for each, and make reviewing the past commitments a second nature for this group.

By providing a recurring forum for giving candid feedback and shaping requirements as one unit, surprises decrease while team alignment strengthens. Consistency is fundamental, and the bi-weekly cadence enables seamless handoffs between product strategy and development velocity, balancing short and long-term decisions to encourage future innovation, resulting in a cohesive partnership between product and technical leaders who know to respect each other and work together to make business products thrive.

Although these ceremonies between product and engineering leaders lay the foundation and remove unnecessary noise from the groundwork, gathering insights from the broader teams executing the work is equally vital. The engineers closest to implementation can help surface crucial constraints and dependencies early. Their perspective helps shape requirements grounded in daily experiences and realities, not just leadership assumptions. Also, it contributes to building a more profound and shared understanding of the "why" behind priorities and transforming the plan into actionable plans across groups. Finally, it enables earlier preparation of resources to support upcoming work based on open communication of timelines and staffing needs.

Building great products starts with creating great partnerships between these two distinct but mutually dependent teams—approach roadmap planning as an opportunity for both leaders to be force multipliers. Respecting differences, leverage complementary strengths to combine innovation with pragmatism, and keep the long-term vision for your users and your business at the center—not individual agendas. Make collaboration a habit; success depends on consistency. Institute ceremonies and recurring touchpoints that strengthen alignment over time through mutual understanding, and you and your counterpart can move away from a transactional relationship to become true partners united by a common purpose—turning great ideas into valuable products through aligned and realistic execution.

Leading Remote Teams: Adapting to the New Normal

The COVID-19 pandemic accelerated a monumental shift in the working world—the transition to remote and hybrid teams. As remote and hybrid models have proven themselves as viable and productive options for many engineering teams, people started embracing them not as temporary solutions anymore, but rather, they are quickly becoming the new normal.

While some companies have traditionally promoted in-office perks like game rooms, snacks, and parties as central to their cultures, the pandemic demonstrated that these are not the most important factors for today's workforce. With remote work now fundamental to many roles, company cultures must evolve to retain talent and to focus on elements that matter more to employees—flexibility, empowerment, and genuine connection with coworkers.

Moreover, remote work is here to stay, and you play a crucial role in evolving company cultures for virtual teams beyond trivial perks. Seamlessly adopting this model requires focused attention on communication, transparency, relationship-building, and empathy across distance and time zones. By adapting purposefully, you can lead distributed teams that collaborate effectively and efficiently, drive innovation anywhere, and accomplish shared goals through aligned vision and values. You must embrace a growth mindset, adapt yourself, and get prepared to extend your influence globally.

Surpassing Key Challenges of Leading Remote Teams

Remote leadership has proven more challenging than traditional office environments. Although the intrinsic flexibility of the remote work model offers greater autonomy, this model requires proactive leadership to avoid misalignment and isolation. Without the organic visibility of a shared workspace, critical aspects of team cohesion are easily eroded—communication suffers, goals become unclear, and relationships weaken. People thrive on connection, sharing common values and principles, and a sense of community. But building trust and camaraderie from a distance proves to be much more complex, and those who can't keep up with this paradigm shift will preside over disengaged and fragmented teams, producing mediocre results.

Maintaining Strong Communication and Collaboration

For leaders of remote engineering teams, maintaining open, frequent, and meaningful communication and collaboration is more critical than ever. Virtual teams can quickly become siloed and misaligned without organic interactions and visibility. Communication breakdowns that may go unnoticed when working side by side could completely derail projects in distributed teams. That's why purposeful, structured communication that builds connections among remote team members is crucial to increase inclusion, transparency, and alignment. However, achieving this cohesion with remote teams requires leaders to be more intentional about their approach.

With video meetings, promote a culture of active participation by encouraging team members to keep cameras on. The nonverbal cues enabled by video foster stronger interpersonal connections and collaboration, allowing you to evaluate your audience's response and reset the tone whenever needed to keep the engagement. Chat tools

CHAPTER 3   COLLABORATION AND TEAM DYNAMICS

empower decentralized, flexible conversations that balance the need for meetings. They streamline workflows when quick questions and updates are more efficient than long email threads, contributing directly to your team's empowerment and autonomy. Project management tools provide a centralized view of who is working on what and where things stand, which is extremely valuable for keeping remote team members aligned.

Given the array of digital communication channels available, it's vital to establish consistent rhythms and protocols around meetings, updates, and information sharing. For example, short 15-minute standup meetings over video at the start of each workday may help maintain face-to-face connections. Weekly 30- to 60-minute team meetings provide a regular cadence for discussing status, face-to-face brainstorming, issues, goals, refinements, and building deeper relationships. Clear documentation practices using shared drives and wikis ensure the entire team can access the most up-to-date information and historical context anytime.

Moreover, standardizing the team's reliance on specific platforms and schedules provides stability. For instance, having a shared channel in your chat tool as the go-to place for ongoing conversations and questions enables transparency. In contrast, conducting sprint retrospectives and planning meetings for each iteration at set days/times maintains alignment and consistency. Reliable communication structures like these bring much-needed cohesion and clarity across distributed teams. Of course, you must still be flexible and adapt to changes and needs to accommodate global team members. Overall, the more consistent communication rhythms, the less confusion and isolation remote workers will feel.

Another crucial communication aspect is recognizing cultural differences to avoid getting lost in translations. You may encounter communication complexity from cultural and language variances across global teams. It's crucial to be patient to understand accents and phrasing. Speaking a nonnative language all day may be stressful and drain energy, so refrain from using slang or regional expressions and facilitate others to understand your message. Seek clarification whenever anything seems unclear rather than making assumptions, and respectfully highlight instances where improved clarity would help alignment. It's your mission to turn language diversity into an asset.

Building Trust and Relationships Virtually

When working with distributed teams, you must get creative in relationship-building without regular face-to-face contact. Intentionally make time for personal connections, not just project talk. Schedule one-on-one video chats to learn who team members are as people—their passions, quirks, families, and dreams. Ask thoughtful questions, then truly listen. Share your own stories and vulnerabilities. Individual care and concern go a long way. We will explore this topic in-depth in the next section of this chapter.

Sprinkle in informal virtual water cooler chats to enable natural human moments in offices. Before meetings, execute ice-breaking exercises and spend a few minutes catching up on weekend plans, sports, pets, favorite TV shows, or anything beyond work tasks. Have team members share fun photos from their weekends in your chat channel. On Friday afternoons, host a team happy hour over a video where everyone grabs a drink and talks about their plans. Celebrate team member milestones like birthdays or work anniversaries with virtual events where people can swap stories and express appreciation. Laughter is a language that strengthens connections everywhere, and taking time for these casual social interactions, even remotely, builds the relationships that make work enjoyable and boost morale.

Ultimately, coordinate online team-building activities to create shared experiences and inside jokes that bond groups over time. Set up regular virtual game nights where people play multiplayer games together—be mindful of one's availability and plans to avoid making this a burden. Host a virtual escape room event where teams race to crack codes and solve puzzles. Organize a virtual cooking class led by team members, with ingredients delivered so everyone can participate from their kitchens. Set goals like collectively logging miles walked or books read and track progress in a shared spreadsheet to motivate one another. These kinds of creative activities strengthen connections and culture.

Ensuring Transparency and Clarity on Goals and Expectations

Regular in-person contact can lead to better alignment and clarity on priorities, expectations, and project specifics. Without sitting together in the same room, details are easily miscommunicated or lost across emails and messages. Consequently, this breakdown in transparency often manifests in duplicated work, frustration over unclear responsibilities, and projects veering off-course.

Furthermore, providing excessive autonomy without appropriate context also hampers remote workers. The inherent distance makes it easier for teams to end up working in silos or heading in different directions. Conversely, a lack of direct and consistent communication may make managers falsely assume that expectations are clear when remote team members need more guidance and insights. The consequences of this ambiguity include declining morale, missed deliverables, and products not meeting user needs.

As a countermeasure, collaboratively build shared repositories using wikis, documents, and project management tools to create single sources of truth accessible to everyone, preventing confusion from details getting lost across scattered emails and conversations and allowing you to share extensive context and visibility into goals, plans, and priorities. Also, comprehensively documenting roadmaps, requirements, success metrics, timelines, and dependencies in these centralized places establishes clarity on direction and specifics, enabling remote workers to reference plans rather than relying on vague memories or fragmented communications.

Supporting Employee Engagement and Well-Being

Remote work's flexibility can enable longer working hours and connection outside regular times. This constant accessibility can contribute to burnout—the physical, mental, and emotional toll of prolonged work stress. Remote team members may lack opportunities to disconnect and recharge without commutes providing natural buffers. Signals of burnout include irritability, lack of motivation, feelings of ineffectiveness, and self-doubt. Whenever you identify a team member exhibiting one or more behaviors, you must reach out to them and have candid but empathetic conversations about providing support without judgment. However, be prepared that the initial reaction may be denial. As a leader, you need to gently discuss practical evidence of changes you've observed, keeping the focus on the team member's health and well-being.

Once you identify burnout, you can lean on existing pragmatic solutions to improve unhealthy work patterns, and promoting sustainable work habits is vital. Discourage off-hour emails and weekend work by instituting core collaboration hours for meetings and questions, outside of which people can focus intensely. Ensure you set expectations for taking minimum vacation days and fully disconnecting. Remember to follow the Lead by Example principle—don't ping team members outside regular hours, and ensure you properly recharge. Shift cultural mindsets through training on time management, goal setting, and work-life balance. Implement collaboration tools with scheduled send features to allow composing responses whenever productive but delivering during office hours. With deliberate policy changes and role modeling, you can influence more sustainable work rhythms and help prevent burnout.

CHAPTER 3   COLLABORATION AND TEAM DYNAMICS

Taming Remote Work Distractions

One of your most important responsibilities is serving as a buffer for your team against constant distractions and interruptions. Without the physical separation of an office environment, remote teams face a barrage of digital disruptions like chat pings, emails, unnecessary meetings, and frequent context switching. These distractions have a high cognitive cost, breaking individual focus and fragmenting team momentum. Consequently, productivity drops at a fast pace.

However, you can establish practices and workflows to protect your team from excessive noise, such as assessing which incoming requests warrant the team's time versus those you can handle yourself or defer. As a leader, you should take on as much direct work as possible—reviewing documents, corresponding with stakeholders, and preparing presentations—rather than simply passing every task to your team. This hands-on approach enables you to consolidate and refine requests, resolve issues independently, and ensure that only the most high-value activities reach your team. The best leaders dig into the critical but less glamorous "tasks in the trenches" alongside their team members, protecting their focus while displaying their commitment to executing the engineering work, not just overseeing it.

To help your team keep focus on what matters, you can establish clear communication protocols that streamline inquiries and limit ad hoc pings. For example, implement a daily standup over chat for questions and priority alignment rather than constant impromptu messages. Discourage expectations for 24/7 availability by modeling offline periods yourself. You must also help team members create distraction-free home office setups and schedules. These include promoting practices like muting notifications during focus blocks, establishing quiet workspaces, and recognizing the routine of each team member. Lead by example by displaying these behaviors yourself.

Furthermore, you must also offer flexible scheduling to accommodate out-of-work obligations. Empower team members to establish routines that maximize personal productivity by aligning with their chronotype and energy levels. Aggressively prune unnecessary meetings to free up focus time, question recurring meetings' true purpose, and pare down attendees. Make "saying no" something normal for you and your team.

Bridging Office and Remote Employees

Hybrid teams combining remote and in-office members represent a complex leadership challenge. Without thoughtful attention to inclusion, transparency, and documentation, hybrid setups risk creating a disconnected employee experience and culture. By purposefully avoiding a split between remote/and in-person work experience, you can foster unified teams that innovate through diversity, not despite it. With the right strategies, hybrid models unlock access to broad talent pools and flexible work arrangements without sacrificing cohesion. Thoughtful adaptation of workflows, documentation, and social activities allow remote and office staff to collaborate equitably.

Firstly, actively including remote team members in brainstorming sessions and social events is crucial, rather than limiting participation to those physically present. Without purposeful efforts for inclusion, they end up at an information disadvantage, unable to contribute fully or make informed decisions, leading to isolation, silos, and remote staff becoming disengaged over time. However, you enable equal participation by having folks join collaborative whiteboard sessions via video conference and assigning someone on-site to capture images and notes to share later. Brainstorming with Post-its may be fun and work fine physically, but it's far from a good experience for those remotely.

Moreover, avoid in-person side conversations that lead to business decisions, excluding remote team members. If impromptu office conversations trigger impactful ideas, promptly loop in remote team members for opinions. It's easy for hallway chats in the office to spawn plans and solutions without distributed colleagues' input. This indirectly signals that on-site employees are more critical for decisions than remote ones. Instead, shift in-person brainstorms to videoconference calls with remote folks included, discourage offline debates, and point people to digital forums and team channels.

Finally, document all decisions, plans, and action items from meetings and collaborations, regardless of whether remote team members are present. Ambiguity breeds misalignment across hybrid teams. For rapid in-person debates, have someone live-type notes in a shared document, and discourage letting outcomes remain "in our heads." The more documentation flows through channels accessible to the entire hybrid team, the less remote workers feel out of the loop. Thorough documentation may feel excessive initially, but it pays off hugely in clarity.

As remote and hybrid models become the new normal, engineering leaders are crucial in guiding this workforce transformation. Avoiding misalignment, strengthening virtual relationships, ensuring clarity, and supporting employee well-being enable distributed teams to thrive. You must maintain open communication through thoughtful use of video, chat, documentation, and project tools and proactively build personal connections and camaraderie online. Radical transparency should increase through centralized knowledge sharing, and you must set clear expectations to empower autonomy and focus. Yet, keep an eye on engagement and burnout.

Leading a remote team requires a complete change in mindset to adapt to your team's needs, which sometimes may be challenging and foggy. But by adopting the strategies explored in this guide, you can surmount any obstacle and amplify possibilities to build high-performing, unified teams across the globe. *Be bold and embrace this change.*

CHAPTER 3   COLLABORATION AND TEAM DYNAMICS

One-on-One Meetings: An Essential Leadership Tool

In engineering leadership's fast-paced and complex domain, strengthening trust, communication, and interpersonal bonds with your team members is imperative yet challenging. Your numerous responsibilities and hectic schedule limit opportunities for meaningful individual engagement. However, investing dedicated time in recurring one-on-one meetings with each of your direct reports is a high-impact yet straightforward way to foster these critical connections.

Think of one-on-ones as periodic touchpoints to calibrate your leadership approach, support, and messaging to each person's unique needs. These private conversations build psychological safety that unlocks candor and surfaces insights you would never gain otherwise. While group meetings serve a purpose, leadership happens one relationship at a time. You can tailor your coaching and resources by understanding motivations, passions, and pain points. That's why regularly scheduled time with each team member is invaluable, and the consistency demonstrates your care and commitment to their growth and well-being.

The Purpose of One-on-Ones: Strengthening Bonds and Communications

One-on-ones enable transparency, early issue detection, and clear communication, ultimately helping you lead with greater wisdom, empathy, and effectiveness. Now, let's explore why you should make them a cornerstone of your leadership.

First, the privacy and uninterrupted focus of these conversations cultivate an environment of trust and psychological safety between you and the team member. You make it clear that nothing leaves that room. With guaranteed confidentiality, they feel comfortable letting their guard

CHAPTER 3   COLLABORATION AND TEAM DYNAMICS

down and being vulnerable and truthful with you, enabling you to gain candid insights into their authentic needs, concerns, frustrations, and mindset without filters or sugarcoating. By encouraging such transparency and reassurance-seeking while issues are still small, you help prevent frustrations from silently swelling into significant pain points that hurt morale. Your team trusts you as an empathetic, nonjudgmental outlet who will protect their interests. This safety valve is invaluable.

Furthermore, dedicated one-on-one attention forges deeper individual understanding than group settings allow. You gain invaluable context regarding their motivations, eccentricities, and growth opportunities by patiently exploring their background, passions, pain points, and aspirations. They open up about private topics such as past experiences, sensitivities, anxieties, or interpersonal conflicts. Gradually, their full story emerges, exposing their preferred working style, sociability, and support needs—*revisit the 4-session framework in the first section of this chapter to help you map these individual preferences.* This trust-driven openness enables you to discern the areas where they lack confidence and need developmental support or coaching to unleash their full potential as a person and professional.

Additionally, the meetings become a judgment-free space for candid, two-way communication. Your team members can share disagreements, tensions, mistakes, or requests for support that they may hesitate to voice publicly. You make clear that these conversations are blameless—airing concerns won't have negative repercussions, and as an empathetic, nondefensive listener, you become a trusted outlet. Rather than growing resentful, your team gains your wisdom and reassurance to work through challenges themselves. Your staff trusts you have their back, even if it means respectfully disagreeing with leadership on their behalf, and you gain visibility into problems you can quickly act on.

Finally, regular one-on-ones allow you to tailor your leadership style whenever needed. Equipped with an understanding of their innate capabilities and limitations, you can adjust your approach to play to their

CHAPTER 3   COLLABORATION AND TEAM DYNAMICS

strengths while providing opportunities to improve weaker areas through projects and training. This intimate knowledge also empowers you to handle situations promptly and effectively as they arise. By being aware of each team member's skills, temperament, and pain points, you can quickly assess if they can handle a particular challenge independently or need greater guidance and development. Over time, your leadership agility, emotional intelligence, and ability to motivate each person rise exponentially.

Conducting Impactful One-on-Ones: Preparation, Collaboration, and Accountability

Even though one-on-ones create space for meaningful connection, thoughtfully preparing for each meeting is key to realizing their benefits fully. As the leader, your mindset going into these conversations is vital—recognize that their primary purpose is addressing your team member's agenda and concerns, not yours. By diligently preparing to prioritize their experience over your own agenda, you cultivate an environment where trust, transparency, and constructive progress flourish.

Thorough preparation demonstrates genuine care and commitment and enables more meaningful dialogue, not just surface-level check-ins. We live in an era where we have too many meetings and too little time, so before each one-on-one, reflect intentionally on how to make the time as worthwhile for your direct report as possible; ask them to come prepared to share recent wins, roadblocks, new ideas, career aspirations, or anything else on their mind; make it clear the meeting belongs to them—your role is to listen, not direct the conversation actively.

Block off quality time in your calendar and eliminate potential disruptions. Turn off notifications and ditch aside anything distracting from the session, review any notes from your last one-on-one, and craft thoughtful, open-ended questions to continue uncovering their unique story from multiple angles. Look for opportunities to follow up on key details they shared previously, but let them lead and be comfortable with silence as they gather thoughts.

Rather than jotting down notes privately, share your screen on a note-taking platform or use a shared document to capture highlights jointly. Explain that this practice promotes transparency, accuracy, and active involvement from you both to align on what is documented. Invite their input to verify that you correctly capture their perspectives' essence and ensure they feel comfortable keeping you honest. This collaborative style strengthens trust and communication as you can clear up any misunderstandings on the spot. Strive not just for precision but to demonstrate your focus on their voice. However, keep this approach from distracting you, and ensure you're practicing presence and empathetic listening to the person. After all, the goal of this session is to build meaningful relationships rather than complete reports.

Furthermore, this active documentation reinforces your shared commitment to progress, removes any ambiguity in communication, and creates an invaluable record so conversations continue seamlessly meeting-to-meeting. Rather than just going through the motions, it keeps you fully engaged in their narrative. The deeper context you jointly document far surpasses what you could recreate independently later from memory. For optimal transparency, share the notes afterward for their validation.

While collaborative note-taking during your one-on-one meetings allows you to capture key insights from the discussion, it's equally important to clearly define and document any concrete action steps, commitments, or decisions that emerge. Deliberately outline each subsequent step in the shared notes, along with who will be responsible for it and when. For example, if you both decide a team member should shadow a colleague to expand their skills, document who will arrange it, when they will start, and how long they will shadow for. If you agree to provide them coaching on a specific leadership capability, note the frequency you will meet and the metrics you will use to track their progress. Consistently assigning clear ownership and timelines provides visibility and alignment so everything is clear post-meeting.

Thorough preparation, collaborative note-taking, and clarifying the next steps are integral to extracting maximum value from each one-on-one meeting. You empower meaningful dialogue and continuous improvement by approaching these interactions with an employee-focused mindset, documenting insights jointly, and defining clear accountabilities. Although one-on-one provides critical time to connect, remember the power of consistent follow-up between meetings. Checking in on progress and barriers regarding action items demonstrates your shared commitment to growth. It also strengthens trust and transparency exponentially.

Now, let's explore best practices for establishing a consistent cadence and scheduling one-on-ones optimally to maintain engagement in the long run.

Optimizing One-on-One Consistency, Frequency, and Scheduling

Establishing a consistent cadence for one-on-one meetings fosters familiarity and comfort between you and your team members, unlocking openness and vulnerability and exponentially deepening trust. When these conversations occur regularly without cancelations, your team gains confidence that you will make the time to transparently provide a judgment-free space for addressing their needs, strengthening your relationship.

Even though urgent matters compete for your time, fight to protect your regular one-on-one cadence. While additional meetings may seem a burden, recognize that your team values this time with you to share concerns, ideas, and disappointments lingering on their minds. Despite your crowded calendar, these conversations carry tremendous weight.

CHAPTER 3   COLLABORATION AND TEAM DYNAMICS

Don't underestimate their significance or let one-on-ones become "just another meeting." Prioritize these productive outlets and your team's needs over other demands. Your team craves your undivided attention.

You may feel lost, tired, or in a bad mood, but don't skip these meetings, and try to bring your best self. Automatically, your brain may send signals to avoid talking to strong personalities or to be patient to get information from quiet members, promoting every little opportunity as a perfect chance to postpone it. But like any habit, consistency strengthens the relationship—progress accrues from meeting-to-meeting. Embrace these sessions as a cornerstone, not a luxury.

Determining Ideal Meeting Frequency

While consistency matters most, smart frequency lets you maintain rapport without overburdening schedules. Therefore, a logical question arises: *What frequency optimally balances meaningfulness and manageability?*

In most cases, weekly or bi-weekly one-on-ones hit the sweet spot. Meeting every 1–2 weeks minimizes the gap between connections, allowing you to keep a pulse on emerging concerns and provide timely coaching. It also communicates your genuine care through dedicated touchpoints.

Shorter intervals between meetings foster a relationship rooted in trust and transparency where team members gain confidence in sharing their thoughts candidly, knowing you'll circle back soon to follow up, making any concerns rarely linger unaddressed for long. Furthermore, this cadence communicates your genuine care through dedicated and unrushed touchpoints and demonstrates that their growth and collaboration matter to you week after week, not just monthly. You make them feel valued by sharing the world's most coveted resource: time.

CHAPTER 3   COLLABORATION AND TEAM DYNAMICS

For managers with a large team, monthly one-on-ones allow you to feasibly meet with each person, whereas weekly or bi-weekly meetings with numerous reports could prove challenging to accommodate back-to-back. In these cases, a monthly cadence with each person provides more breathing room in your calendar to make the rounds. Additionally, monthly check-ins give you and your team members more time to gather substantive feedback, ideas, or challenges, removing the pressure of always needing something new to discuss weekly.

Yet, weigh these advantages against drawbacks. Infrequent meetings allow too much time to lapse between connections, failing to provide real-time support when your team members need it. Since some individuals tend to accumulate topics until their scheduled one-on-one, imminent concerns or escalating issues often spiral during the lengthy gap between monthly check-ins, making you lose visibility and momentum. As a month passes between meetings, potentially mounting worries have festered within your staff without a productive outlet. Smaller concerns mature into larger problems without timely attention, forcing you into a reactive mode instead of spotting concerns proactively through more frequent touchpoints.

Although weekly or bi-weekly meetings may be best, remain open-minded once the ideal cadence shifts as team size, responsibilities, and challenges change, and the personal needs of each person from the team; what works today might need reassessment tomorrow. The best strategy to mitigate potential pitfalls from frequency is to solicit occasional feedback from reports on what timing they find most compelling, considering their actual scenario. These consistent evaluations enable the understanding of whether your current frequency still provides maximum value for your team and you. Remember, the goal is maximizing the value of these touchpoints, not adhering to a rigid or permanent schedule.

CHAPTER 3   COLLABORATION AND TEAM DYNAMICS

Crafting an Optimal One-on-One Meeting Framework

Establishing a purposeful framework for one-on-one meeting duration and frequency is vital to maximizing their immense value amid your endless responsibilities. Consider implementing the following structure:

Aim for 45–60 minutes per meeting. Thoughtfully break this down into 15 minutes for rapport building and personal check-ins to show you care about them as a whole person. Allow 10 minutes for them to download key updates and surface pressing concerns. Dedicate 15 minutes for you to provide coaching, developmental feedback, and resources. Use 10 minutes to outline action items and next steps collaboratively. Finally, reserve 5 minutes to wrap up and allow time to transition to the next meetings.

Given a 60-minute recommended meeting length, initially cap one-on-one time at 4 hours per week. This guideline supports weekly meetings with up to four direct reports. If you manage multiple people, carefully tailor the duration to 30–45 minutes or less to stay within 4 hours.

For teams above eight, consider bi-weekly meetings to keep within the framework, and strategically supplement with monthly 15-minute check-ins for lower-risk members or more introverted staff less comfortable frequently voicing concerns. Customize meeting frequency and length based on new hire onboarding ramps, challenges or growth areas requiring extra support, and direct report preferences based on their responsibilities and temperament.

Schedule recurring meetings well in advance using calendar blocks to protect this precious time, and consider leveraging auto-scheduler tools to find optimal timing across multiple busy calendars efficiently. As discussed in the previous sections, you must approach each meeting within the framework with rigorous preparation and follow-through on action items after.

While this meeting framework sets clear guidance, remain open-minded and consistently seek feedback from your team on what meeting length and frequency optimizes value for them based on their workload, energy levels, and preferences; for some, 60 dedicated minutes may feel too long or unnecessary.

Check how your reports respond to the current approach and be ready to adjust duration, frequency, or format accordingly. The goal is to maximize the quality of your one-on-one interactions, not rigidly adhering to a prescribed structure. That said, adapt over time to keep your framework aligned with your team's needs and your capacity as their leader.

Avoiding Common One-on-One Pitfalls

One-on-one meetings provide a valuable opportunity for managers to foster trust, support growth, and strengthen relationships with team members. However, without conscious effort, it's easy to fall into common traps that limit the meetings' impact. Avoid these missteps to ensure your one-on-ones are as productive and collaborative as possible:

First and foremost, don't let your one-on-one become a monologue dominated by your voice. Remember, this meeting is for your team members, not you. It's natural to get excited about sharing your own updates. But avoid talking their ear off about your agenda. Actively foster two-way dialogue by frequently pausing, asking thoughtful questions, and reflecting on their perspectives, and keep pulling the focus back to their needs. Your goal is an equal exchange where they feel fully heard.

Equally important, show up prepared and reflect in advance on what you need to do to make the meeting worthwhile for them. Lack of preparation signals apathy and invites superficial discussions. In contrast, investing time upfront demonstrates care and enables more meaningful interactions. Prepare by reviewing past conversations and intentionally formulating developmental, thought-provoking questions.

Additionally, avoid turning your one-on-one into just a status meeting. While asking about progress on tasks is natural, redirect the focus to connecting with them on a deeper interpersonal level. You can easily cover status updates through email, chat, or weekly team meetings. One-on-ones present a unique opportunity to engage individually. Rather than asking, "What's the status of X project?" have them share their challenges, ideas, and development goals related to the work. Keep the emphasis on collaborative problem-solving and growth.

There are other detrimental pitfalls as well. Don't distract yourself with multitasking during the meeting or let your eyes wander—you may think you're still listening, but your inattention signals disrespect; practicing active presence shows you value their time. Equally important, maintain complete confidentiality of private conversations—sharing personal details destroys trust instantly. Additionally, follow up consistently on action items so meetings lead to impact. Finally, balance discussing their work with individual check-ins to nurture your relationship holistically. With intention, you can avoid these traps and keep your one-on-ones supportive, meaningful, and productive.

Takeaways

1. Investing time in one-on-one conversations to understand each team member's motivations, passions, and development needs is invaluable for tailoring your leadership approach.

2. The 4-session framework of ground rules, life story, dreams, and expectations conversations enables building authentic leader-team member partnerships.

3. Regularly uncovering both established and evolving values provides insights into team members' motivations to guide personalized growth opportunities aligned with their priorities.

4. Discussing preferred communication mediums builds an understanding of how each individual processes information and feedback best.

5. Explaining your intentions upfront sets clear expectations around investing in their growth through your leadership approach.

6. Values can shift over time as engineers experience new responsibilities and environmental changes that reshape motivational priorities.

7. Like a tree's extensive root system providing stability, an individual's values and principles cultivated over time inform their attitudes and observable behaviors.

8. Asking targeted questions focused on "What is important to you?" helps surface evolutions in team members' motivational values over time versus when they started.

9. Respecting boundaries around private topics and rebuilding trust requires patience when aiming for candid life story conversations.

10. Outlining tangible next steps for dreams demonstrates support for team members' professional and personal growth and ambitions.

11. Promoting shared ownership and constructive handling of mistakes is vital for transforming accountability into an empowering cultural norm versus a blaming exercise.

CHAPTER 3   COLLABORATION AND TEAM DYNAMICS

12. Cultivating peer accountability through caring yet candid feedback and rotating retrospectives broadens team responsibility.

13. Restoring broken trust requires confronting issues openly, dedicating time to understand all perspectives, and outlining actionable steps to rebuild bonds.

14. Leading by example amid stress requires emotional discipline to uphold values instead of taking convenient shortcuts that contradict principles.

15. Responsibility groups with autonomy yet oversight foster leadership growth for junior and senior members alike.

16. Admitting limitations humbly and being vulnerable enables receptivity to feedback, which is critical for trust.

17. As a facilitator during conflicts, you optimize information flow, ensure all voices are heard, and guide constructive dialogue focused on mutual understanding.

18. When mediating conflicts, impartiality, deep listening, uncovering root causes, establishing ground rules, and identifying mutually beneficial solutions are key.

19. Promoting openness through modeling receptivity to feedback and transparency makes you more approachable for early surfacing conflicts.

20. Stepping in as a mediator or facilitator requires discernment regarding when it will help versus strain relationships further.

21. Simple rules, like one person speaking at a time and maintaining constructive language, create a framework for productive conflict dialogue.

22. Encouraging empathy during conflicts builds mutual understanding of differing perspectives and recognition of unintended harms.

23. Intervening swiftly but compassionately when conversations spiral into unconstructive hostility and resetting the tone.

24. Documentation of mediation outcomes, action plans, and follow-ups demonstrates a long-term commitment to restoring team harmony.

25. Immersive collaboration between engineering and customer-facing roles builds firsthand empathy for user needs versus just seeing users as data points.

26. Tight customer feedback loops through support tickets, churn drivers, reviews, etc., directly inform continuous improvements and pain point resolution.

27. Publicly celebrating customer-centric behaviors fosters culture change by linking user focus to growth and peer admiration.

28. Involving engineers directly in customer research and feedback analysis cements customer focus at a visceral level.

CHAPTER 3 COLLABORATION AND TEAM DYNAMICS

29. Reframing engineering priorities using data on user needs and business impact pushes teams to solve real human problems.

30. A long-term customer perspective focused on loyalty and retention often reveals the right trade-offs despite potential short-term costs.

31. Breaking down silos through proactive, immersive collaboration focused on exceptional user experiences regardless of role.

32. Maintaining frequent video-based communication with consistent rhythms and documentation practices preserves cohesion across distributed teams.

33. Virtual team-building activities create shared experiences, while proactive 1:1 relationship-building nurtures interpersonal bonds.

34. Bridging remote and in-office staff through inclusive meetings, discouraging offline decisions, and extensive documentation avoids misalignment.

35. Actively including remote staff in brainstorms and social events rather than limiting participation to present team members physically.

36. Identifying early signals of burnout, like irritability, lack of motivation, and self-doubt, enables candid yet caring conversations about solutions.

37. Taming distractions through structured communication protocols, offline periods, focus blocks, and flexible scheduling empower individual productivity.

CHAPTER 3   COLLABORATION AND TEAM DYNAMICS

38. Standardizing team reliance on communication platforms provides stability and clarity for distributed team members.

39. Assessing which incoming tasks you can handle directly versus delegating consolidates requests and protects team focus.

40. Recognizing and bridging communication complexities stemming from cultural and language differences across global teams.

41. A purposeful one-on-one meeting framework balances rapport building, updates, coaching, action planning, and transitions within a consistent weekly or bi-weekly cadence.

42. Seeking feedback on optimal meeting length and frequency tailors your framework over time to changing team needs.

43. Customizing one-on-one time allotment based on ramps, challenges, and preferences of each direct report.

44. Collaborative note-taking strengthens trust, reinforces shared commitment to progress, and creates a record for consistent follow-up.

45. Consistently assigning clear owners and timelines for the next steps provides post-meeting visibility into accountabilities.

46. Blocking off uninterrupted quality time and eliminating distractions demonstrates care and enables meaningful dialogue.

CHAPTER 3   COLLABORATION AND TEAM DYNAMICS

47. Preparing in advance by reviewing past conversations and crafting thoughtful questions tailored to their needs.

48. Redirecting from status updates to deeper interpersonal conversations focused on their challenges, ideas, and goals.

49. Maintaining confidentiality and consistently following up on action items avoids detrimental pitfalls.

Time to Practice

1. Think of a time when you uncovered a shift in a team member's motivational values based on changes in their life. How did you realign their responsibilities or support to nurture their growth in alignment with their evolving priorities? What coaching questions helped raise their self-awareness?

2. Reflect on an experience where you had to restore trust after a breach within your team. How did you confront the issues compassionately yet courageously? What steps did you take to thoroughly understand all perspectives before outlining a path forward?

3. Recall a conflict situation where you stepped in as a mediator. How did you maintain impartiality when listening to each side? What ground rules and time expectations did you establish to foster open and productive dialogue?

CHAPTER 3   COLLABORATION AND TEAM DYNAMICS

4. Reflect on your relationship-building approach and communication rhythms when leading remote teams. What practices best enabled you to nurture trust and clarity across distributed teams?

5. Consider your one-on-one meeting framework and preparation. What practices work well for strengthening individual connections? How might you improve areas like consistency, focus, or collaborative note-taking?

6. In what ways have you tailored your leadership style and one-on-one support based on a deep individual understanding of team members' needs and motivations? How has this personalized approach impacted their performance and growth?

CHAPTER 4

The Art of Mentoring

The mentoring relationship represents one of the most profound and rewarding connections a leader can establish, as it allows you to shape the next generation of professionals, transfer wisdom to rising talent, and experience the deep fulfillment of unlocking others' potential. By guiding teammates to develop their skills and achieve their ambitions, you facilitate their success and multiply your impact through their future accomplishments.

After exploring crucial leadership principles like embracing feedback, clear communication, and leading by example, you arrive at a pivotal point in your journey: choose to become a mentor. The core lessons from previous chapters, such as the importance of soliciting others' input to refine approaches, ensuring clarity in discussions, and modeling desired behaviors through your actions, have equipped you with foundational skills to guide and develop your staff. These capabilities allow you to listen attentively, communicate expectations clearly, and exemplify the leadership qualities you wish to impart. However, to become an effective mentor, you must go deeper.

Mentorship stems from genuine care, empathy, and understanding of your people as unique individuals. Recall from earlier chapters that investing time to know your team members' motivators, ambitions, and dreams establishes stronger connections and trust. As a mentor, you must go beyond superficial knowledge to understand what drives each person. You must understand their values, passions, and vision for their futures and recognize that every individual has diverse needs and aspirations, which enables you to deliver tailored guidance that helps them grow professionally and personally. These personal insights prove invaluable because you can adapt your mentoring approach to align with mentees' journey and empower them to achieve their full potential. Your empathy, support, and commitment to knowing your people at a deeper level allow you to establish the confidence and openness for a transformative mentoring relationship.

Moreover, as you progress in your leadership journey and establish yourself as an empathetic, insightful mentor, expect to receive growing requests for mentorship from within and beyond your team. Your reputation as a thoughtful mentor will organically spread when you demonstrate deep care for colleagues and commitment to their growth. People at all levels across departments may approach you to become their mentor as they recognize your expertise in leadership or technical domains. Receiving these requests is a privilege and reflects the trust you have built. Be prepared to make time for mentoring relationships while balancing your other responsibilities, and approach each new opportunity with genuine care for the mentee's aspirations and an open mind to learn from their experiences.

Yet, asking someone to become your mentor requires vulnerability. It means admitting you lack specific skills or knowledge and exposing uncertainties about the future. This discomfort deters many from seeking out mentorship. People may hesitate to voice their professional and personal gaps or struggles. Some worry about judgment or appearing incompetent. Others fear wasting mentors' limited time. Several believe they can figure things out themselves. However, suppressing the need for guidance stunts growth. As a leader, recognize these nuances. Make it clear through your words and actions that sharing vulnerabilities represents strength, not weakness. Foster an environment where they can voice their needs without filters or fear of judgment.

When people ask for mentorship, you have the ethical obligation to carefully evaluate if you can guide them effectively in the areas they asked before accepting this commitment. Great leaders recognize when others may be better equipped to mentor in certain domains; this is far from a reason to be ashamed of. A solid self-awareness of your expertise allows you to assess the mentor-mentee fit honestly. If a mentee needs technical or soft skills coaching outside your wheelhouse, introduce them to specialists while still providing overall mentorship. Your goal is truly nurturing their development, not stacking mentees to build a portfolio based on quantity. Understand that mentoring is not like a soccer game where whoever scores more points wins the match. Your program has the power to change someone's life or career, so understand your limits and always seek excellence to make your mentee progress and thrive. If you can handle ten or one at a time, great. But do it gracefully.

Understanding the Nuances Between Coaching and Mentoring

As you guide teammates' growth, you will draw upon two complementary development approaches—coaching and mentoring. Both are valuable for nurturing others' potential. However, failing to recognize the key differences between coaching and mentoring can limit leadership effectiveness. Many use these terms interchangeably, but they address distinct needs. While one focuses on tangible skills and near-term goals, the other takes a broader, long-term professional and personal growth perspective.

As we explore the nuances between these two methods, remember that to become a great leader and mentor, you must fluidly blend coaching and mentoring as situations require, and distinguishing their unique roles empowers you to make the right call and maximize your team's success. Keep this crucial distinction top of mind.

CHAPTER 4   THE ART OF MENTORING

Coaching centers on building specific skills and overcoming tactical hurdles, and it does not require creating a deep connection at the individual level due to its near-term duration. For example, if a developer on your team struggles with mastering test-driven development (TDD), you coach them through focused training. You may walk through TDD principles in hands-on sessions and provide instructional materials to solidify concepts and facilitate troubleshooting exercises tailored to common TDD pitfalls they face. Another compelling alternative is to pair programming with them on actual feature work, enabling real-time guidance as they implement TDD.

This targeted approach focuses on sharpening their abilities to plan incremental tests, write test cases before implementations, and leverage tests to guide development, rapidly expanding their tactical knowledge and hands-on skills with TDD through your guidance. Unlike open-ended mentoring, coaching has a defined scope and duration, focusing on delivering structured knowledge transfer to expand capabilities in the short term and concluding once the developer achieves the desired competency; in this case, sharpening their skills using TDD as part of the development process.

In contrast, mentoring involves an expansive and long-term investment in someone's holistic growth. As a mentor, you guide across technical areas and soft skills, sharing insights on mastering new languages, frameworks, patterns, communication strategy, persuasion and storytelling, and techniques to continue expanding your mentee's capabilities over time. You offer wisdom forged from experience in navigating work relationships and politics, warning mentees of potential organizational landmines and power dynamics. You inspire and motivate.

Another responsibility is to give candid feedback on personal blind spots and areas for improvement that may hinder advancement. Through your observation and investment, you help them identify and address areas for improvement and, at the same time, affirm their strengths. You understand the better resources and connect mentees to networking opportunities, high-visibility projects, and leaders who can accelerate their careers. They see you as an ally for brainstorming creative solutions when facing crossroads involving significant trade-offs between prestige, compensation, responsibilities, work-life balance, and intrinsic fulfillment.

In conclusion, unlike regimented, time-bound coaching, mentoring focuses on nurturing lasting excellence and fulfillment through a trusted relationship cultivated over time. As vulnerabilities and unconscious needs arise, you devote time, energy, and emotional commitment to helping your mentees chart ambitious yet grounded career and personal growth paths. You both recognize that progress doesn't come overnight and commit to crossing the finish line with your best selves.

Reaping the Rewards of Mentorship

As a mentor, you must fully commit to your mentee's growth, devoting focused time and energy to guide them through technical and interpersonal challenges. You care deeply on a personal level, taking their struggles as your own, but you also challenge them directly by illuminating blind spots and providing candid feedback. Although sometimes exchanges may get uncomfortable during the mentoring process, they lead to breakthroughs.

Your commitment and energy throughout the process are rewarded with the feeling of making part of someone's progress. Your mentees flourish in skills they may have never dreamed about, and you set the stage for them to thrive in their careers. Yet, it is okay if you question yourself about the benefits of mentoring someone. At the same time, suggesting coaching or mentoring for your team members may not be as linear as you think due to our natural defensive way of reacting when someone illuminates some of our vulnerabilities and opportunities for improvement. Consequently, you may have to explain why mentoring is a good option and how people benefit from it, and when this time comes, you must be ready to provide the answer confidently.

CHAPTER 4   THE ART OF MENTORING

The Benefits for Mentees

People's motivations for seeking mentorship will vary widely and evolve naturally. For instance, an early career engineer may initially want tactical guidance in navigating new technical responsibilities or learning specific coding standards. In contrast, rising leaders may look to mentors to shore up gaps in business acumen and management skills in hopes of being promotion-ready to higher leadership roles, while others desire greater visibility on high-impact projects or want mentorship focused on accountability, motivation, and support in reaching ambitious goals.

As the mentoring relationship matures and mentees experience significant growth and self-discovery, their priorities and goals for the mentor and mentee relationship often shift. What mentees need from the mentor six months in may look very different from when they started. Yet, regardless of their situation and initial objectives, the core benefits of being a mentee remain constant through all stages of the process. These benefits will vary in priority, but in most cases, they will relate to career guidance or advice, leveling specific skills, improving performance, building confidence, getting new perspectives, shortening their learning path, establishing and sharing a solid network, or even getting emotional support to make tough decisions in their life or career.

Let's start with career guidance and advice. You can provide career guidance to help your mentees navigate their major professional decisions and crossroads and help them gain clarity on their best path forward. Your outside perspective allows you to help assess options more objectively without emotion clouding judgment. When they feel unsure about charting their course, you can illuminate the path by sharing hard-earned lessons from your own experiences, providing practical clarity to help them make informed decisions. Your counsel helps weigh trade-offs holistically, cautioning against tempting shortcuts that could sabotage their vision, effort, and progress. This career guidance directs mentees toward opportunities that stretch their capabilities while aligning with their values.

Another significant benefit is sharpening existing skills and acquiring new ones. Through a well-rounded program, you can connect mentees to ideal training and opportunities tailored to their growth needs and recommend enriching books, podcasts, and resources that align with their learning styles and ambitions to master new skills, both technical and interpersonal, effectively. For example, beyond technical guidance within your domain, you may guide mentees in understanding their impact on business by mapping the value chain between their work and other departments, communicating with impact to pursue others, influencing without authority, and creative problem-solving by outlining best practices.

Furthermore, you give your mentees accountability and encouragement, building their confidence and improving their performance. This vulnerable modeling from someone further along their career path empowers them to recognize that self-doubt is common yet surmountable, unlocking them to move past their doubt with emotional support.

Also, you can provide a refreshing perspective to help them avoid learning through trial and error alone. By candidly recounting experiences earlier in your career, you equip your mentees with critical insights so they can anticipate potential pitfalls and navigate around them strategically, allowing them to bypass the frustrating process of solely learning from their own mistakes over an extended timeframe. Your guidance exposes potential hidden workplace dynamics and politics, equipping your learners to read situations, understand intrinsic implications when making decisions, and avoid common mistakes. The tools you share as part of your mentorship program serve to educate on formulating work philosophy and principles to guide choices and priorities using your system as a blueprint. Rather than reinventing the wheel, they can build upon your lessons and knowledge to make conscious decisions throughout their careers.

CHAPTER 4   THE ART OF MENTORING

Finally, you can provide exposure to your professional network, accelerating their advancement. Introductions to your colleagues, former coworkers, clients, vendors, and other contacts give mentees visibility with respected industry players and accelerate building their networking, providing insider knowledge that helps them make assertive career decisions over time. Interfacing with your network develops relationships that can lead to new opportunities and sponsors, allowing your disciples to gain knowledge and connections and advance their careers far faster than going alone.

The Benefits for Mentors

When considering mentorship, we often focus solely on the valuable benefits to the mentee's growth and overlook how it dramatically contributes to our development as leader and mentor. Guiding others is also highly beneficial for mentors professionally and personally. The commitment and care required to mentor well fundamentally strengthens character, expands skills, and increases empathy at all levels.

You build discipline, active listening abilities, and emotional intelligence by pushing yourself to provide thoughtful guidance tailored to mentees' needs. Embracing the commitment to preparing mentees for success forces you to sharpen your mastery of subjects and reflect on transmitting knowledge effectively. Their fresh perspectives challenge stale assumptions, enriching your worldview and reinforcing leadership virtues like patience, selflessness, and dedication to a purpose larger than oneself.

One of the most rewarding mentor benefits is that teaching others significantly strengthens your learning. As you strive to share wisdom clearly, you gain new insight into subjects you thought you had mastered. Mentees' questions force you to view topics from fresh angles and reexamine concepts you previously took for granted; distilling complex ideas requires revisiting fundamentals more intimately. When mentees struggle with the techniques offered, the process of demonstrating them repeatedly until mastery sticks sharpen your skills. Their novel perspectives reveal blind spots in your knowledge, allowing you to gain as much from mentees' viewpoints as they do from your experience.

Also, serving as a caring mentor greatly expands your empathy and emotional intelligence, which are essential leadership skills. Yet, getting this level of intimacy requires perspective-taking, where you envision challenges from their vantage point, not just your own. It means active, nonjudgmental listening to grasp motivations and goals without projecting. The mentees' diverse backgrounds expose you to rich life experiences that contradict biases, strengthening sensitivity and letting you absorb fresh worldviews that challenge stale assumptions. Adopting this mentee-centric focus strengthens essential human skills such as compassion and adaptability, making you socially and emotionally better.

Last but not least, as you progress as a leader, mentoring others becomes a natural part of your responsibilities. And over time, people around you start seeing you as an authoritative and trusted reference professionally and personally. As you accumulate stories of successful mentorships to your portfolio, don't be surprised as you begin hearing feedback about how your time investment and dedication have impacted people beyond professional growth. They will speak of how your advice guided major life decisions, confidence building, and vision for their futures. This respect and status as a wise counselor on career development, leadership, technical abilities, and life become part of your reputation, driving executives to take note of your strategic leadership abilities, contributing to expanding your influence in promotion processes, sway critical decisions, and receive exciting assignments.

CHAPTER 4   THE ART OF MENTORING

Cultivating a Mentor Mindset

After exploring the professional and personal benefits of mentoring for mentors and mentees, you likely feel inspired to embrace this practice as your next step. However, becoming an impactful mentor demands you push yourself beyond your comfort zone to deliver more than good intentions; it requires cultivating a mindset rooted in foundational attitudes and attributes.

Although sharing your knowledge and experience with an eager mentee may be tempting, taking the time to adopt particular perspectives and principles is essential to genuinely elevating your mentoring experience. Simply imparting wisdom without a solid and motivating framework limits your potential to facilitate the growth of others. Mentoring should be anchored in a deliberate approach, focused on serving your mentee, not stroking your ego. Internalizing this mindset allows you to establish a meaningful connection with your pupil to maximize your impact as a guide.

One of the biggest misconceptions among people who choose to become mentors is relying solely on expertise in a domain and interpersonal skills as quality indicators. If you pick this path, it's essential to understand that embracing philosophies that put mentee needs first, pursuing constant learning, letting go of ego, and leading with compassion are more impactful than any expertise. If you make your mentorship program a stage where the spotlights are on you, you will fail. Acting as the protagonist instead of the coadjuvant, you will fail. If you force people to embrace a practice or try something not appealing to them just because you think it's the right way to achieve something, it will lead you to fail. If you focus your efforts on analysis or evaluations instead of observations and needs, well, you got the point.

Instead, to make your mentorship program a success, you must cultivate a mindset where you seek to understand your mentee's motivations and needs, communicate compassionately to influence them positively, reflect on your actions and behaviors, enhance your cultural sensitivity, and assume a selflessness posture. Additionally, you recognize that you are the navigator instead of the driver and that you are the mentor, not the boss. Let's dive into these enabling attitudes that separate mentors who teach versus those who transform lives and careers.

One of the most significant causes that breaks a mentorship program is to make it too personal for you. You care so much that you want to make the program succeed at any cost, even if it means stepping on your mentee's toes. You must firmly understand that you must act as a navigator, not a driver, in your mentee's development journey. You provide guidance and direction without imposing directives or forcing your preferred path. Avoid commandeering their growth experience based solely on your biases, tastes, or agenda. Rather than specifying prescriptive steps, share your knowledge and experience to outline potential routes and trade-offs, but let them evaluate independently to acquire autonomy in choosing their direction.

You can't and shouldn't attempt to force your rigid choices or expectations without regard for their needs and goals, which leads us to the next attitude. Unlike some eventual daily situations where you must drive decisions to break paralysis or mitigate business risk, you are the mentor, not the boss, in a mentoring relationship. It's vital to have this difference in mind. As a mentor, your role is to guide, support, and empower, not dictate. You aim to enrich their decision-making by providing insights and enlightening possibilities. But the choices remain theirs. This attitude highlights the importance of humility and celebrates that you don't need to be the most intelligent person in the room just because you are the mentor. After all, effective mentorship thrives as a collaborative partnership, not a dictatorship.

Adopting the previous attitudes makes you well-equipped to embrace a selflessness posture. Dedicate your time, effort, and energy beyond self-promoting, and be prepared to give more than you receive—mentor for intrinsic rewards, not extrinsic validation. Avoid letting your pride, control issues, or rigidity create silly and unnecessary distractions. Get away from instincts to gain credit or praise; the relationship exists to serve your mentee's development on their terms, not to stroke your ego. Foster an environment where your mentees feel you truly care by making them the priority. Be their ally, not judge. Summon the courage to share power and relinquish the need to be the expert with all the answers and last words.

Another vital aspect of your journey as a mentor is recognizing that people have different personalities and behaviors. You may get a satisfactory result using a particular technique with one but get a completely different outcome using the same practice with another. Being open and discussing vulnerabilities may be daunting for many people, making it challenging to identify their needs and requests, and adopting a compassionate communication style is essential to manage these situations. You must be open and aware that behind any self-doubt, demotivation, or unclear messages, there are often unmet needs that could undermine the entire mentoring relationship if left unaddressed. These may relate to confidence, past failures, competence gaps, or trauma that inhibits skill development. With compassion as your guide, you can foster the trust and psychological safety for mentees to voice these unspoken gaps and inhibitions. Then, your wisdom and care can empower them to conquer inner obstacles and unlock their potential.

Furthermore, exposure to different cultures and beliefs is more common as the world becomes more remote, making cultural sensitivity a vital element for inclusive mentorship. Respectfully understanding diverse backgrounds and perspectives allows you to help mentees better. Do not make assumptions based on your worldview, and recognize how different cultures influence communication, values, and needs. Educate yourself on the mentees' cultural context to adapt your guidance appropriately. Ask open questions to gain insights about their experiences and how they perceive advice, and recognize that some may be reluctant to challenge your suggestions over the journey. Highlight common ground and emphasize you want to collaborate. Remember the principle of Communicate Clearly discussed in Chapter 1, and avoid idioms as phrases may translate oddly or offensively across cultures.

Finally, adopt a regular self-reflection practice and improvement to remain an effective mentor amid evolving needs. Reflect on your mentoring practices, shared advice, and interactions. Instead of sugarcoating your self-analysis, try to get yourself out of your perspective and imagine you are a flying bug sitting on the wall, observing your actions and behaviors during a mentor session. How do you see yourself? Did you listen attentively and avoid assumptions? Were discussions thought-provoking? Did body language convey care? Were you guiding on behalf of your ego or for your mentee's welfare and progress? Could patience and compassion increase? Imagine mentee perspectives on your guidance to check for tone-deafness. Do not rest on your laurels or assume your approach needs no adjustments. Also, assess whether your energy and commitment are unwavering and guard against mentor fatigue.

No mentor is perfect, and that is okay. What matters is having the humility and wisdom to regularly self-analyze and grow. View continuous improvement itself as a core competency and commit to making each mentee relationship more substantial than the last. Reflection ensures you adapt to serve every person's emerging needs at their highest level.

Mentorship Program Structure: A Blueprint to Success

When establishing a mentorship program, avoid improvising sessions based solely on mentees' immediate needs once a lack of structure risks losing momentum, failing to address core competencies, and sending mixed signals on expectations. Instead, develop a multi-phase program flow that methodically progresses through establishing rapport, aligning on goals, imparting knowledge, and closing out the engagement.

CHAPTER 4   THE ART OF MENTORING

Matching and Orientation, Profiling, Developing and Learning, and Closing and Celebrating represent these phases. Each stage aims to facilitate your pupil's growth while ensuring a consistent, productive cadence. Although situations may require flexibility in pacing or focus areas, retaining the core four phases lends credibility through a proven framework anchored in mutual understanding.

In the Matching and Orientation phase, you will understand mentees' aspirations and how you can assist them. Also, you will explain the program structure and establish your boundaries so both sides can consciously evaluate the mentor-mentee relationship compatibility. Next, the Profiling phase involves mapping needs, values, principles, and motivations through exercises that identify areas for improvement and the likelihood and determination to progress on each so you can define the optimal approach to tailor the program. The following stage, Developing and Learning, supports growth via personalized Individual Development Plans and tailored goals based on mentees' core needs and motivators while directly helping with their ad-hoc needs. Finally, the Closing and Celebrating phase conducts final goal evaluations and retrospective assessments of what went well and areas for improvement through open dialogue.

With this strategic four-phase blueprint in place, you gain a proven framework for maximizing your mentoring impact and efficiency. The structured cadence lends credibility and consistency, so you can focus entirely on nurturing advancement rather than worrying about ad-hoc logistics. Gradually progressing through milestones ensures momentum continues, core competencies get addressed, and expectations remain aligned. Consequently, your time and energy stay concentrated on facilitating growth through a personalized approach tailored to mentees' needs and styles. Moreover, steady evaluations and celebrations of incremental progress keep engagement high and flowing. This framework equips you with tools to elevate the relationship from transient coaching to lifelong mentorship.

Now, let's explore each phase to equip you with a strategic approach, supporting you in organizing your mentorship program. Yet, as you embark on this section, remember your role is to illuminate, not dictate. The path and the success depend on a two-way commitment to growth.

Phase 1: Matching and Orientation

The Matching and Orientation phase lays the foundation for the entire program, where you will gain clarity on mentees' aspirations and how you can support their growth. Additionally, you will explain the program structure, logistics, commitments, and boundaries to align with expectations. This open communication allows both sides to evaluate compatibility and determine if the match enables success. Be transparent if you identify a mismatch ahead of time, as deciding not to move forward and illuminating the reasons can be an act of caring. Run this phase deliberately, as adopting a stance rooted in transparency will facilitate mutual understanding and strengthen your relationship. Invest time upfront to understand motivations and ensure proper fit before dedicating your time, effort, and passion to the project.

Start by understanding their backgrounds and ambitions, and schedule an extended session focused solely on their story. Explore their career path, accomplishments, difficulties, lessons learned, and future aspirations. Grasp what they are willing to get from this relationship with you as their mentor. Listen intently to facts and emotional undertones revealing passion and drive. Identify the inflection points that shaped their development and perceptions. For example, a mentee may feel devastated after failing to complete an unrealistic project timeline set by a previous manager. They observe that they didn't contribute to the goal setting, and while persistence is essential, goals must also align with current capabilities to be achievable. From this experience, you can extract the mentee's values of resilience and learning from challenges, the principle that goals must be realistic and match skills, and the motivation to pursue

CHAPTER 4   THE ART OF MENTORING

self-improvement and belonging. This fuller context illuminates work styles, motivations, and support needed to excel. While you can't absorb someone's full complexity quickly, striving to view their professional journey through their lens fosters empathy and insights into fit.

Furthermore, while learning their background is insightful, directly explore why they are seeking guidance as understanding the motivation behind the request reveals its importance to growth and illuminates the level of potential commitment. Ask how much time and energy they can dedicate to sessions, assignments, and working on development areas. Gauge their discipline and determination. In addition, have the mentee comprehensively describe your profile, capabilities, experience, and approach that made you stand out as a potential mentor. This exchange highlights areas of alignment and any mismatches between the mentee's developmental needs versus your expertise, communication style, and strengths. If misalignments emerge, transparently discuss viability or suggest alternative mentors before proceeding. This honesty is paramount to allow you to tailor the relationship for maximum impact.

Although knowing your potential mentee on a deeper level is paramount, ensure you share your background, career journey, challenges overcome, and motivations for becoming a mentor in a way that highlights alignment with their needs. Explain how you deliver value and can contribute to their growth through providing strategic advice, networking, crafting personalized development plans, guiding goal setting, contributing to problem-solving, offering candid feedback, or other ways that fit into your reality. The focus is to illustrate that your knowledge and approach can guide them toward realizing their potential and achieving aspirations through your mentorship program.

Now that you've introduced one another, it's time to explain the program structure. Start by emphasizing that your mentoring approach is tailored to their needs and values, not a one-size-fits-all formula, and explain that each session and exercise has clearly defined goals to provide focus and track progress. Based on experience, recommend an

CHAPTER 4 THE ART OF MENTORING

ideal program duration of 16–24 weeks while allowing flexibility based on mentee needs. This timeline allows for tangible growth and skill development without losing momentum. Also, reinforce that the efficiency and effectiveness of the program require a substantial commitment from both sides. It's worth mentioning that there are no shortcuts to meaningfully expanding one's capabilities.

Then, define the typical meeting cadence bi-weekly for 45- to 60-minute sessions. This cadence balances consistency with flexibility to accommodate schedules. The week between meetings provides time to absorb concepts and practice applying new skills. This combination of personalized content, clearly defined session goals, committed duration, and consistent pacing comprises a strategic framework optimized to unleash your mentee's potential.

Next, provide an overview of the program phases, including the Matching and Orientation, Profiling, Developing and Learning, and Closing and Celebrating stages. Explain that each step has defined goals and outcomes; Matching and Orientation establish rapport, alignment, and fit; Profiling maps strengths, needs, motivations, and objectives; Developing and Learning executes the personalized growth plan through knowledge sharing; Closing and Celebrating reflects on progress and cementing lessons learned. Highlight that despite this structure, there is flexibility to address their immediate needs, like reviewing a presentation, getting advice on a workplace challenge, or supporting in resolving conflicts. Outlining this phased approach provides a strategic framework while allowing customization to their priorities, ensuring they see you as a partner and not as a one-off guide.

Additionally, have an open discussion to align on boundaries, as this transparency can make or break the mentoring relationship. Define appropriate personal topics that relate to professional growth versus off-limits areas like family or personal relationships. Cover your availability for meetings and impromptu contact like emails or texts. Share which communication mediums you prefer, such as email, phone, video calls, etc. Explain your feedback style involves objectively describing the situation, the observable behavior, and its impact. Establish that everything shared in confidence will remain strictly confidential—for instance, discussions around workplace challenges, interpersonal conflicts, or performance issues.

In closing this foundational alignment discussion, solicit your mentee's genuine feedback on the program overview. Unfortunately, sometimes you will hear vague statements like "sounds good." Although well-intentioned, these superficial responses provide little substantive value for tailoring an optimal experience. Gently push past the temptation to accept pleasantries by explaining that you want to ensure the program resonates with their needs and style. Instead, draw out richer perspectives by asking targeted follow-up questions. What elements resonated most or caused concerns? How does this approach fit your needs and reality? Are there adjustments to boundaries, pace, or style that would maximize comfort? Listen intently for implicit cues revealing more profound thoughts. Reflect on their emotions and priorities. This approach confirms your commitment to a mentee-centric partnership, not a one-sided dynamic. Adapting based on continuous feedback demonstrates your dedication to their growth and welfare, establishing the trust and mutual understanding essential for impactful mentorship.

Phase 2: Profiling

The Profiling phase delves deeper to map your mentee's needs, values, motivators, and goals. As discussed in Chapter 3 on Uncovering Individuality, this understanding spotlights areas for development and behavioral tendencies. Profiling works because people's past experiences shape future performance and reactions. Recall my pivotal moment from the book's introduction, where a toxic work culture revealed my motivation to become a more empathetic leader focused on unlocking others' potential. However, the profiling exercise is only possible if you create a safe environment nurtured with trust where safety is the cornerstone.

Once you establish this connection, you will notice that gaining a chronological view of your mentee's life story provides invaluable context for this process stage. Have them share experiences from childhood to the present day while respecting their comfort level regarding sensitive topics. Listen intently for themes revealing core values that formed over time, such as dedication, curiosity, or community. Note challenges faced and resilience built through hardship, from bullying to health issues. Identify when interests first sparked and motivations took root that still drive them now, whether a lifelong passion for technology or a desire to help others. Look for pivotal moments that profoundly shaped their outlooks, like a mentor who instilled confidence. Observe their emotional responses and what experiences left lasting impacts or scars. This comprehensive narrative helps map their developmental arc across personal and professional dimensions, empowering you to adapt your mentoring approach based on more profound empathy and insights into their behaviors, needs, and potential blind spots.

After developing a deep understanding of your mentee's life story, core values, motivations, and principles, the next vital step is connecting these insights to their goals, aspirations, and reasons for seeking mentorship. Have an in-depth discussion where they unpack their desired goals and what they hope to achieve through this relationship. Listen for objectives tied to career advancement, skill development, work-life balance, and overall well-being. Ask probing questions to unearth parallel development areas that could enable their goals. Identify both near-term milestones and longer-term ambitions. Discuss obstacles and where they most need guidance to break through and link these goals back to the motivations and experiences that shaped them. This linkage provides essential context to personalize an approach that accelerates their progress.

CHAPTER 4   THE ART OF MENTORING

The Roles and Scaling Exercise

Even though the idea of unfolding parallel areas of improvement may sound complex, the exercise Roles and Scaling may facilitate this process for you. This technique explores the mentee's roles in their professional and personal life, enabling deep reflection on where they are in given roles, where they want to get, and the level of their self-awareness and determination to progress—visual support will make the exercise easier to digest and more effective, so incentivize the mentee to take notes throughout the discussion.

After listing their roles—for instance, father, leader, brother, son, mentor, writer, volunteer, etc.—select each individually and have the mentee visualize a satisfaction scale from one to ten related to that role, and ask them to describe both ends in their own words, as perceptions vary based on personality. What does one look like to them? How would they define a ten? Understanding how they define fulfillment and dissatisfaction lets you understand their needs and motivations. Next, invite them to close their eyes, imagine where they currently fall on the fulfillment scale for a particular role, and have them share the reason for such a score. Then, based on their definition of one and ten, ask where they want to be on the scale for that role to feel fulfilled and if they can list what needs to be done to drive them to achieve the desired score on the scale.

Have them walk through this scaling visualization for each significant role in their life and identify roles where they rank themselves low and which represent the highest sources of energy and meaning. The gap between their current and desired state reveals priorities for development. You will notice that sometimes the gap between how they perceive reality versus where they dream to achieve is large, like a current score of four and a desired score of nine. In this situation, avoid setting the far goal initially once they may need to develop more self-awareness or maturity on the incremental steps to get there. Instead, ask what they recognize necessary to do to reach the next couple of levels on the scale. Break larger goals into smaller ones and highlight that establishing realistic interim objectives keeps motivation high while building capabilities over time is vital.

To conclude the exercise, for a few minutes, have the pupil reflect on where they currently rank for each role, where they want to be to feel fulfilled, and what's necessary to get there. Then, ask them to draw one final one to ten scale representing their level of determination and motivation to move the needle and achieve the desired score. Ask where they fall on this motivation scale, with one being low motivation to do what's required and ten being incredibly determined to get there. This insight exposes potential gaps between aspirations and willingness to put in the effort. If it ranks low, explore resistance. If determination is high, brainstorm incremental objectives.

For example, they may rate their leadership skills at a five but desire a nine, with a motivation of seven. The solid determination is promising, while the gap may signal the need to adjust their expectation in reality and work incrementally to cross the finish line. For instance, suppose they recognize the need to become more influential as part of the definition of nine. In this case, you may work in impactful communication or bridge the gap between the Engineering and Support teams as smaller objectives to progress over the next levels. Alternatively, they may rank their health as a four but with motivation only a three. Here, you would compassionately dig into their reluctance to change habits before targeting goals and help them address these obstacles.

This multilayered scaling assessment provides insights into their goals, needs, and motivational outlook. Revisit it periodically to track evolutions as your relationship and their self-awareness deepen.

After the Profiling stage, you will have a customized roadmap to guide this individual toward their best self. By understanding their values, motivations, principles, and goals, you can tailor an approach that aligns with who they are. The insights gained into their various life roles, current

CHAPTER 4   THE ART OF MENTORING

fulfillment levels, desired states, and determination to progress spotlight priority areas for growth, allowing you to comprehend their needs and nature at a foundational level.

Their story illuminates the "why," while their goals define the "what." Bridge these together to maximize your mentoring impact by bringing skill-building to life in a way that resonates with their unique passions and priorities. Concluding this phase equips you to propel them to the next step of the mentorship program.

Phase 3: Developing and Learning

The Developing and Learning phase represents the core of the mentorship journey, where growth takes flight through practical and structured guidance and real-time support. This phase entails two interconnected facets—personalized development plans to build capabilities methodically over time and on-demand advising to tackle immediate needs.

Using the Profiling Outcome to Drive Objectives

Start by analyzing the outcomes from the Profiling phase to determine which insights carry the most potential to drive success for the mentee's primary goals stated earlier. Together, reflect on which roles and scaling score targets may contribute directly to their central ambitions around career, skills, and overall well-being, and identify definitions of excellence versus mediocrity that revealed unmet expectations and motivations. Then, channel these key understandings to establish focus areas to guide your knowledge-sharing sessions throughout the mentorship program.

At the same time, while structure provides consistency, never lose sight that this relationship centers on your mentee's needs. Be agile in shifting focus to address obstacles or questions arising in their work. Shed light on ongoing issues by asking thoughtful questions to encourage a solution-driven mindset rather than solving the problem yourself. Fostering autonomy and ownership remains key. Though you may provide advice or resources, the mentee must drive their development. It is paramount to remember that you are the navigator, not the driver. By balancing executing a tailored roadmap and readily available support when needs emerge, you demonstrate commitment to their ongoing advancement and empowerment, enriching the mentee's experience and trust in you.

Setting Goals: The Fuel for Effective Mentorship

Once you set the stage for handling ad-hoc and planned necessities and with key focus areas identified, you are ready to bring the mentee's goals to life. A pivotal step is co-creating Individual Development Plans outlining tangible objectives tailored to their motivations and growth needs spotted during profiling.

While we will discuss a blended approach later, being aware of different goal-setting models enables mixing and matching as needed. These include SMART (Specific, Measurable, Achievable, Relevant, Time-bound) goals; OKRs (Objectives and Key Results); GROW (Goals, Reality, Options, Way Forward); BHAG (Big Hairy Audacious Goals); VISION (Valuable, Inspiring, Specific, Intentional, Natural); and many others. Yet, the core idea behind any IDP is to create a practical roadmap guiding the mentee to achieve an objective through tailored, incremental goals reflecting their motivations. For example, SMART establishes incremental progress indicators by making Specific, Measurable, Achievable, Relevant, and Time-Bound plans, bringing focus and accountability. OKRs define how goals will be accomplished through concrete Objectives and measurable Key Results, structuring execution. VISION delineates longer-term targets fostering motivation. BHAG sets bold, daring ambitions driving breakthroughs. GROW provides a systematic structure of Goals, examining Reality, identifying Options, and clarifying the Way Forward, enabling thoughtful planning.

Even though each of these frameworks has a proven track of effectiveness, in the upcoming section, you will learn how to blend SMART with OKRs into a robust approach that leverages the strengths of

CHAPTER 4   THE ART OF MENTORING

each. Together, they provide the what and the how to turn ambitions into realities. While OKRs give the roadmap, SMART goals fuel the engine to stay on track. By following this recommendation, you equip your mentees with a comprehensive structure to systematically guide efforts toward self-improvement and personalized plans.

However, setting short-term goals as part of your program is as important as working on long-term ones. Although IDPs provide a structure for broader development goals, these small-sized goals help maintain engagement and momentum. Set specific objectives for each mentoring session, such as preparatory homework, researching concepts from your discussions, or summarizing key takeaways. These mini-goals stimulate deep thinking, accountability, and commitment while keeping development top of mind. Celebrate these achievements with the same enthusiasm as for achieving more significant milestones. They will set the pace, make progress tangible, and serve as a refreshing fuel when procrastination comes to light. Then, set the next steps collaboratively and ensure these near-term objectives align with longer IDP milestones to build confidence and excitement to pursue bolder ambitions.

Furthermore, as progress becomes tangible, action points will inevitably arise, and following up on open actions and exercises from previous sessions needs to become second nature to support the program's success. Perceive them as part of the short-term goals mentioned before.

Delivering Feedback: Objective Observations Instead of Shallow Statements

Additionally, provide prompt, constructive feedback using the Situation-Behavior-Impact (SBI) model grounded in objective observations. For example, ineffective feedback may be "You don't seem very committed to our mentoring sessions and don't follow through on your action items." In contrast, SBI-framed feedback would be, "In our last few mentorship meetings (Situation), I've noticed you've come unprepared without completing agreed action items (Behavior). This makes our discussions less productive and hinders your development progress (Impact)." Avoid unhelpful criticism targeting the person versus actionable behaviors.

Conversely, praises require the same level of commitment and structure to go beyond tapping shoulder. Many leaders and mentors overlook the importance of sharing compliments based on concrete observations, making a powerful tool a useless resource. For instance, an empty appraisal may sound like, "You did a great job on that project!" Observe that the receiver can't extract what went well and will not know what they should keep doing or the standard for quality or success you are using to evaluate their performance. Let's reframe this compliment using the SBI model, "When you led the team to deliver that complex project under tight deadlines last month (Situation), I was impressed by how you kept morale high with your positive attitude while ensuring meticulous attention to detail (Behavior). This resulted in us delighting the client with high-quality work delivered on schedule (Impact).

The first example is vague, subjective praise that lacks actionable details. In contrast, the SBI-framed praise specifically cites the situation, behaviors that stood out, and the impact on the project's success. You moved the needle from a generic and ineffective approach to a meaningful and impactful one that calls out exactly which actions had an exemplary impact so the person can replicate success.

Sharing Resources: The Food for Thoughts

In addition to feedback and advice, an impactful part of the Developing and Learning phase is sharing relevant resources that contribute to the mentee's growth, including books, online courses, TED talks, articles, podcasts, and other materials aligned with their goals, needs, and optimal ways of learning.

Yet, when providing supplemental resources, it's important to be sure to follow up in the next session about whether the materials were useful and resonated with their learning preferences. For example, if you recommended an insightful but lengthy book, check if a concise video summary or interactive course may have been more digestible. Despite their applicability on paper, you must recognize that not all resources will be impactful or practical in real life.

Demonstrate openness to adapt recommendations based on the mentee's feedback and demonstrated engagement. If certifications energize them, explore options to deepen their technical expertise. If podcasts got a lukewarm reception, curate inspiring speeches and share vivid stories instead. There is no one-size-fits-all approach to knowledge sharing—personalize resources to fit the individual.

The Power of Networking

Expanding your mentee's professional network is a pivotal part of their growth. Strategically integrating them into your network creates opportunities for mutually beneficial collaboration. Your contacts can provide insider expertise that complements the knowledge you impart through mentorship. Meanwhile, the pupil contributes fresh perspectives and abilities in engagements with your network.

These connections accelerate their advancement through access to people, skills, and experiences otherwise unavailable at their current stage. Working alongside respected industry veterans boosts their credibility while contributing value develops confidence. Together, brainstorm creative ways for the mentee to interact with your network, whether through informational interviews, shadowing experienced members on projects, taking on short-term work, or providing pro-bono services to gain exposure.

This real-world experience allows them to strengthen competencies and gain visibility rapidly. Guide them through classes and conferences to widen their circle, and when the time is right, leverage your relationships to endorse their readiness. A strong network is lifelong social capital; their world progressively expands with your guidance.

Through structured guidance and on-demand support, you provide the means to empower mentees to pursue knowledge and practice lessons learned. Customized IDPs offer a personalized roadmap for development while short-term goals maintain momentum between meetings. Constructive SBI feedback accelerates growth, along with sharing curated resources. Expanding professional connections opens doors. With commitment and care, you supply tools for advancement. Your role is to uncover hidden potential, whereas their role is to realize it through dedicated effort. This phase equips them to chart their course, yet the destination depends on their determination. Once they have found their way and achieved their objectives, you are ready to move to the program's final phase.

Phase 4: Closing and Celebrating

The Closing and Celebrating phase provides meaningful closure through final evaluations and reflection. In this culminating meeting, the mentor and mentee review the journey, assess goal achievement, share feedback, express appreciation, and set intentions going forward. This is a celebration of both tangible advancement and intangible personal growth.

Discuss what goals have been met through deliberate effort. For unfinished goals, identify contributing obstacles and lessons learned. Exchange honest feedback on the relationship using the Situation-Behavior-Impact model focused on productive improvement. Convey genuine gratitude for the privilege of guiding their development. Outline intentions for informal engagement as needs arise. This phase honors the relationship that made progress possible.

While formal mentorship concludes, an opportunity for lifelong impact emerges. The personal bond forged enables future informal engagement as needs arise. However, the most significant closing gift is intangible—being part of someone's growth, directly and indirectly, will fuel your purpose indefinitely. Honor that your guidance facilitated, but their determination actualized the transformation. Beyond skills gained, the greatest achievement is expanding their vision of what is possible. As renowned poet Maya Angelou wrote, "We delight in the beauty of the butterfly but rarely admit the changes it has gone through to achieve that beauty." Through your mentorship, you contributed to their metamorphosis. Be proud and cherish that privilege as you both transition to bold new chapters.

Crafting Impactful Individual Development Plans

An Individual Development Plan is a personalized roadmap portraying the shared commitment between mentor and mentee to nurture advancement. It captures targeted goals, accountable metrics, and development timeframes designed collaboratively to help mentees achieve their full potential. Unlike informal coaching, which often tackles short-term needs, an IDP provides an intentional, strategic scaffolding for sustaining long-term growth tied directly to the mentee's motivations and ambitions.

A well-rounded IDP shifts the focus from loosely defined development areas to breaking down concrete, measurable objectives. Together, you transform lofty but vague aspirations into clearly defined incremental milestones, delineating tactical and sequenced action steps to make abstract goals feel actionable and attainable, leading to achievement. You progress from dreaming big-picture outcomes to mapping out manageable steps to make those dreams a reality. An IDP illuminates the direction and pace of the path to turn ambitions into achievements.

Yet, a common misconception is that many mentees and mentors handle the IDP artifact as a one-off document once created. In reality, an impactful IDP must remain a living, breathing blueprint, requiring consistent follow-ups and check-ins to review progress on goals and key milestones. Anchoring development to a static, outdated plan contradicts the spirit of mentorship. It stifles growth once assumptions made early on may become invalid over time and don't align with your mentee's needs. Maintaining openness to recalibrate timeframes or modify steps is essential when life circumstances or mentee priorities shift, and you must build it in flexibility to add new enrichment opportunities that align with their passions as they evolve.

SMART Goals and OKRs: Uncovering the Foundation

Even though the Individual Development Plan provides the overarching structure for the roadmap, adopting a goal-setting framework may support you with well-rounded strategies to make the document more relatable and compelling. Yet, combining some of these frameworks still provides you with a more robust structure to support a long-term journey while maintaining a satisfactory level of personalization.

Moving forward, you will learn a blended approach based on the SMART and OKR models. This combination channels the strengths of each to accelerate the mentee's advancement throughout their growth journey. However, before deep-diving into this strategy, let's better understand the nuances of each of these frameworks separately.

OKRs stands for Objectives and Key Results. Objectives are memorable, qualitative descriptions of the overarching goal you want to accomplish. For example, an Objective could be "Become an expert and certificate professional in Project Management." Observe that it captures the essence of the desired outcome in a short, inspirational phrase that energizes mentees.

Key Results are quantitative metrics tied to initiatives that measure incremental progress toward achieving the Objective. For the example Objective mentioned earlier, Key Results could be "Read the PMBOK and highlight key concepts," "Create a distilled summary from the PMBOK manual," "Pass the PMP exam," or "Acquire 100 PDUs (Project Development Units) through training." OKRs intentionally separate the aspirational "what" from the executable "how" to maintain focus on the end goal while clarifying how to achieve it through specific Key Results defining initiatives.

On the other hand, we have the SMART goals framework. SMART is an acronym for Specific, Measurable, Achievable, Relevant, and Time-Bound goals. Specific defines that the goal must have a clear, detailed definition of what you must accomplish to avoid ambiguity and lack of focus. Measurable sets the standard that the objective must have tangible metrics and indicators to track progress, providing visibility on achievement and gaps. Achievable preaches that you should stretch capabilities but be realistic, given available resources, knowledge, and timeframes. Relevant defines that you must align with the individual's values, motivations, and development needs identified during mentoring. Time-bound is the guardrail for commitment, meaning you must have clearly defined timeframes and deadlines, fostering accountability and urgency.

Let's convert the previous example into a SMART goal:

Specific:

- Complete a project management certification program by passing the Project Management Professional (PMP) exam to gain formally recognized skills for leading engineering teams and projects.

CHAPTER 4   THE ART OF MENTORING

Measurable:

- Study for the PMP certification exam for at least 15 hours per week.
- Read the PMBOK guide and make chapter summaries.
- Take practice exams, scoring at least 80% correct before registering.
- Schedule to take the PMP exam by December 30, 2023.

Achievable:

- Research PMP prep courses and schedule one within the next month.
- Block out consistent time in my calendar to study.
- Utilize practice exams and other PMP exam resources.
- I have the available time and focus needed to prepare.

Relevant:

- Gaining formal project management skills will strengthen my capabilities to lead larger engineering initiatives in my current role and align with my two-year goal to become an engineering manager.

Time-Bound:

- Complete a prep course within two months.
- Be exam-ready within five months.
- Pass the PMP exam by December 30, 2023.

A quality indicator of how a SMART goal is defined comes from the ability to consolidate it into a single statement encapsulating all criteria. As illustrated in the example, with a sufficiently detailed SMART goal, you can capture the whole ambition in one insightful sentence:

CHAPTER 4   THE ART OF MENTORING

To strengthen my project management skills to become an Engineering Manager within two years, I will complete a PMP certification program by studying for at least 15 hours per week, summarizing the PMBOK guide, scoring 80% on practice exams, and passing the PMP exam by December 30th, 2023.

This comprehensive statement hits all components—specific certification and skills targeted, measurable preparation and exam details, achievable execution plan, relevance to career goals, and the time-bound deadline.

OKR + SMART: A Personalized Approach to Growth

In the previous section, we explored the power of both the OKR and SMART goal-setting frameworks. But you can still elevate your strategy for goal setting to another level. By blending SMART's structured process with OKRs' inspirational vision, you can empower people to pursue meaningful objectives in a structured yet adaptable way. You keep the strategic and long-term visions close enough to provide direction and purpose and ensure your goals are well-defined, relevant, and achievable.

Although inspirational on their own, OKRs, with their qualitative objectives and aspirational key results, risk becoming too vague or abstract without clear, measurable plans for execution. The ambitious vision alone lacks the tactical details and the necessary incremental steps to ground goals and translate aspirations into reality firmly. Conversely, SMART criteria provide helpful structure, but adhering rigidly to incremental milestones can cultivate narrow thinking that loses sight of the big-picture vision, and focusing solely on the precise measurable steps, it becomes easy to forget why the goal matters. Simply fulfilling a timeline risks an empty "check box" mentality.

However, merged, they balance vision with structure. Incorporating SMART metrics as part of Key Results under an ambitious OKR objective counteracts vagueness with concrete execution plans. Let's convert the previous example into this metamorphic approach.

Objective: Become an Expert and Certified Professional in Project Management

Key Result 1: Obtain PMP Certification Within Six Months

Specific:

- Understand the eligibility requirements and an exam syllabus.
- Read the PMBOK guide and make chapter summaries.
- Research what preparation resources the PMP community recommends.

Measurable:

- Study 15 hours/week.
- Complete 70 hours (PDUs) of study with the PMP exam prep course.
- Take three practice exams, scoring 80%+.
- Create a mindmap of concepts per area of interest.

Achievable:

- Block two hours daily for studying.
- Enroll in the prep course within one month.
- Conclude any self-served course in less than two months.
- Use provided materials and practice exams.

Relevant:

- PMP aligns with my goal of becoming an engineering manager and strengthening my project management skills to become more effective and efficient for my team and company.

Time-Bound:

- Take the exam by the end of Q4'2024.

Key Result 2: Attend Two Project Management Conferences in the Next Year

Specific:

- Identify two relevant conferences by the end of Q1'2023.
- Primary topics should cover Agile methodology.

Measurable:

- Create a checklist of target conferences and track registration/attendance.
- Gather 5+ insights per event.
- Publish two articles related to the conferences, highlighting the key takeaways.

Achievable:

- Discuss the conference budget with the manager and get the budget approval to attend the event.
- Buy conference tickets in advance and register in the desired tracks.
- Book travel/accommodations early.

Relevant:

- Conferences will expose me to the latest trends in Agile project management, expand my network, and allow me to exchange experiences related to the field, supporting the adoption of new concepts and processes to optimize team performance and business growth.

Time-Bound:

- Attend both conferences by the end of Q3'2023.

This IDP example demonstrates the power of blending OKRs and SMART to create a robust goal-setting framework tailored to the individual. The aspirational objective provides a qualitative vision—becoming an expert and certified project management professional, encapsulating the end ambition in an inspirational manner. The key results then break this down into three central quantifiable outcomes to make the objective concrete—obtaining PMP certification, attending conferences, and publishing insights. Defining these measurable targets maintains focus on the big-picture vision. Finally, the SMART details under each key result structure the execution plan, outlining specific actions, metrics, resources needed, and deadlines to accomplish each outcome.

Together, the aspirational objective, measurable key results, and tactical SMART plans combine to form a comprehensive IDP. The OKR components provide direction and purpose, while SMART grounds it with achievable milestones—this blended model leverages complementary frameworks to motivate and empower customized advancement.

Technical skills may be taught, but the inner potential is unlocked through connection. By intentionally dedicating your time, passion, and energy and adopting a tailored approach, mentors inspire the path for mentees to come into their own. Although the formal journey ends, bonds developed allow lifelong impact. Equipped with new wisdom, your mentees can continue ascending, transformed from within.

CHAPTER 4 THE ART OF MENTORING

To conclude, as you progress through each phase of your mentorship program, approach this relationship deliberately yet adaptable to emerging needs. Establish trust and psychological safety first as a foundation for growth. Listen intently to understand, not merely respond—co-create ambitious yet attainable goals fueled by the mentee's motivations. Share knowledge creatively tailored to their learning preferences. Introduce opportunities aligned with their passions. But above all, commit to their development with care, wisdom, and empathy. The technical mentoring competencies explored here serve as means, not ends. Keep the mentee's holistic advancement and fulfillment central always.

Takeaways

1. Mentoring is a privilege that allows you to shape others' potential and growth. Approach it with care, wisdom, and empathy.

2. Mentoring stems from understanding people's motivations, ambitions, and dreams at a deeper level. Invest time to know your mentees.

3. Mentoring differs from coaching. Coaching focuses on tactical skills and is short-term. Mentoring is long-term and holistic.

4. Effective mentors adopt principles like selflessness, openness to learn, letting go of ego, compassion, and cultural awareness.

5. Successful mentoring requires a structured approach with defined phases: Matching, Profiling, Developing and Learning, Closing and Celebrating.

CHAPTER 4   THE ART OF MENTORING

6. In Matching, align on goals, needs, style, and boundaries. Assess fit. Be transparent about mismatches early.

7. The profiling phase maps mentees' motivations, values, needs, and goals through exercises like the Roles and Scaling technique.

8. Developing and Learning executes the growth plan through knowledge sharing, feedback, goal setting, and addressing real-time needs.

9. Share feedback using the Situation-Behavior-Impact model. Praise and critique should be objective and actionable.

10. Set ambitious yet realistic SMART goals aligned with motivations and needs spotted during profiling.

11. Expand mentees' network strategically through introductions, collaborations, and visibility opportunities.

12. In the Closing phase, review progress, exchange feedback, and discuss ongoing informal engagement.

13. An impactful Individual Development Plan (IDP) captures goals, metrics, and timeframes personalized to the mentee.

14. IDPs should evolve as mentee priorities and needs change. Build in flexibility.

15. Blending SMART goals with OKRs creates a robust structure—SMART grounds the vision, and OKRs inspire.

CHAPTER 4   THE ART OF MENTORING

16. Adopt a "navigator verses driver" mindset—guide, but don't impose. Mentees must own their development.

17. Be a mentor, not a boss. Empower mentees to evaluate options and make their own choices.

18. Let go of ego. Make mentees the priority, not seeking credit or validation for yourself.

19. Approach mentoring with cultural sensitivity and humility. Avoid assumptions based on your lens.

20. Regularly self-reflect and get feedback on your mentoring skills. Strive to continuously improve.

21. Establish trust and psychological safety before diving into vulnerability and change.

22. Ask insightful questions to uncover motivations, resistance, and needs versus solving problems yourself.

23. Recognize mentoring takes substantial time and energy. Assess availability before accepting mentees.

24. Tailor knowledge sharing and resources to mentees' learning styles and interests.

25. Celebrate small wins and completion of "mini-goals" between mentorship meetings.

26. Follow up consistently on action items from previous sessions. This builds accountability.

27. Openly discuss boundaries and commitments early on so expectations are clear.

28. Listen more than speak during sessions. Draw out perspectives through targeted questions.

29. Help mentees gain visibility and experience through collaborations with your network when ready.

30. Inspire an ambitious vision while setting realistic incremental goals to get there.

31. Focus on unlocking potential, not accomplishing tasks. The mentee's advancement is the goal.

32. Adapt advice and guidance based on continuous feedback, not a one-size-fits-all approach.

33. Mentor for intrinsic fulfillment, not external validation.

34. Cherish that you get to facilitate mentees' journeys of growth and self-discovery.

35. Formal mentorship may end, but lifelong bonds enable ongoing impact when needs arise.

Time to Practice

1. Reflect on when a mentor once gave you advice that transformed how you approach leadership. What specifically did they share, and how has it shaped your perspective? Consider the mindsets, principles, or insights you learned from them that still guide your leadership style today.

2. Think of a time you felt stalled in your career development. What three areas would you have wanted guidance from a mentor to gain clarity and momentum?

CHAPTER 4   THE ART OF MENTORING

3. Consider a colleague you see potential in. How might you build rapport with them to understand their goals and motivations? What mentoring opportunities or introductions could support their growth?

4. If you were to craft a personalized mentoring program for a team member, what core values, strengths, and development needs of theirs would shape your approach? How might you adapt advice and growth plans based on their unique personality, work style, and ambitions?

5. Recall a time you received feedback delivered ineffectively. How could framing it objectively using the Situation-Behavior-Impact model have improved the experience and enabled you to apply the insight?

6. Think about your next objective. Create your IDP using OKRs and SMART to support your long-term vision and delineate a practical and tangible execution plan.

CHAPTER 5

Fostering Growth and Innovation

As a leader in engineering, you are often overwhelmed with projects with tight deadlines and multiple stakeholders with different needs and expectations. In the relentless push to deliver outcomes and be impactful, you can lose sight of the people who make it all possible. Without meaning in, you view your team members as resources—cogs in a machine—rather than individuals. Over time, this leads to a broken culture where people feel expendable, growth feels forced, and innovation stalls.

When engineering cultures become too task-oriented, they often develop a mentality of *"people come last."* With the focus on delivering features and meeting deadlines, you forget a vital truth: your products begin and end with people. Every line of code and every elegant solution comes from your team's human insight and effort. Your people are responsible for exploring interdependencies with adjacent departments and cross-functional partners to make requirements feasible and value tangible. Without sustaining your people's drive and creativity, the well runs dry. Likewise, every business goal depends on pleasing customers and users with your offerings. If your business succeeds, rest assured it's not because you had a tremendous idea that might work or solve an issue for you and please your ego. However, instead, it's because you are addressing a customer need that leads their business to success—a human customer!

CHAPTER 5   FOSTERING GROWTH AND INNOVATION

Yet, it's quite common for many companies to choose the path where high revenues dictate the definition of success and focus on outcomes at all costs, creating a culture where productivity and conversion rules. The market's fast pace requires an aggressive posture from executives to reduce lead time and make the company better positioned compared to competitors to the detriment of quality. The relentless pressure and top-down focus on productivity blur your perception as a leader. You start modeling behaviors prioritizing short-term outputs over long-term innovation and employee well-being. You follow prescriptions instead of experimentation. The pressure influences your leadership style, and your team operates in the same sense as you.

Consequently, your team gets burned out trying to meet unrealistic deadlines and unempathetic demands. Talented individuals leave to find more supportive environments, and those who remain become disengaged. You start treating people as means to company ends rather than the ends themselves. You forget that solutions come through people, and products serve people. You stifle growth and innovation. The incremental gains you eke out through extreme productivity can't bridge the chasm between what your company offers and what the market demands next. You dig your own grave by neglecting your people's need to experiment and create.

However, the key is orienting your culture toward the people generating ideas and those needing solutions. It means making their skill growth, sense of purpose, and happiness the ultimate measure of success instead of productivity metrics and deadlines. With people placed first, innovation and customer loyalty naturally follow. Your team will feel energized and supported to meet expectations through lightning-bolt insights and a willingness to defy the status quo. With the human feeling flowing into your business veins, your people will feel inspired to understand and embrace customer pain points and drive exponential solution value by iterating passionately on them.

When you demonstrate internal empathy to your people, they pay it forward externally by bonding more deeply with customers and addressing subtler emotional needs alongside functional ones, creating a ripple effect of understanding and goodwill between your brand and community. Yet, adopting this mindset is only possible by fostering a human-centric engineering culture.

Cultivating a People-Centric Culture

At its core, people-centric engineering leadership means elevating your team's growth, fulfillment, and well-being as central pillars alongside your business ambitions, not coming at their expense. It recognizes that sustained innovation depends on people feeling psychologically safe to create and drive breakthroughs.

A study of 72 hospital teams by Nembhard and Edmondson found that when team leaders demonstrated more inclusiveness by listening openly, being accessible, and inviting all input, team members felt psychologically safer to speak up and try new ideas. In precise terms, the analysis showed leader inclusiveness directly predicted team psychological safety in 33%. Additionally, teams with greater psychological safety implemented more process improvements and innovations, demonstrating the link between safety and risk-taking behavior.[1]

This people-first ethos transforms how you approach significant decisions, systems, and structures. When reviewing productivity policies, you ask, *"How could we provide more support?"* rather than *"How can we enforce more control?"* When team tensions arise, you seek win-win resolutions through open dialogue rather than top-down decrees.

---

[1] Nembhard, Ingrid M., and Amy C. Edmondson. "Making It Safe: The Effects of Leader Inclusiveness and Professional Status on Psychological Safety and Improvement Efforts in Health Care Teams." Journal of Organizational Behavior 27, no. 7 (October 2006): 941–966.

CHAPTER 5   FOSTERING GROWTH AND INNOVATION

In resource allocation, you weigh psychological safety as important as output efficiency. Even when shifts demand painful changes, you ease uncertainty by overcommunicating context and showing genuine care for each person affected. You judge the rightness of difficult calls based on balancing the sustainment of your people and their needs alongside market realities. You aim for mutual success at every turn—enabling an ownership culture and honoring human priorities beyond the job.

You still empower autonomous risk-taking but anchor it in empathy for both employee growth and customer experience. For example, you encourage rapidly prototyping inventive solutions, measuring success based on learning rather than short-term financials. You also enthusiastically elevate engineers' ideas to leadership once vetted as applicable, understanding that sticking your neck out for their innovations pays dividends in engagement. Moreover, seeking out dissenting voices avoids misalignments and unlocks creativity, as individuals closest to problems often have some of the clearest insights on improvements. Even when past executive experience makes you cautious, remain open and honor the wisdom from the ground up.

A research led by Hirak and colleagues covered thousands of executives to evaluate the influence of inclusive leadership to build psychological safety to spark open team exchange. The study quantitatively found leaders who actively seek out dissent and diverse input foster 54% more idea-sharing between teams[2]. By suspending assumptions and listening with fresh ears, people feel confident discussing new ideas without fear of embarrassment or cancelation from early missteps, accelerating game-changing innovations.

---

[2] Hirak, R., Peng, A.C., Carmeli, A., & Schaubroeck, J.M. (2012). Linking Leader Inclusiveness to Work Unit Performance: The Importance of Psychological Safety and Learning from Failures. The Leadership Quarterly, 23(1), 107-117.

CHAPTER 5   FOSTERING GROWTH AND INNOVATION

Fundamentally, people-centric leadership architects an environment nurturing both human flourishing and business effectiveness. Motivation to achieve great things develops organically when a caring culture secures individual growth. Let's see examples in Microsoft's cultural transformation under Nadella, moving from Ballmer's aggressive business-oriented approach toward a radically people-centric model empowering innovation.

Turning the Ship Around: A New Era at Microsoft

The shining example of people-centric leadership fueling innovation comes from Microsoft's renaissance under Satya Nadella. When he took over from Steve Ballmer in 2014, Microsoft struggled to shed its legacy identity from the PC era despite solid revenue growth. As CEO since 2000, Ballmer prioritized competition and aggressive deadlines. His intense, productivity-obsessed style had created a cutthroat culture where employees felt drained and insecure, with endless stack ranking keeping them on edge.

Although revenues grew steadily from $25 billion to $86 billion under Ballmer, Microsoft stock languished and largely traded sideways for 14 years—a shocking stagnation given its past meteoric rise. Investors worried the company relied too heavily on traditional software licenses rather than subscription models that could ensure recurring revenues aligned to long-term success. They saw nimbler competitors like Google eating market share across emerging categories like mobile, cloud services, and machine learning. Ballmer struggled to convince shareholders that he could fuel innovation beyond the core PC business in the face of these threats. Calls grew to take bolder risks in the future through M&A and R&D across new domains like social, video, and music.

Since taking over, Nadella has enacted a radical cultural shift centered on empathy, collaboration, and growth. He trusted employees' judgment and decentralized decision-making to ignite creativity rather than dictating

CHAPTER 5   FOSTERING GROWTH AND INNOVATION

a fixed vision from the top. He invested aggressively in R&D for cloud computing and AI, encouraging teams to build new capabilities through a high rate of experimentation. By giving engineers room to take risks without jeopardy, Nadella ensured that major innovations came to life.

At the same time, Nadella focused intently on genuine employee care to combat previous burnout. He revamped HR practices worldwide to nurture well-being, implement extensive parental leave policies, empower work-life balance through flexible hours, and provide a wide array of learning opportunities from online courses to classroom workshops. His fundamental goal was to support employees at all levels to develop more skills, discover fresh passions, and chart fulfilling careers. Nadella's more humanistic philosophy manifested in a renewed *"customers love it, employees love it, investors love it"* mission permeating every level of Microsoft. The clarity of this purpose tied to benefiting all stakeholders motivated teams and oriented their creativity toward big, bold bets. Initiatives like LinkedIn's $26 billion acquisition aligned perfectly with ambitious targets because employees intrinsically shared leadership's drive for industry dominance through integrating professional data and cloud services.

The results have been undeniable: Microsoft enjoyed its most successful run ever under Nadella, with immense growth continuing for eight years. Its stock price rose steadily from $34 to all-time highs of over $323 in late 2022—a more than 900% increase—signaling market enthusiasm for long-term strategy. Plus, the company continues to innovate fast, directly challenging rivals with cloud products like Azure while expanding into future niches like immersive mixed reality.

Nadella's holistic focus on employee experience proved that when human potential is unleashed by care and trust, business performance reaches unprecedented heights through nonstop innovation. Where Ballmer's commanding leadership led to stagnation, Nadella's people-centric emphasis compounded significant gains year after year.

CHAPTER 5 FOSTERING GROWTH AND INNOVATION

Microsoft's epic rise, fall, and comeback clarify one lesson: technology companies must stay obsessed with constant innovation to maintain dominance. In the digital economy, complacency is deadly, no matter your current market share. As smartphones gave way to AI and software went to the cloud, Microsoft's transformation showed the foresight required to preempt seismic changes or risk defeat.

Yet, you can't foster innovation through force of will alone. It blossoms from people feeling individually and collectively empowered to create. By architecting an empathetic culture that liberates human potential, you prime your organization for nonstop metamorphosis. However, the future unfolds. Sustaining morale, nurturing daring ideas across teams, and welcoming dissent and experimentation are the ultimate drivers of prolific innovation year after year.

Technology will keep exponentially evolving. To stay ahead of revolutionary shifts, companies must continually revolutionize culture and leadership strategy as well. Without satisfied and empowered employees, even the most powerful technology company faces an uncertain path, but with a human-centric approach, seemingly modest innovations can shift the industry's future.

Pillars for Creating an Engineering Culture Rooted in Growth and Innovation

Microsoft's reinvention story begs the question: How can you drive this level of empowerment-fueled innovation within your own engineering teams? The ingredients exist to replicate their cultural overhaul. By cementing key pillars throughout your organization, you can transform engineers from task-oriented executors into entrepreneurial trailblazers blazing new trails.

It starts with reimagining your strategic vision around unlocking human ingenuity versus dictating outcomes. You must lay the foundations of psychological safety that replace inhibition with conscious risk-taking. Building bridges between teams through collaboration and knowledge sharing compounds idea diversity. You create highly motivated owners rather than passive implementers by further championing autonomy and grassroots empowerment. Most importantly, instilling a growth mindset so every effort feeds the next round of learning and success.

When these pillars structurally support your organizational architecture, employee fulfillment and hard problems drive themselves to infusion. People build self-reinforcing momentum that perpetuates creation. The same force multipliers that reinvented Microsoft from the stagnant status quo into a continuous innovation machine can transform engineering dynamism within your culture. Let's explore the core pillars for enacting this self-sustaining level of growth and ingenuity.

Craft a Compelling Strategic Vision

The foundation for transforming engineering culture starts with reimagining strategic vision as a platform for maximizing human potential rather than an endpoint. Your vision should spark teams' imagination, not constrict it. When people connect to an inspired future story, they feel part of creating versus disconnected edicts, and their discretionary efforts compound. Here are the keys to bringing a bold innovation vision to life:

Tell Compelling Narratives

Tell compelling narratives using engaging stories that spark teams' imagination of future innovations while tying to a higher shared purpose. People naturally seek the sentiment of belonging and impact. They want to be part of something bigger. Help people feel the problems they'll conquer and the lives and businesses they will change. Appeal to hearts and minds by showing how each project ladders to grander aspirations.

Instead of defining an engineering strategy rooted in generic statements such as "provide the best AI tools to support clinical analysis," anchor your vision in narratives spotlighting your efforts as vehicles for improving human lives and solving business needs. Draw the narrative where people can imagine a future where diseases rarely turn terminal thanks to your new AI tools that can synthesize subtle clues human practitioners may miss and algorithms comb through millions of pages of medical research in seconds to prompt checks for elusive yet critical risk factors. Envision software that scans the body layer by layer, generating enhanced internal maps flagged for the slightest anomalous signals. By investing time and effort in building this solution, your team may radically contribute to patient longevity and quality of life by augmenting doctors' capacities and bringing scientific precision to the imperfect yet profoundly human healing arts.

This strategic narrative, enriched with human detail, ignites creative momentum. Even small progress ladders to positive outcomes because teams know who they're innovating for. They feel the weight and meaning of work unlocked when leadership grounds the abstraction in human stories. Visions manifest when people see their future selves benefitting others through advances, large and small.

Get Specific with Milestones to Invite Participation

Anchor ambitious visions with achievable milestones so all teams grasp realities presently hindering progress. Whether pursuing telemedicine granting global access to top-tier expertise or autonomous vehicles safely navigating sans drivers, outline incremental tiles needed to pave the way. Ask: How many rural clinics still lack reliable electricity and Internet for powering remote diagnosis? Do current maps provide precise localization and semantics for self-driving cars to interpret dense environments reliably? Does AI have sufficient labeled training data across diverse traffic scenarios to enable safe decisions? Fit visionary puzzles together by first enumerating and addressing vital nuts and bolts.

For example, product teams may first need to deliver easy-to-use interfaces that enable subject matter experts to rapidly label massive volumes of images, video footage, and audio snippets. Curating these vast training resources is essential for Machine Learning teams to accelerate the development of accurate computer vision, speech recognition, and predictive capabilities. Computer architects could provide optimized chipsets enhancing simulation capacities to stress test future smart city models with millions of projected variables. Policy experts could prepare regulatory-approved frameworks allowing remote diagnosis and prescription across borders.

With a shared line of sight translating the long-term vision into present possibilities, spur participation by soliciting ideas to chart the course ahead together. Ask your AI experts which modeling advances seem most promising for transforming prediction capabilities in areas like healthcare and sustainability. Inquire sensor engineers on which embedded systems innovations could enable the continuous collection of precise environmental and behavioral data to inform intelligent interfaces. Engage quality assurance teams on test automation solutions addressing new risks as services scale up in intricacy and mission-criticality.

Lead with Actions Aligned with the Vision

With your vision and strategy backed with short-term milestones defined collaboratively, it's time for you to lead decisively through actions that show the desired cultural behaviors. Celebrate customer-obsessed teams running rapid prototype sprints to uncover latent needs. Cheer quality assurance engineers relentlessly stress testing new environments before finalizing requirements. Champion innovation labs to serve as internal incubators to the organization, questioning legacy operating methods to uncover new business models. Lay the foundations for agile teams to rapidly experiment with unconventional commercial ideas in parallel while being shielded from bureaucratic barriers that could quickly snuff out their radical thinking.

Additionally, to pull people toward a bold vision, celebrate small but symbolically significant steps demonstrating movement in the intended direction. Recognize engineering groups not traditionally spotlighted to signal values around rigor and quality ownership. Make visible how unsung efforts weave together to inch toward the greater vision. Trust that by putting a stake in the ground on priorities, momentum concentrates resources naturally to combine gains over time.

However, in environments with more fear than faith in unconventional ideas, put yourself on the line first to shift culture. Attend hackathons overflowing with unfiltered creativity to select a couple of breakthroughs for investment. Sit in on a design review where provocative concepts face heavy scrutiny and lend your vote of confidence to fuel promising but risky directions. Plant seeds that prove fresh innovations blossom when teams feel psychologically safe to experiment. Soon, business units begin proactively ideating around your North Star vision, knowing leadership intent. As culture transforms from compliance to co-creation, people align efforts to avoid duplication, maximize resources for the boldest ideas, and accelerate synergies. The vision manifests tangibly when you model the desired behaviors before asking others to follow suit. But it takes you first walking the walk for the path to reveal itself.

Continually Adapt and Reinforce the Vision

An innovation strategy cannot remain fixed but must keep pace with market dynamics and learnings. As vision meets reality through execution, humility and flexibility become vital to bridging gaps. Gather ongoing feedback at every level—through pulse surveys, forum discussions, and anonymous input channels—on how well you and other leaders communicate the vision, how clearly priorities translate into product roadmaps, and how genuinely the strategic narrative resonates across the organization. Listen intently, with openness, not defensiveness, to discover where misfires happen between inspirational intent and how teams interpret goals at the points of delivery. Identify where portions feel misaligned with values or lack feasible empowerment structures for manifesting the vision.

Furthermore, you must quickly and honestly adapt top-down directives, which inevitably lose voltage as they cascade through organizational layers. You must promote revisiting the visions frequently through collaborative frameworks welcoming cross-functional perspectives and allowing fluidity in revising messaging, structures, and plans to keep the vision interconnected to those upholding it daily. Most importantly, your ego can't interfere with how you process candid feedback from your people that reveals where alignments got lost between leadership intent and ground-level implementation. Instead, recalibrate through transparency, granting teams latitude to reinterpret visions within their domains versus just dictating orders to operationalize.

In parallel, continuously infuse vision into the employee experience—from evaluating skills that align with the vision through the hiring process to onboarding training positioning individual roles within the bigger picture; from agile ceremonies keeping backlogs mapped to vision to performance reviews evaluating alignment to vision-enabling behaviors like creativity and collaboration. The vision persists dynamically when made ubiquitous through everyday channels, interactions, and milestones.

Psychological Safety

Setting a compelling strategic vision is fundamental to energizing your team but requires open and direct collaboration. The challenge begins when many team members make the fear of speaking up candidly their primary behavior. Yet, this fear may come in different flavors, such as fear of facing reprisal, making "silly" questions, or demonstrating undesired vulnerabilities or lack of knowledge in specific areas. Consequently, engineers may hesitate to propose daring ideas outside perceived norms. Teams get hesitant to experiment beyond well-trodden paths, knowing failure risks criticism. Over time, this inhibition to stretch boundaries leads to stagnation.

By committing to create a culture focused on growth and innovation, you must proactively nurture psychological safety. Without people feeling secure enough to express ideas openly, creativity stagnates on the vine from self-censorship, preventing growth velocity in the long term. When slight missteps in exploration risk harsh responses, teams logically avoid stretching into breakthrough thinking or voicing gut concerns about flaws. Let's understand how to mitigate the culture of fear.

Ignite the Change by Role Modeling

Start with your own leadership, and foster safety by first modeling openness that invites belonging for teams. Disclose thought processes on current tensions, navigate complex innovation decisions, and be authentic about uncertainty. Explain inhuman constraints and trade-offs you wrestle with instead of projecting a misleading aura of omniscience. Make it feel normal to surface dilemmas jointly rather than bear the load in isolation. Ask teams directly where visibility falters on balancing priorities—from short-term targets versus long-term, transformational bets to supporting bold ideas versus pragmatism. Bring groups into collaborative priority setting and direction aligning to strategic vision. They will reciprocate candid co-ownership of wise decisions rather than leave leaders alone accountable for direction.

Equally, demonstrate receptiveness if teams illuminate unintended negative ripples from past problematic structures. Welcome this constructive criticism with appreciation, not ego or defensiveness. Thank those bringing systemic issues forward. Explain contextual pressures that influenced previous policy while acknowledging the suggested changes better align with cultural goals. Then, realign based on feedback. Model this nonjudgmental reflection first, and teams will step forward to help improve things together versus hiding flaws to avoid blame.

The more leaders radiate approachability over authority, a joint crusade over one-sided perfection, and understanding over accusation, the more the teams feel psychologically safe being candid themselves, moving the needle through transparency. But it starts from the top down. Leaders who initiate vulnerability get staff to open up trustingly.

Conducting Blameless Failure Postmortems

Conducting blameless postmortems requires nonjudgmental inquiry focused on learning over finger-pointing. For example, ask open-ended questions inviting teams to share uncertain considerations along the way, obstacles faced, and thought processes on key decisions. Make it feel safe to unpack intentions without negative scrutiny. Separate contributors' efforts from suboptimal results to understand root causes versus attacking work quality prematurely. For instance, if an innovative feature misses the mark, openly discuss resourcing barriers faced or UX assumptions made first before critiquing engineers. Additionally, outline process insights without attributing incompetence retroactively or forcing simplistic conclusions. Recognize multiple valid perspectives likely existing in ambiguous situations and model intrinsic learning motivation post-setbacks rather than punitive reactions.

Implementing blameless retrospectives shifts dialogue from toxic to constructive by promoting inquiry over assumptions. As a result, this slowly builds trust that it's safe to air messier realities, which in turn drives prevention. Teams feel comfortable surfacing costly missteps early to mine progress from them when you react with understanding, not anger. Over time, groups intrinsically push toward excellence, feeling secure and supported, not anxious and inhibited, fearing overreaction.

Enable Anonymity Expanding Contributions

Finally, allow anonymity in idea-sharing channels to mitigate social anxieties about speaking up. Introverts or those from underrepresented groups may hesitate to participate equally to extroverted or dominant colleagues; identity exposure limits input. Provide venues for safely proposing ideas in smaller trusted cohorts like innovation soundboards, quality circles, etc., where a noncompetitive environment builds trust over time, and people eventually self-identify when ready.

Additionally, institute anonymous online submission forums and open feedback channels on policy roll-outs. Provide the right to anonymity even in wider meetings. This expands the funnel for unfiltered insights on everything from early-stage product enhancements, process streamlining, and automated solutions to customer feedback highlighting real pain points.

Give space for remote asynchronous contributions. Many will only anonymously provide raw, unvarnished perspectives rather than sanitize face-to-face feedback or by name attribution. This gives transparency into problems needing remedy hidden under the false calm of harmony bias. Trends also emerge faster from candid data otherwise obscured by reluctance in nonprivate environments due to career jeopardy.

While anonymity risks some loss of context or follow-up clarity compared to direct conversations, if you respond in understanding nonjudgmental ways and implement suggestions judiciously without overreacting, the benefits outweigh the costs as contributors see the outcome. Soon, psychological safety spreads confidence in speaking transparently, even directly, over time once cultural incentives realign from political to progress-focused through actions.

CHAPTER 5   FOSTERING GROWTH AND INNOVATION

Collaboration and Knowledge Sharing

Gone are the days when focused specialists could keep expertise walled off. In the modern business age, ideas compound fastest through cross-functional and cross-organizational pollination. Even though high autonomy is crucial for initiative, siloed teams become islands unable to take advantage of new perspectives, access needs across units, or leverage work done by other groups. Conversely, fluid collaboration mitigates duplication, diversifies thinking, and unlocks emergent value, making joint efforts and knowledge sharing another key pillar to sustain a culture of growth and innovation.

You must execute three must-have strategies to facilitate cooperation across team members with different skills: create communities with similar interests, evangelize internal models that enable resource reuse, and build diverse and cross-functional teams. Let's explore each of them.

Create Communities of Practice

The motive for fostering *"Communities of Practice"* goes beyond elevating capabilities—their cross-pollination prevents reinventing wheels across siloed teams. You can organize these cohort groups around shared specialties like data science, backend development, frontend, and quality assurance rather than specific business projects. Provide dedicated time for these distributed expert networks to brainstorm new ways to create solutions across the company and collectively advance techniques. Although engineers should remain embedded in agile product teams, these secondary self-managed communities diffuse skills broadly across groups who can apply learnings through their specialty lens.

For example, backend engineers may collaborate on building next-gen microservices architecture foundations for distributed systems. Frontend developers share ways to lift and shift legacy UIs to modern reactive frameworks. Quality assurance leads co-author test automation APIs any evaluator can leverage when assessing new systems. Provide online community platforms so insights gained solving challenges in one context readily cross-pollinate into others, preventing duplicate efforts over time while amplifying strengths and accelerating individual growth.

Through diverse experience and motivations, these communities actively seek to exchange information and define guardrails to guide the technological evolution and self-determine priority knowledge gaps or external benchmarks to close based on the actual product or architecture. Then, set improvement goals; your mission as an engineering leader is to get the buy-in to add these technical initiatives to your product roadmap, ensuring human power and time to make them feasible. They determine what to workshop, document, or standardize next to magnify effectiveness across the organization's domain of focus. Some may prepare reference architectures while others collect optimization learnings. Trust their intrinsic motivation and self-direction, balancing both project and community contributions.

Establish an Inner Model Philosophy

Suppose one of your product teams encounters complex requirements to create a feature focusing on data transformation to create a next-generation product that processes operational activities in real-time to allow customers to make proactive decisions in their inner teams instead of reactive ones. The team thought out of the box and created an agnostic layer that allowed client applications to connect and execute several data operations, facilitating data consumption. Still, the project has been developed strictly under the Data Team's context with low visibility to other teams. In a short period of time, this application became the heart of the entire new product.

However, due to this lack of visibility, whenever a product team had to create a new feature requiring extensive data consumption to generate reports or execute complex processing, their default action was often to reinvent wheels, creating custom ETL, warehousing, connectors, and adapters inside their context without broader input. Consequently, the team was constantly recreating one-off data tools, wasting resources while forcing fragmented experiences across competing business systems and inflating new capability timelines.

An alternative is adopting an inner source model, where the Data Team would act as *producers* responsible for providing high-quality documentation, communicating the technical nuances and available resources to educate other teams about intrinsic interdependencies. On the other hand, these other teams would act as *consumers*, responsible for researching existing functionalities as part of the technical planning before creating new ones. The result is a win-win situation, where producers can gather feedback from other teams to evolve their features to accommodate different scenarios and facilitate the development of upcoming product needs, and the consumers can streamline their development cycle, shortening the lead time and fastening the time-to-market for new features.

Build Cross-Functional Teams

Even though communities of practice and reusable code accelerate knowledge share within specialties, building cross-functional teams is vital in contributing to growth and innovation. These teams are composed of specialists from different departments with a common goal within a shared domain. Product managers are responsible for the product vision and guide the business priorities. Engineering leaders ensure the engineering strategy aligns with the product vision and orchestrate the development cycle. Product designers bring concepts and research outcomes to life through intelligent UI/UX. Engineers bring the idea to life. Consequently, engineers gain visceral user insights, designers understand technical feasibility constraints, and strategists learn about deep implementation considerations.

Together, this team collaborates in a single cohort, owning a product or domain experience, bringing the best of each department to create solutions that solve customers' needs and help drive them to success. Make them full-time feature teams co-located physically and/or virtually through always-on collaboration tools.

Despite having the team members working directly in their areas of specialty throughout the development life cycle, they contribute indirectly to all areas of the team, stimulating the collaboration from understanding the *whys* to implementing the *hows*. Every perspective adds a fresh layer of understanding on how the product evolves, creating a common sense of accountability and commitment, creatively leveraging each other's superpowers based on contextual needs and passions, not rigid roles.

Growth Mindset

Yes, once again, a growth mindset. An innovation culture requires the perpetual progression of skills to keep pace with emerging technologies. But beyond professional development, prioritizing comprehensive personal growth unlocks the full spectrum of human potential needed to fuel original thinking. Fixed mindsets believing abilities are static debilitate aspiration. By contrast, embracing self-betterment as an endless journey cultivates the versatility and creativity that change-making demands.

Adopting this principle in a broader context starts with reversing legacies that pitted individual capability against team cooperation, instilling values where peers feel invested in each other's improvement. Instill the mantra of *"I get your back, and you get mine."* Institute regular feedback cycles for constructive suggestions on sharpening technical, business, and interpersonal abilities, yet remember to educate your team with the SBI model. Cultivate an environment where healthy competition is welcome, but collaboration is the rule. Curiosity and desire to explore are second nature instead of reigning on fear. You must frame development as a lifelong journey with periods of achievement and challenge, both advancing the collective mission.

Stimulate Team Curiosity

Additionally, cultivate curiosity as the engine powering skill progression. Defy the paradigm where people avoid asking to avoid *"making silly questions,"* and evangelize that those who prefer not asking are the silly ones. You must foster an insatiable desire across teams to question *"why"* and *"how"* things work and label curiosity as an opportunity to confirm an assumption or learn something new. Also, you must promote that making problems evident only reveals gaps in understanding, not failures of intellect.

Furthermore, push beyond skepticism to uphold the collective benefits of tossing old paradigms. If something seems off, dig deeper into root issues or alternatives. Progress follows the curious—help teams step forward by making it psychologically safe, not knowing, only seeking. Recognize that curiosity is the catalyst for everything to come.

Encourage Reciprocal Team Development

Catalyze skills progression by making teammate investment in each other's growth a cultural requirement, and institute peer mentoring programs for collaborative coaching relationships, where technical leaders or engineers strong in areas like system design guide colleagues looking to gain those capabilities. Make aiding team capability advancement a recognized contribution—not just an informal favor—during performance evaluations, and spotlight team members dedicating coaching time for their peers.

Furthermore, you must provide learning resources and incentives for individuals focused on self-driven development. Highlight engineers expanding coding languages on passion projects or taking external courses to become more influential. Track personal growth in training portals through individually authored development plans outlining capability and exposure goals and then log courses/activities pursuing them.

Finally, reinforce that opportunity expands when you lift others up the talent ladder alongside and make engagement with team members grow intrinsic to what leadership means. And help those aspiring to acquire leadership skills set examples through their own transparency, working through skill gaps or knowledge limitations via emerging leader programs while maintaining latitude to contribute.

Autonomy and Empowerment

This pillar is slightly different from the other ones. While the others focus on stimulating the power of collaborative thinking to feed ideas for thoughts, autonomy and empowerment are responsible for cementing the ideation with the execution and converting ideas into reality by dismantling bureaucratic barriers to experimentation. Yet, often, companies sacrifice or create unnecessary barriers to justify controlling risk-taking with a negative impact in the long run, not only for the engineering team but for the business growth overall.

To mitigate the impact of overcontrolling engineering resources and limiting innovation, you must foster a decentralized decision-making environment where people are empowered to plan relevant initiatives and self-organized to deliver their best with guidance and support instead of rigid controls throughout the company. Remember, your job is to empower people to unleash their potential, directly impacting business growth, not babysitting.

Amplifying Engineer Perspectives in Planning

Fuel innovation velocity by incorporating engineering lens early influencing product roadmaps and planning cycles. Too often, technically complex initiatives get defined devoid of implementation realities, accumulating disconnects once coders decompose granular needs after the fact. As discussed in the section "Collaborating with Product Teams" in Chapter 3, you can bridge this through formal mechanisms elevating engineer perspectives, including directors or representatives from R&D groups in planning committees plotting experience maps, drafting capabilities backlogs, and framing initial hypotheses around novel concepts. Make their membership both sanctioned and consistent throughout cycles rather than ad hoc guest appearances.

Moreover, engineers bring invaluable judgment on interpreting early-stage ideas about pragmatic restraints around tooling and technical trade-offs, latency thresholds, regulatory boundaries, reliability demands, and adjacent dependencies. Their inputs identify infeasible initiatives early, saving months of duplicated effort realigning after teams receive rigid delivery orders, ignoring real-world constraints. Enable them to voice developmental considerations, concerns, risks, and upside breakthrough potential while priorities still remain somewhat fluid before manifesting as prescribed delivery timetables. Catching disconnects upfront prevents a deficiency from plan interpretation varying across siloed teams.

Foster Agile Team Formation

Innovation benefits immensely from fluid team structures aligned to opportunities and strengths rather than isolated groups. Promote engineers proactively evaluating projects needing staffing help based on skill relevance, rotating between different product domains to expand experience and perspectives. Reduce existing bureaucracy delaying bespoke squad assembly targeting promising concepts or customer needs.

Catalyze this through light-touch processes facilitating visibility into initiatives seeking specialized talents so interested individuals can self-nominate without prolonged approval chains. The broadcast must transparently allow people to pursue collaborators across the org based on passion, not decree. For example, an engineer studying advances in

CHAPTER 5   FOSTERING GROWTH AND INNOVATION

machine learning model training may see a forecasting service effort and volunteer to participate in the project, providing new ideas and designing the model to provide more accurate estimates.

Additionally, sponsor regular cycles where teams reconfigure based on updated priorities, and participants map strengths to the most resonant business challenges. Engineer-led formation keeps groups intrinsically engaged around opportunities they opt into, not problems they get handed. Assignments last from project duration to a quarter, allowing fluid reformulation, balancing continuity with fresh combinations, and addressing emerging needs.

Creating an Environment to Support Growth and Innovation

Imagine a fertile farm remaining stubbornly barren for years despite farmers continually sowing seeds using sound agricultural practices—plowing soil, watering adequately, and so on. After years of struggling to get positive results and the accumulated failure of others, one resident decided to explore the problem deeper. He tested soil samples from across the land, discovering several vital nutrients severely lacking due to abnormalities like high acidity or low organic matter. Any seed hazards sprouting in such conditions would practically guarantee crop failure from the start, no matter how perfectly other factors aligned. By researching ways of improving the soil quality and methodically augmenting missing elements, bountiful crops flourished where none had emerged previously.

This metaphor applies fittingly to organizations striving yet struggling to spark innovation through even well-formulated cultural building blocks. Demonstrating a willingness to enact a growth mindset or targeted principles to promote experimentation is not enough to yield intended results in a structural *"soil"* lacking specific underpinnings those seeds

CHAPTER 5   FOSTERING GROWTH AND INNOVATION

require to bloom. Like the farming resident, you, as an engineering leader, must understand and fill the environmental gaps holding back innovation to progress.

However, just as crops translate essential elements into growth engines organically, innovation practices manifest most vigorously when backed by systems and processes that remove obstacles while actively enabling teams through knowledge, platforms, policies, and purpose-built tools to transform ideas into market impact.

This section will explore five environmental elements for inspection—and conscientious adaptation where necessary—to ensure your organization's climate remains primed to convert innovative sparks into thriving business solutions.

Centralize Knowledge to Avoid Reinvention

The first environmental action for conscious innovation optimization focuses on centralized knowledge. Recognize that every experiment yields learnings—from successes demonstrating what resonates in the market to failures spotlighting techniques to refine. Ensuring this discovery and proven solutions get strategically logged, organized, and made discoverable for reapplication instead of stranded in product silos improves your team's efficiency, reduces the discovery process when refining technical solutions, and contributes to tame technical debt over time.

In the absence of systems channeling intelligence exchanges across business lines, staggering amounts of duplicative efforts emerge, producing wrong usage of time, resources, and effort, consequently leading to increased time-to-market and dangering, losing momentum and market space to competitors. Without accessible archives of designs, architectures, algorithms, and code from past initiatives, every team puzzles through identical obstacles and blind alleys. At scale, teams grind, solving challenges colleagues conquered perhaps weeks ago but keeping insights confined locally.

However, you can accelerate innovation velocity organization-wide by instituting accessible knowledge bases codifying assets from completed projects for company-wide leverage. For example, construct searchable repositories detailing business capability designs, data models, delivery plans, microservices frameworks, coding standards, architectural decisions, resource dependency maps, and other modular artifacts—every document in a single place, built collaboratively. Still, ensuring each artifact has accountable groups for maintaining, reviewing, and publishing new versions is essential. Remember, an outdated document may be worse than not having a document once it may lead your team to make severe unconscious mistakes, affecting the company's reputation, customer experience, and team morale.

Cultivate Creativity Through Idea Portals

There is no right time or place to have an insight with enough power to become a promising idea. Your mind constantly processes personal and professional information related to your daily activities, and suddenly, what is foggy becomes clear. Yet, many of these insights never get wings. Introverts may feel uncomfortable sharing their ideas, fearing the spotlight and the pressure to pitch their thoughts to other audiences. Junior developers may lack confidence and avoid expressing themselves to avoid asking *"silly questions"* or making *"pointless statements."*

However, bad leaders and broken cultures are another root cause of silent employees. Who wants to work with leaders more preoccupied with appearing as solo innovation heroes who dismiss collaborative inquiries in self-interest than actively listening and promoting collaboration as part of their ethos? Or working in companies with cultures that provide opportunities only for senior roles and centralize critical product development decisions only to executive people, ignoring the diversity of thoughts or experiences? Over time, the compound silence speaks loudly!

CHAPTER 5   FOSTERING GROWTH AND INNOVATION

Stimulating your team to share hidden ideas must not be a cumbersome process when merely establishing idea portals helps unlock more comprehensive innovation funnels regardless of level, tenure, or department. A simple web form allows confidential submission of suggestions on anything from new products to efficiency enhancements. From feedback to ideation. Extroverts and introverts, directors and juniors, speak in the same tone and at the same influential level. Comment streams let peers discuss nascent proposals, providing constructive refinement, and a voting mechanism may help you identify common areas of interest across the company, signaling hidden motivations and potential opportunities to create new business cases.

Nonetheless, reviewing and following up on these thoughts is as important as creating an environment where people can voice their ideas. Implement review cycles, then judge ideas by alignment to customer needs, business aims, and group preference rather than submitter's seniority. Route shortlisted proposals to appropriate specialized units for feasibility analysis and functional roadmapping and make the exploration progress visible to increase transparency so that concepts gain real consideration, further stimulating participation.

Finally, equally incorporate data input like usage metrics, product analytics, and changing market insights for factoring objective signals into proposal viability alongside executive hypotheses. The more ideas surface and then are shepherded responsibly through structured evaluation, the more quality submissions accumulate as intrinsic motivation to participate drives volume.

Leverage Sandboxes to Safe Experimentation

Sandboxes provide invaluable testing grounds where your teams can freely explore innovative ideas without real-world consequences. These isolated environments mirror production systems—spanning hardware, software, data stores, and interfaces—creating a risk-free representation. Teams build creative features, models, and algorithms, then assess functionality, resilience, and performance without directly touching live systems or risking business continuity. Hypothesis validation builds confidence needed before considering integration with higher-risk production systems. Still, constructing complete and mirrored environments requires heavy upfront resource investment—no small tax for most companies.

Alternatively, you can implement proxy sandbox alternatives using automated cloud tooling that simulates software conditions and provides lighter-weight on-ramps addressing core stability, scale, and performance validation needs. Even simple canary testing of experimental code in quarantined pools is worth the price, unlocking exploration velocity otherwise severely hampered by production obligations and iterative development over monolithic change sets less prone to disruption. The key lies in sticking ROI above extravagances, providing clear advancement of future capabilities over present duties alone. Gauge innovation lift, then build just enough playgrounds to meet accelerated learnings rather than perfectly mirrored production.

Support Creativity with Processes and Governance

Many see governance as inhibiting agility with oppressive controls. However, implementing a wise governance system to support your team's innovation provides safe guardrails for experimentation. It establishes a reliable foundation for engineers to confidently build new solutions with autonomy without needing to endlessly validate compliance with processes and policies and evaluate unnecessary risks that can be intrinsically mitigated as part of the product development lifecycle.

Defining and introducing such development guidelines early in the process directly impacts the innovation pace and potentially the time-to-market if the assumptions and business value are confirmed. Suppose your company is SOC2 certified, and you have defined specific development guidelines to ensure security compliance for experimentation, such as using updated and checked libraries and ensuring the team properly handles sensitive data. Then, you define an experimentation policy, ensuring the understanding of such a premise and everyone is onboarded and accountable for it. In this case, you end up with a win-win situation: Innovative solutions are compliant by default with the company's needs and engineering standards, reducing sales friction and maximizing market receptiveness.

Conscious governance liberates innovation by embedding continuity considerations intrinsically across the product lifecycle and empowers engineers with conscientious duty, benefiting all stakeholders through shared diligence frameworks. It fosters privacy, ethics, sustainability, and accountability intrinsically alongside security, reducing retrospective alignment burdens upon delivery. Still, you must keep awareness of the thin line between surrounding your team with positive guidelines and unnecessary restrictions and bureaucracies. Over time, these barriers undermine team engagement and stagnate product evolution. It's vital to ensure that processes are relevant to the business and that you create them to support, not block. Ensure your processes are constantly reviewed to accommodate seasonal changes so you can adapt to get the most value from them and identify areas for optimization.

Foster Innovation Through Diverse and Unbiased Hiring

Implementing a strategic and ethical approach to sourcing and selecting talent must be a top priority if you seek to embrace innovation as your team's motto. Many leaders pour endless time and resources into reshaping existing teams with the latest techniques, expecting innovation to follow. Yet, transformation is pointless if people's practices fail to attract, hire, and onboard talents capable of pioneering change. The roots of innovation begin with recruiting, and as an engineering leader, you have a responsibility to shape processes that remove bias and give equal opportunity to all candidates, regardless of gender, ethnicity, age, or other factors unrelated to skills and cultural fit.

In 2018, McKinsey conducted extensive research examining the relationship between executive team diversity and financial performance across over 1000 companies in 12 countries.[3] The study specifically looked at gender, ethnic, and cultural diversity among top leadership. The results revealed a clear correlation between diversity and profitability. Companies in the top quartile for executive-level gender diversity were 25% more likely to outperform the bottom quartile on earnings. Even more striking, enterprises with the most ethnic/cultural representation financially outperformed industry averages by a remarkable 33%.

Additionally, the innovation and decision-making lift from inclusive hiring plays out across organizational levels. In 2017, Cloverpop published results from a study of over 200 businesses in the United States and United Kingdom.[4] They assembled sample project teams where members represented diverse genders, ethnicities, ages, education levels, and work backgrounds. These heterogeneous groups were then presented with a series of decisions involving new market entry, resource allocation, HR policy, and other complex business topics. When compared to control groups lacking diversity, the inclusive teams reached better decisions up to 87% of the time. Researchers concluded bringing together professionals with varied backgrounds and perspectives leads to more thoughtful vetting of alternatives, constructive debate weighing merits and risks, and integration of insights that homogeneous groups readily overlook.

---

[3] Hunt, V., Yee, L., Prince, S., & Dixon-Fyle, S. (2018). Delivering through Diversity. McKinsey & Company. https://www.mckinsey.com/business-functions/organization/our-insights/delivering-through-diversity

[4] Cloverpop. (2017). Hacking Diversity with Inclusive Decision Making: How To See What Matters and Fix What's Broken. https://www.cloverpop.com/hacking-diversity-with-inclusive-decision-making

CHAPTER 5   FOSTERING GROWTH AND INNOVATION

The compounding impact of these studies highlights why building diverse engineering teams must be an urgent strategic priority. Implementing equitable and ethical hiring practices provides a competitive edge through financial gains, mitigated risk exposure from better decisions, and increased innovation fueled by a greater diversity of ideas and solutions.

However, most organizations default to convenient sourcing channels, opaque evaluation methods, and subjective hiring criteria that propagate homogeneity. This defeats innovation from the outset by forming homogeneous teams aligned with the status quo rather than customer needs. Instead, you must challenge assumptions permeating existing recruitment practices and reset mindsets around the type of talent required to invent the future.

Reset Constraining Beliefs Around Recruiting

Before exploring the specifics of equitable and inclusive hiring, take a moment for introspection around your current mindsets. Many accepted truths about recruiting top talent actually constrain your ability to build genuinely innovative teams. Traditional practices propagating homogeneity often reflect lazy assumptions and confirmation biases instead of facts.

If you sincerely aspire to diversity's demonstrated innovation lift, several constraining beliefs must be challenged:

First, recognize that an engineering hiring process is more than system design discussions and code challenges. While those activities demonstrate immediate skills, you must equally evaluate the whole individual and your alignment around values, work styles, and priorities. Your assessment should determine not just competency but long-term compatibility. Consider recruiting akin to seeking a marriage partner rather than a transactional role fill. Qualities like curiosity, growth mindset, communication style, and response to conflict reveal compatibility just as much as syntax proficiency. Yet, few engineering leaders invest in behavioral interviewing or evaluating cultural contribution because legacy paradigms claim coding correctness is the only worthy barometer. Have the wisdom to gauge the entire person.

Next, avoid seeking the perfect candidate profile that checks every imaginable box and gold stars across diverse technologies. Such unicorn hunting inherently limits possibilities and diversity by arbitrarily filtering those with nontraditional backgrounds yet high potential. Instead, scope requirements focused on must-have capabilities for day-to-day work, keeping them simple, straightforward, and accessible to professionals with more varied experience. For example, do not automatically require 4+ years with niche frameworks as a blanket expectation for all roles. Only call out less common skills like Kubernetes expertise if genuinely mandatory for a specific team. Also, amplify opportunities to candidates from boot camps and code academies if their drive and foundations show promise despite lacking elite pedigrees. Setting unrealistic gates on previous experience prevents discovering those with untraditional paths that could become stellar contributors.

Additionally, avoid conflating culture fit with only onboarding those who align with existing norms. That restricts diversity by automatically filtering candidates that seem atypical compared to current staff. Check tendencies to gravitate to applicants with shared experiences or backgrounds. While some affinity is human, consistently favoring similarities entrenches homogeneity. Instead, evaluate each candidate's potential to assimilate and enrich your culture through a unique perspective. Assess what new dimensions they may bring to understanding users or sparking original solutions. Determine if they embrace the organization's values creatively, challenging assumed applications of things like trust or innovation. Rather than just affirming *"good culture fit,"* determine whether applicants align with principles while complementing gaps that constrain current teams. Strive for *"culture add"* through diversity over fit through conformity.

Finally, understand that retention begins long before an offer gets accepted. Candidates form distinct impressions throughout sourcing, screening, and interview interactions that shape eventual engagement as an employee. Those feeling tokenized, disrespected, or probed about personal traits leave with doubts about cultural inclusion. Once hired, lackluster onboarding and hazy career development plans exacerbate doubts.

Set the foundations of retention through an exceptional candidate experience showcasing your genuine commitment to equitable opportunities and onboarding support. Define specifics around ramp-up training, mentor pairings, future growth prospects, and leadership's direct investment in their success. Share how engineering priorities came to focus on specific strategic domains to provide context around project staffing and technology choices.

Adopt the ABCs Mindset to Attract and Assess Diverse Talent

While challenging constraining beliefs, you must also adopt constructive mindsets permeating the hiring process. Consider these the ABCs—forming the basis of positive candidate interactions that attract diverse talent pools and evaluate them objectively. Structuring evaluations around agility, positivity, phenomenal experiences, and values confirmation conveys through actions that candidates from all backgrounds can thrive and belong. This mindset model transforms recruiting from a transactional chore into a strategic opportunity to reinforce your commitment to diversity and inclusion.

The model helps candidates reduce anxiety through transparent timelines, warm reception, and relevance of discussions to role expectations. Instead of feeling like a number, their skills get assessed fairly in an engaging process. For hiring teams, structured milestones, calibration guidance, and values-based interview practices mitigate unconscious bias risk while allowing efficient finalist comparisons. For the business overall, the ABCs approach curates highly qualified talent pools tuned to the specific capabilities and cultural contributions needed to drive innovation and growth. The ABCs elements are as follows:

Agility: Breed agility through a structured yet rapid hiring process with clear milestones, real-time feedback loops, and transparency. Set expectations upfront around the 4-6 week timeline from application to offer. Notify candidates when advancing each step, explain the following steps, and provide timing updates. Nothing disengages promising talent faster than disjointed communication after they apply.

Be Positive: Broadcast engaged positivity by ensuring hiring managers, recruiters, and interviewers portrayed the team's inspiring mission and collaborative climate. Ask values-based questions to assess cultural fit beyond technical skill. Share growth opportunities from training programs to global mobility that reinforce retention. This shapes what daily work life, career trajectories, and advancement could entail.

Craft Phenomenal Candidate Experiences: Architect a phenomenal interview experience through responsiveness and transparency on role expectations, technology direction, and cultural attributes. Maintain ongoing dialogue welcoming candidate questions. Disclose challenging aspects of key initiatives without exaggeration that could undermine credibility. Ultimately, sell them on the role aligned to strengths while objectively assessing mutual fit.

Sell Your Values: Bake themes of diversity, equity, and inclusion throughout screening. Explore previous experiences working across cultures. Evaluate receptiveness to respectful debate of dissenting views. Set the stage for candidates from all backgrounds to feel welcome to contribute unique perspectives.

Uncovering Bias

Beyond outdated assumptions, unconscious bias is another enemy sabotaging equitable and innovative hiring. At its core, bias causes you to feel or demonstrate an inclination for or against someone arbitrarily. In recruiting, bias manifests through quick perceptions about talent based on demographic affiliations like gender, ethnicity, age, or cultural background rather than the neutral evaluation of skills against role needs. These prejudices become highly problematic when unrelated factors are allowed to influence the assessment of candidates' potential contributions.

However, the resulting bias is usually not conscious or intended, and it constantly manifests in the unconscious level of your mind. You are exposed daily to subtle evaluations or stereotypes that affect your impressions, judgments, and behaviors. This exposition contributes to creating these rooted and undesired predefined perceptions, activated automatically without intentional control or awareness, and wires your brain to generate automatic associations that manifest instinctively.

Let's check some scenarios where the unconscious may break your perception and sabotage your process:

First impressions, whether sparked by viewing candidate photos or browsing public social media profiles, may color subsequent evaluations long before skills are assessed objectively. Within milliseconds, you may form subconscious perceptions about tenacity, creativity, leadership potential, or team orientation just from appearances that match common stereotype biases for groups frequenting tech. For example, an engineering manager may assign elevated intelligence or work ethic assumptions simply by noticing degrees from globally renowned universities or brand names like Google or Apple on a resume. Seemingly logical deductions based on talent magnet affiliations quickly trigger overgeneralized expectations separate from the person's actual achievements or experiences.

Once first impressions take hold, they often anchor subsequent judgments due to confirmation bias, even when conscious values reject allowing demographics or background to unfairly influence hiring decisions. Subsequent interview missteps get magnified. Answers contrary to established expectations feel jarring. Skills downplayed as idiosyncrasies when reinforcing initial impressions get flagged as warning signs otherwise. Without realizing it, candidates may receive misaligned scrutiny or inadequate consideration based on review materials or photos introducing imprecise preconceptions—and never receive a fair, bias-free opportunity to demonstrate competence.

Stereotyping represents a lethal form of bias where interviewers automatically expect candidates to exhibit behaviors or technical capabilities tied to group affiliation rather than individual accomplishments. It stems from false preconceptions about shared traits across genders, ethnicities, national origins, or academic backgrounds. For example, an engineering leader may unconsciously assume Asian candidates possess superior math proficiency or that women will demonstrate stronger empathy but weaker assertiveness than men. Despite consciously rejecting stereotypes, first impressions get shaded when screening resumes or observing initial body language during introductions.

These learned biases cause an instinctive tendency to amplify responses aligned with stereotypes as confirmatory evidence while critically flagging misaligned behaviors as outliers. Without balance, candidates receive misconstrued scrutiny for failing imagined stereotype criteria unrelated to real job requirements while getting the undue benefit when exhibiting behaviors an interviewer arbitrarily associates with a demographic.

Nonverbal cues like a dress, eye contact, the physical distance between speaker and listener, or variations in tone/volume of speech account for most of the communication, often subconsciously. Thus, misinterpreting culturally diverse nonverbal behaviors as formal instead of modest or nervous rather than disinterested leads to biased, unfair candidate assessments. For example, candidates from certain Asian cultures may demonstrate avoiding prolonged eye contact out of respect rather than disengagement or dishonesty. However, through conditioned Western norms valuing direct eye contact as confident and trustworthy, an engineering manager may conclude better rapport or communication ability in those maintaining such gaze despite what gets verbally conveyed.

Additionally, you may negatively perceive a candidate wearing a suit seemingly misaligned with the casual dress code as too rigid or formal for the open culture. Yet, that interpretation embraces conformity over individual preference diversity. Rather than guessing meanings behind nonverbal signals, adopt practices clarifying intent to determine attributes directly from candidates before risking unfair characterization based on misconstrued body language, appearance, or speech patterns biased by the observer's own norms.

The halo or horn effect represents another insidious bias where a single positive or negative quality demonstrated early in an interview eclipses all other attributes, preventing a balanced assessment. Instead of weighing strengths and weaknesses equally, impression formations from an initial exchange or moment anchor opinions distort remaining interactions through confirmation bias. For example, if an engineering manager highly appreciates a candidate's answer on leveraging artificial intelligence for user insight mining, a reflexively positive halo effect may form around technological vision. Subsequent responses then get

CHAPTER 5 FOSTERING GROWTH AND INNOVATION

evaluated favorably, such as connecting agile deployment practices back to robust data collection or discussing trade-offs balancing complexity and accuracy when training ML models.

In contrast, a single fumbled system design question on cloud architecture principles may cast a horn effect, painting the applicant as generally incompetent on technical fundamentals. Even when answering code maintenance scenarios flawlessly afterward, scrutiny sharpens attempting to validate broad deficiencies suggested by the initial struggle. In both cases, isolated interactions set runaway first impressions oblivious to contradicting objective evidence in either direction. Mitigate such bias by weighing all interview segments equally against defined skills benchmarks.

Recalibrate Hiring Practices to Combat Bias

Hiring processes remain anchored in assumptions and convenience, perpetuating the status quo and stifling the seek for diversity. Practices like listing niche skills over principles in job descriptions, tapping the same talent channels oblivious to exclusion elsewhere, and over-indexing credentials first in interviews optimize for conformity, constraining innovation by devaluing differences that challenge groupthink. However, growth requires ingredient diversity as the catalyst. With urgency, you must scrutinize existing recruiting funnels for barriers arbitrarily filtering qualified candidates, consciously reforming biased stage gate traditions unaligned with inventing the future.

This audit starts by overhauling job descriptions, intentionally expanding sourcing pipelines, and reframing interview processes with equity guardrails, destroying blind spots early on. While only initial steps, deliberately addressing each establishes momentum for tangible transformation, not allowing known issues to continue silently

CHAPTER 5   FOSTERING GROWTH AND INNOVATION

Rethink Job Descriptions and Qualifications

Just as recruiters spend seconds scanning resumes to form initial impressions of candidates, this same dynamic occurs in reverse. The job descriptions and qualification criteria you convey shape candidates' initial perceptions of their roles and, by extension, how you perceive and implement diversity and inclusion. Still, unfortunately, most job descriptions follow compliance-driven models, emphasizing checklists of tactical competencies at the expense of principles, values, learning potential, or creativity. This stems from legacy philosophies that label the number of technologies mastered and years of experience as directly correlated to the competence to perform a role.

For example, a typical software engineering role might list preferences like:

- 5+ years in a similar role
- Expert in Python and Java
- Proven experience with Redis, Elasticsearch, Docker, CI/CD, AWS, PostgreSQL, MySQL, PHPUnit & Codeception, Agile Scrum, Restful, Kafka, and clean and event-driven architectures.
- Familiarity with GCP or AWS services
- Strong verbal and written communication skills

By adopting such a tactical and exclusionary approach, the pools of qualified candidates arbitrarily shrink, filtered into demographic segments that are unlikely to enrich the diversity of perspectives. Interestingly, few question the assumptions behind requiring every niche database and coding language out there. Could an eager developer learn on the job? Does your team truly leverage the entire technology spectrum on a daily basis, or do they only get involved based on project needs? Do you prefer a solo master of all technologies or a team player eager to learn?

Considering this, it is necessary to challenge these legacy paradigms that value conformity over creativity. The solution depends on carefully reformulating the description of your team, and the project needs to highlight transferable skills rather than checking for tactical ones. Evaluate each technology and ability requirement through a diversity perspective before including it in this distorted market standard, and understand that even though certifications and years of experience still provide signals, you must not filter candidates solely on their technical prowess, as this is no guarantee of success or quality.

Therefore, change how you formulate your job descriptions and highlight your needs more agnostic but assertively. Remember that creating an innovative and diverse environment requires effort even before hiring. So, make your values and principles evident to potential candidates, obtaining a better market positioning to attract talents with diverse backgrounds and experiences. You can reformulate your needs as per the following example:

- Passion for quickly mastering new languages and frameworks
- Hands-on experience optimizing system performance
- Resourcefulness in debugging complex interdependencies
- Willingness to break down complex problems into smaller problems
- Desire to uplift others through guidance and clear communication
- Embrace respectful debate of divergent points of view during decision-making and collaboration
- Commitment to empathetic engineering practices that build user trust

CHAPTER 5   FOSTERING GROWTH AND INNOVATION

- Defense of transparency and democratization of information

- Curiosity to understand the diverse needs and challenges of users

- Commitment to share timely and compassionate feedback, helping others improve

- Promote connection between technical and nontechnical colleagues

Much more attractive, right? You backed your technical necessities with a growth mindset. You opened doors for high-potential professionals from different niches and backgrounds, focusing on the problem you want to solve instead of the formulaic approach to how to solve it. For instance, a dedicated developer may easily transition from one programming language to another if they have a strong engineering foundation. Despite the lack of proficiency in the primary technology, they can quickly add immediate value from the behavioral standpoint and transition to the new programming language. After all, software engineering is software engineering, regardless of the development language used. Conversely, finding or aligning a *"cultural add"* is much more complex and expensive. Setting your expectations in the early stages ensure your job descriptions mirror the future of your business and team, and avoid short-term disappointments.

Broaden Sourcing Pipelines to Attract Talents

Even though job descriptions broadcast initial impressions, sourcing processes translate intent into action by determining what talent pipelines actually get tapped. Unfortunately, this stage often suffers from unconscious biases undermining diversity and innovation efforts before evaluating skills fairly. Research quantifying these trends offers sobering evidence that culture-add candidates face an inclusivity gap long before any interviews occur.

A poignant example of how unconscious bias permeates sourcing is a 2004 study by economists Marianne Bertrand and Sendhil Mullainathan.[5] They investigated callback discrimination in the labor market by responding to over 1300 help-wanted ads in Boston and Chicago newspapers using fictitious resumes manipulated only by name to signal race and ethnicity. Specifically, they created sets of resumes equal in qualifications but used names like Emily, Brendan, Jamal, and Lakisha to cue visual characteristics. Across industries, identically qualified applicants with Caucasian-sounding names received 50% more interview callbacks than those with African-American-sounding names. Alarmingly, having a name indicative of white racial affiliation was equivalent to eight additional years of experience.

This systemic discrepancy highlights how bias taints candidate evaluation long before skills are assessed fairly. Well-intentioned, merit-based notions of finding *"best players"* give way to homogeneity directives when resumes from underrepresented groups get discounted on sight.

Nonetheless, purposefully broaden channels and partnerships to reach qualified candidates across backgrounds early rather than just lamenting sad and sobering statistics. Establish partnerships with your People Operation department to set metrics expanding diversity within initial application funnels such as *"Percentage of applicants identifying with underrepresented ethnic/racial backgrounds"* or *"Percentage of applicants identifying with underrepresented gender identities,"* then work backward assembling sourcing plans reaching untapped communities. Additionally, promote voice to these communities by creating your internal communities to keep the fluids flowing to promote diversity across the business.

---

[5] Bertrand, M., & Mullainathan, S. (2004). Are Emily and Greg More Employable Than Lakisha and Jamal? A Field Experiment on Labor Market Discrimination. American Economic Review, 94(4), 991-1013.

CHAPTER 5   FOSTERING GROWTH AND INNOVATION

Proactively targeting underrepresented talent pools begins rewriting narratives that opportunities exist for all, not just dominant demographics who have achieved insider access through cycles of homogenous hiring. Have the courage to form new alliances with organizations like *Women Who Code, AfroTech,* or *Out in Tech*, who have already built trusting ecosystems, and attend local chapter events to build authentic relationships while showcasing the humanity behind your technical roles. Such proactive investment sets ripples, expanding reach to candidates who've rightly felt excluded based on experiences like those that Bertrand and Mullainathan quantified. But connection starts with showing up. So, show up!

Additionally, emphasize themes of creativity, empathy, and inclusion throughout sourcing communications, conveying your uniquely supportive innovation culture. For example, have engineers share career narratives highlighting autonomy over solutions, the camaraderie within teams, the diversity of thoughts, and leadership support trying bold ideas without reprisal for failure. Such authentic artifacts symbolize freedom, often lacking at platforms obsessing over scale above all. Let artifact storytelling affirm you reward skills applied creatively far more than credentials accrued conventionally. Remember that talented candidates from all backgrounds seek destinations enabling impact; your colleagues provide the proof.

Reframing the Interview Process

Typical software engineering interview funnels overemphasize technical skills before exploring cultural fit and are processes optimized for quantifying skills rather than nurturing potential. This model misses the opportunity to raise awareness and educate everyone involved in the process of evaluating cultural and behavioral traits that align with business and team values and principles, as well as promoting the misaligned view that you value the completion of tasks rather than commitment and attitude.

Although this model facilitates the assessment of the project's immediate technological needs, understanding essential behavioral gaps, such as collaboration, communication, team dynamics, work methods, responsibility, and engagement, takes a back seat and creates a real challenge, which, if not identified early, may trigger the need to replace hired talent over time, requiring additional investment of time and financial resources, in addition to impacting the morale and efficiency of your teams.

However, defying this conventional hiring paradigm lies within reach. The mechanisms exist to reframe evaluations around potential rather than just qualifications. This realignment involves initiatives like forming balanced hiring committees to mitigate individual biases, creating structured interview guides that calibrate assessments consistently, setting equitable ground rules for panel members, and emphasizing criteria focused on coachability over specific requirements. Adjustments like these allow room to assess different hard and soft skills and the cultural fit throughout the process instead of targeting isolated knowledge areas. Ultimately, these changes aim to promote continuous equity improvements versus allowing embedded traditions to perpetuate blind spots.

Convene Cross-Functional Hiring Committees

Balanced hiring committees infuse diverse perspectives into evaluating candidates, mitigating individual biases that isolated assessments allow to permeate. Too often, single hiring managers or narrow departmental teams own screening fully, limiting objectivity through homogeneous viewpoints. Forming committees with members across functions like Product, Design, Engineering, and Customer Success brings different voices to frame capability priorities, guide structured interview practices, and inform final talent recommendations.

CHAPTER 5   FOSTERING GROWTH AND INNOVATION

Product and Design partners particularly help set context on the user challenges future hires aim to solve. Understanding those human needs and nuanced use cases anchors engineering roles to real-world utility over theoretical proofs. These lenses shape discussions exploring applicants' grasp of the problem space, creative instincts framing solutions, and intrinsic drive to impact customers through programming. Partners immersed in user workflows spotlight valuable signals beyond coding exams. Just their presence during evaluations can help calibrate tech-first panelists prone to over-indexing niche skills fit over collaborative potential.

Make committees both cross-functional and inclusive internally. Promote participation spanning tenures, demographics, and team purviews. Such diversity within assessment teams directly counteracts homogenous notions of ideal talent while exposing different strengths.

Implement Interview Guides to Calibrate Assessments

Structured interview guides foster equitable assessments by proactively aligning strategies and evaluating participants evenly against defined role needs. These documents outline considerations across the hiring funnel to enable panel collaboration by directing capability questions evenly across staged touchpoints and participants instead of relying solely on in-the-moment assessments prone to implicit bias.

For technical abilities, you can precisely describe coding fluency areas to probe, like systems design patterns, test automation approaches, and debugging techniques spanning both initial screening and subsequent role-specific questioning. For collaboration skills, sample scenarios assess abilities working cross-functionally, tailoring complex solutions for nontechnical partners, and showcasing engineering concepts to mixed audiences. Culturally, these guides expand qualifications beyond generic *"team player"* clichés to include demonstrated strengths in resolving group conflicts constructively, internalizing user needs to guide requirements debates, and lifting up peers through coaching and feedback.

By implementing these structured interview guides, you can coordinate critical hiring processes to enhance consistency, bring evidence-based rigor to talent evaluations through aggregated feedback metrics, and support continuous equity improvements over time. Additionally, you secure strategic returns from recruiting investments by curating technically excellent, collaboratively fluid, and culturally contributive new hires ready to deliver oversized impacts aligned with company priorities. Your team's human potential gets built and improved incrementally into each process refinement, catalyzing innovation previously constrained by homogeneity.

Create a Well-Rounded Onboarding Process

Onboarding goes beyond mundane paperwork and bucket list compliance items that new engineers must click through before gaining systems access. Done right, onboarding sets expectations around growth trajectories and establishes a welcoming environment for the newest members to rapidly absorb the company culture and build key relationships. This human-focused immersion fuels retention through purpose transparency, which many often fail due to poor assimilation rather than weak qualifications. Without structured support easing transitions, initial optimism gets displaced by ambiguity anxiety. Who guides career development trajectories? What does the company expect from me? Who can help me with this issue? How do new hires demonstrate competencies? Which training opportunities accelerate my growth?

An onboarding process can make or break someone's motivation and desire to become a *"cultural add,"* and it shapes the vision of how the new member perceives the company. That's why investing in planning the proper welcome in advance is crucial. Ensure to assign peer buddies invested in smooth immersion guiding new hires end-to-end. Right from day one, the buddy helps proactively surface key questions and clarify anything that seems fuzzy on topics like internal mobility, technical stack overviews, and team dynamics. They also facilitate warm introductions within the business unit, easing networking nerves.

Additionally, share your plans for your first one-on-one and reaffirm this supportive ethos by outlining your personal commitment to frequent check-ins, leadership accessibility, and open-door collaboration expectations. Frame your role as a primary advocate invested in their ascent, no matter the questions or struggles ahead. Model vulnerability, recalling moments you felt uncertain years back but found friendly wisdom.

Furthermore, provide a 30-60-90 plan. For instance, define that within the first 30 days, the focus is on culture assimilation, systems access, values fluency, and networking with key peers. The 60-day plan sets the tone to prioritize understanding engineering strategy, product vision, technical documentation, and partner integrations. Finally, the 90-day empowers the team member to apply the learnings through rotations on backlog grooming, feature brainstorms, and releases showcasing capabilities. Allow incremental progress and accountability, and clearly highlight your expectations for each phase. Don't forget to dispel imposter syndrome by celebrating questions!

Embedding Innovation Through Purposeful Rituals

The first step in fostering innovation involves crafting cultural and environmental foundations through people-centric cultural pillars and environment optimization. Still, to drive lasting impact, you must also reinforce desired behaviors consistently through purposeful rituals that make expected cultural traits tangible. Instituting regular ceremonies focused on imagination, creativity, and boundary-pushing cement an agile, empowered engineering ethos over time. On the surface, events like hackathons, design jams, and failure retrospectives may seem routine. However, these recurring rituals unlock inspiration when framed as engaging platforms for teams to connect aspirational goals to actual outcomes through celebration, reflection, and renewed purpose.

Let's explore practical examples you can consciously embed into your organizational culture and ways of working to spark lasting zeal for pushing limits across their organizations.

Sparking Innovation Through Hackathons

Hackathons represent intense yet inspiring innovation rituals, convening diverse technology enthusiasts across days of focused boundary-pushing. These collaborative marathons blend various skill sets and perspectives, becoming cauldrons where fresh ideas emerge and feed into one another. The ticking clock induces a sense of urgency, pushing participants to think disruptively and produce creative breakthroughs aligned with solving specific problems.

As an engineering leader, your hackathon role extends far beyond facilitation to become an innovation catalyst and guiding light. While setting clear objectives aligned to organizational goals provides direction, equally prioritizing allotting creative freedom for teams helps to immerse in solution exploration. Promoting skill diversity in forming groups remains vital, as this variety sparks novelty. Supply all infrastructures for development and discovery but don't constrain tool selection. Often, puzzling through novel options illuminates capabilities a prescribed tech stack would hide.

Additionally, hackathons represent opportunities for participants to embrace roles expanding comfort zones, unlocking unexpected insights from such fluidity. Encourage engineers to manage scoping trade-offs collaboratively while designers prototype human-centric interfaces based on product cues. Quality assurance talent could orchestrate testing innovation solutions at scale while data scientists extrapolate future applications of core concepts. Through briefly transcending day-to-day functions by cross-pollinating specialized lenses, breakthroughs accumulate exponentially.

Ensure hackathon spaces foster psychological safety for sharing embryonic ideas without judgment. Seed concepts need room for unfiltered debate and iterative refinement to blossom. As a leader, walk the floor asking thoughtful questions, motivate teams, and facilitate cohesion through phases of uncertainty inherent when mentally stretched thin.

Once finished, avoid treating hackathon outcomes as one-off amusements. Gather executive stakeholders across functions to actively evaluate the innovative prototypes and solutions teams produced regarding feasibility and alignment with current product and technical roadmaps. Prioritize concepts for future funding allocations' logical next steps, partition, and integrate elements into existing initiatives. This post-hackathon commitment cements that such visionary exploration efforts connect to strategy and priorities, fueling retention by making people feel their contributions manifest change. It closes the inspiration loop.

Hackathons represent indispensable rituals for catalyzing experimentation, building teamwork, and sparking game-changing visions. As a leader willing to devote hands-on guidance, you turn innovation sparks into blazing organizational momentum. Your active facilitation unlocks the potential for compounding technology breakthroughs and novel solutions tackling customer problems when framed as inclusive ideation marathons versus elite competitions. Participants united by common goals, not titles, become the source material for realizing engineering leadership visions.

CHAPTER 5   FOSTERING GROWTH AND INNOVATION

Embedding Customer Obsession Through Collaborative Design Sprints

Design thinking represents a constructive innovation ritual relying on empathy, assumption challenging, and problem reframing to conceive solutions optimized for human needs. Unlike unfiltered brainstorming, design methodology journeys deep into the minds of target users through iterative prototyping and feedback loops, intrinsically aligning desirability, feasibility, and product viability.

As an engineering leader, actively facilitate collaborative design jams to uplift this user-centric ethos across your teams. Guide participants in embracing key pillars of the design process to unlock novel solutions and retain customer obsession values amid scale:

> **Empathize with People:** Kick-start jams by issuing ethnographic and market research reports to ground upcoming ideation in customer pain points. Task breakouts with profiling distinct personas across analytics-rich *"day in the life"* scenarios spotlighting emotions around user challenges. Such immersion builds appropriate context, steering concepts to tangibly alleviate struggles technology could resolve.
>
> **Challenge Perceptions:** Push teams to question preconceptions on usage models for current or emerging capabilities by spotlighting persona behaviors research revealed. If quality engineers assume automated scripts sufficiently test critical workflows, have them map detailed customer escalation scenarios that simulations could miss. Reframing development constraints through a human lens spotlights innovation opportunities.

CHAPTER 5   FOSTERING GROWTH AND INNOVATION

Redefine Problems: Guide reorientation from solving predefined issues to reimagining what optimum user experiences may require. If the jam focuses on streamlining supply chain processes, have architects envision entirely self-correcting production flows enhanced by sensor data instead of just reactive reporting. Challenge wide-scale thinking first, then reverse engineer technical possibilities.

Prototype Concepts: Maintain quick momentum, moving teams from grounded visions to tangible models, evaluating ideas faster through structured feedback. Push rapid prototyping methods like sketching interfaces or crafting user flow diagrams over exhaustive documentation. Keep the emphasis on translating empathetic understanding into demonstratable solutions for assessment.

Test and Refine: Construct engaging test scenarios, allowing users to experience prototype interactions and provide genuine feedback on usability, understandability, enjoyment, and areas needing refinement. Be willing to iterate without ego as flaws surface, recognizing such vulnerability as growth opportunities and making the right solutions. Measure both qualitative user input and performance data, like task completion rates, to gauge iterative improvements.

Conclude each design jam with showcases allowing groups to share key learnings on breakthrough concepts conceived, gather executive input on viability, and celebrate empathetic engineering success stories when

CHAPTER 5   FOSTERING GROWTH AND INNOVATION

innovations demonstrably uplifted target customers. These ceremonies remind teams that human needs ultimately drive technology requirements ahead of internal priorities. Their solutions impact life and should, therefore, connect back to living.

Standardizing Innovation Recognition with Quarterly All-Hands Meetings

Conveying all-hands check-ins every quarter is an impactful ritual, shining light on the latest software initiatives and accelerating product vision and outcomes. While daily standups remain focused at the incremental/execution level, these events provide ripe moments to tie major deliverables back to leadership aims, sustaining momentum through transparency and celebration. By showcasing launches aligned to strategic pillars with evidence of exponential user and business value unlocked, teams feel collectively motivated toward shared objectives versus siloed efforts.

> **Spotlight Launches Accelerating Product Vision:** Curate presentations on key software launches and enhancements intentionally innovating to propel foundational product roadmap pillars—like the mobile team assessing account security pain points before shipping the revamped two-factor authentication flow, understanding user needs boosts trust and conversions. Or the platform reliability squad proactively refactoring threading logic to resolve found fragility risks plaguing partners, exemplifying how purposeful innovations compound reliability at scale over time. Connecting outcomes clearly aligned to advancing product purpose and customer value rallies staff unity.

Quantify Value in Business Terms: Require teams to detail tangible value created through engineering launches using clear business metrics–including quantifying how dashboard UX improvements increased client analytics usage by 10%, supporting more premium subscriptions. Or how resolving platform inconsistencies minimized revenue loss risks by $600K annually based on renewal data insights. Making technical contributions understandable in financial outcomes and client adoption gains sustains executive support by spotlighting engineering's business value versus just theoretical progress.

Spotlight Values in Action: Importantly, call out engineers across levels who embodied key cultural pillars like creativity, grit, and mentoring, which multiplied project success—from new college grads discovering inventive compatibility solutions when vendor tools limited scope to senior architects voluntarily conducting extra design reviews to unblock juniors, unlocking coding potential sustaining future innovation. Spotlighting such behaviors at all levels cements values-driven progress.

Finally, enable open networking during events, seeding possibilities for cross-functional spin-offs from recent achievements that can inspire fresh innovation quests. Sustain momentum by regularly showcasing engineering efforts collectively building toward audacious product visions.

Accelerating Innovations Through Early Feedback

Consider instituting regular cross-functional *"innovation demo days"* to accelerate early validation of engineering experiments through candid feedback focused on customer needs. Instead of pitching one-way selling concepts, facilitate two-way review conversations, answering, *"Should this move forward and how?"*

Getting specific insights from sales, support, and success around potential product-market fit proves invaluable for steering viability. These teams directly field unsolved user pains that fuel breakthrough ideas while ensuring proposed solutions resonate. Their lens keeps innovations grounded in reality.

These sessions are also great opportunities to review nascent concepts and prototypes. Ask your team to prepare five-minute reviews of early-stage solutions and nascent pilot capabilities intended to address strategic development gaps or untapped market opportunities, focusing on the ethos of *"what can our customers do now that they couldn't a few weeks ago?"*—the idea is not to demo concluded ideas, but rather ongoing initiatives. Keep presentations brief and engaging so the emphasis rests on constructive inquiry—no one wants to spend time discussing bug-solving. Demonstrate enough prototypes and technical context to ground subsequent requirements and business impact discussion.

Additionally, anchor these discussions around customer needs, not on engineering egos. Require innovation teams to lead collaborative reviews oriented by the needs of customer-facing reviewers representing key user segments. Have these partners detail priority jobs to be done and problems that cause friction or churn today, which could inform pilots. Discuss how new technical capabilities may alleviate key issues while also introducing considerations based on supporting diverse users at scale.

Finally, the demo sessions are crucial to increase visibility to guide strategic experiments, making promising innovation experiments more discoverable within the company for leadership support. Groups gain awareness of initiatives potentially aligning with product roadmaps, triggering natural technical collaborations or resourcing discussions. Consider maintaining an insights repository to further inform teams on past strategic priorities when shaping new concepts.

Yet, you must approach these sessions with an open mind, willingness to have initial assumptions challenged, desire to adapt, and increment on any necessary course correction. Your attitude will define how your team perceives these sessions, so ensure that you demonstrate a positive attitude and embrace a growth mindset. Remember the mantra: *"We are all product!"*

Fueling Growth Through Learning Days

A common fallacy among product and engineering teams labels the time invested in professional development as the villain and the most significant cause of delays in urgent product deliveries. However, the opposite is true: Not allowing continuous learning severely restricts the solution vision, adaptability, and relevance of technological changes. Structured not to obstruct operational continuity, assigning distraction-free windows for self-directed skill development ensures teams sustainably gain broader capabilities that match evolving strategic requirements.

Your team's growth must instill consistent, uninterrupted, dedicated learning days. Designate each engineer on your team as having a whole day to experiment or acquire new skills every two to three weeks, and adjust the rotation frequency based on the department size to limit single points of interruption. Furthermore, it is essential to promote this initiative as business as usual, ensuring that there is no impact on employee paid leave or other benefits. The aim is for people to adopt the initiative willingly, with a positive outlook instead of meaningless decrees.

CHAPTER 5   FOSTERING GROWTH AND INNOVATION

To safeguard process efficiency and transparency, set communication guidelines that protect time from typical business requests and unnecessary distractions so people avoid context-switching while absorbing new skills privately. However, confirm full team presence on rituals that require team collaboration, like sprint planning, backlog grooming, or retrospectives. These collaborative workshops rely on full teams present to size work, refine granular requirements, and identify continuous improvement opportunities through candid lessons learned. Missing key engineers or fragmented attendance severely hinders delivering shared outcomes.

Additionally, providing autonomy for engineers to explore passion topics beyond assigned project responsibilities reignites vital personal purpose and healthy work-life balance. Over lengthy periods locked into product delivery, teams risk disengagement as work grows repetitive, strengths remain untapped, and learning plateaus. Without intermittent windows to refresh abilities or follow curiosities, the flame of passion flickering out remains a grave leadership failure, stifling innovation and growth.

Conversely, when organizations actively invest through dedicated days for employees to develop different skills, discover budding personal passions, and explore purpose, they feel valued as holistic professionals, not as company resources. You must allow teams' self-directed space to complement expertise with wider capabilities, boost internal mobility, and build sharper discernment on upcoming strategic priorities based on their intersecting viewpoints.

Most powerfully, when engineers intermittently break from habitual systems to reimagine solutions and play in unstructured ways, creativity compounded across teams intersects serendipitously, birthing game-changing perspectives unconsidered during crowded project schedules. Just as star athletes require substantial rests and cross-training outside repetitive daily drills to perform record-breaking feats, building human potential similarly demands intentional habits entrenching lifetime growth.

CHAPTER 5 FOSTERING GROWTH AND INNOVATION

Learning from Stumbles to Reach New Heights

Productive engineering cultures skillfully transform failures from stigmatized breakdowns into stepping stones toward higher purposes. You can nurture a growth mindset by reframing defeat as necessary for eventual success, viewing iteration as intrinsic to inventive work, especially when exploring unsolved customer challenges. Additionally, setbacks become a shared curriculum by spotlighting stories of persistence through uncertainty, steeling creative resilience across teams. Finally, establishing collaborative failure autopsy rituals extracts hard-won progress opportunities from strained initiatives to inoculate downstream efforts through the conscious redefinition of missteps as shared stepping stones, not endpoints, continuous momentum compounds as groups assimilate accumulated insights into the next bold experiment or launch done right.

Adopt a Failing-Forward Attitude

Recast failures as necessary steps, not permanent endpoints, en route to eventual success. To create a culture embedded in growth, you must recognize that smart experiments sometimes stall out and position teams one pivoted step closer to goals by illuminating flawed assumptions early. So, highlight that inventive work inherently involves iteration over perfection, especially when pioneering unsolved customer challenges.

To reinforce this fail-forward ethos in teams, spotlight stories of creative resilience. For example, share vulnerably how, after multiple prototypes misfired in cracking unmet user needs, pressure mounted as leadership questioned continued investment before finally reaching a breakthrough after systematically isolating impediments blocking wide adoption. Show honesty in revealing moments of self-doubt and uncertainty amid failure before igniting fresh perspectives to move forward. Framing your own rollercoaster persistence through the story lowlights the drama while spotlighting the resilience and momentum shifts.

These reflections humanize that frustrations inevitably arise when repeatedly wrestling with threats or unknowns, yet the steady expansion of knowledge builds bridges, ultimately transcending barriers. When engineering leadership authentically models and rewards fast failure cycles as pathfinders, not reprimands or threats, psychological safety spreads for creatives themselves to internalize this growth mindset. Over time, cultivating this measure of design immunity against the fear of stumbles compounds bolder experimentation velocities, accelerating rates of sustainable innovation and breakthrough.

Humanize Triumphs

Celebrate successful innovations and breakthroughs by recasting launches through compelling human-centric narratives. Rather than just spotlighting features shipped themselves in isolation, showcase the aspiring teams whose creative visions and dedicated collaboration brought the ideas to life over months of designed experimentation. Share vulnerable stories of early stumbles, almost cancelations, long coding nights, honest disagreements, and heartbreaking back-to-the-drawing-board junctures that forged bold solutions. Such storytelling cement that innovations advancing life quality and industry empowerment for many originate profoundly from the human care and creativity of collaborative teams who refused to settle for mediocrity.

Furthermore, showcase behind-the-scenes contributors essential for imparting hard-fought lessons and steering projects right—from quality assurance partners stress testing boundary assumptions before customer dangers to UX researchers urging simplifications helping mainstream usefulness beyond early adopter niches. Making each collaborator's impact visible, both technical mastery and emotional team glue fosters more inclusive cycles of recognition fueling sustainable innovation as groups align efforts to shared outcomes benefitting all stakeholders amid challenges.

CHAPTER 5   FOSTERING GROWTH AND INNOVATION

Distill Failures to Extract the Learnings

Lastly, fuel future success by establishing regular failure autopsy rituals, allowing teams to reflect openly on key learnings from stalled initiatives without judgment. Make it a priority to schedule collaborative retrospectives soon after closing initiatives before momentum dissipates. At the same time, experiences remain fresh and objectively reconstruct timelines identifying fateful turns—from technical limitations encountered to customer adoption barriers arising unexpectedly.

Instead of combing through wreckage seeking individuals to blame, focus dialogues on illuminating faulty assumptions, unknown interdependencies, or priority conflicts that hindered success. Bring together those closest to failed projects to piece together their distinct vantage points into shared understanding. If, despite strong collaboration and planning, foundational requirements shifted left initiatives under-resourced to adapt quickly enough, spotlight the breakdown to realign constraints.

The purpose remains mining processes themselves for latent disconnects versus targeting any person or group. Psychological safety allows participants to unpack decisions comfortably, highlighting risks deemed acceptable that proved not. Once root causes are cataloged without attributing a fault, empowered teams can brainstorm solutions that may have accelerated signals to uncover deal-breaking flaws sooner or prevent key coordination lapses. The emphasis stays forward-moving, so retrospectives cement continuous improvements over finger-pointing.

Embracing Continuous Change

In this era of rapid technological innovation, customer expectations evolve swiftly. If you rigidly stick to legacy systems and philosophies, you risk losing relevance as both markets and optimal strategies to serve them transform. However, as a forward-thinking leader, you can architect a culture that intentionally embraces change as a catalyst to fuel sustained innovation. By using change proactively instead of reacting reluctantly when forced to realign, you unlock breakthrough thinking intrinsic to your teams. Instead of top-down course corrections alone, regularly reexamining assumptions through fresh perspectives precipitates creative friction and progress. As a leader who supports employees through uncertainty, you build resilience to the fluidity successful businesses require. Spotlight and celebrate every team member who models bold adaptations to change. This showcases the inherent creativity transitions enable, inspiring teams to view them as opportunities for innovation and not as drawbacks eroding stability.

When you reframe change as a growth opportunity that boosts abilities instead of an ominous threat, people band together and rally their talents to cross the finish line. They expect frequent improvements, trusting you have their backs during turbulence. You must frame change in people-centric foundations while articulating the business vision to anchor business priorities and decisions in humanity and inclusive values, yielding positive momentum that accelerates market leadership over time.

Modeling Adaptability and Growth as a Leader

Implementing changes without actually believing in the growth opportunities yourself breeds distrust and inflexibility that sabotages progress and morale. Despite your attempts to frame change as an innovation catalyst, your own behaviors betray the authenticity of that message when you ignore it for yourself. Employees hold back from sharing creative ideas or fresh perspectives that could catalyze growth, fearing closed-minded executives will swat down suggestions conflicting with entrenched perspectives. Without air cover for proposing improvements, people learn to keep their heads down, focusing solely on immediate job scope rather than pursuing initiatives that could transform operations but require buy-in from resistant senior stakeholders first.

CHAPTER 5   FOSTERING GROWTH AND INNOVATION

This dynamic demoralizes staff, degrades work quality from lower engagement, stifles innovation pipelines, and directly obstructs business results. Progress stalls while teams balance managing up to appease stubborn leaders averse to change even as they bear the brunt of executing new initiatives handed down as mandates. This, in turn, slows adoption enterprise-wide. People cling tighter to status quo stability the more those resisting change dig in heels from above despite touting new directions. Sensing the turmoil this disconnect between words and actions causes, your best talent quietly transfers off pioneering projects while morale and momentum plummet company-wide.

Yet, if you expect teams to embrace changes, you must first adopt shifts yourself, even when uncomfortable. This builds crucial credibility that you genuinely believe initiatives hold transformational potential versus merely enforcing mandates. For instance, when implementing a new Incident Management process for engineering teams unused to structured on-call rotations, resistance or skepticism may bubble up given personal life impacts. Though you spearheaded designing the streamlined response protocols for faster resolution, you similarly adopted every aspect yourself first.

You personally undergo the same training as team members for using new escalation platforms and diagnosing issues. You schedule yourself for overnight and weekend shifts as the initial incident commander. You join the first incidents even if you are not scheduled directly and guide the team through investigating the issue to resolve it actively.

In retrospectives, you discuss your own frustrations acclimating to fragmented sleep while reassuring teams of the lessening disruption once everyone gets cross-trained as a backup. You share when your family expressed annoyance but ultimately understood that some disturbance enables preventing worse customer-impacting failures. This vulnerability and willingness to endure the same uncertainties motivate teams through initial transition pains. They know you genuinely believe in the collective commitment despite costs. Peer accountability cements, accelerating competency gains across all responders.

Leading by example during change management paves the way for adoption and commitment. However, your responsibilities do not end after initial implementations. True adaptability means actively eliciting ongoing feedback—especially dissenting perspectives—to refine direction perpetually. Resist only surrounding yourself with supporters reaffirming your viewpoints. Instead, intentionally create safe channels welcoming contrarian input without backlash. Seek to understand divergent opinions truly through curious inquiry. Ask what blinded you from seeing objections yourself so you can expand your perspectives. Then, demonstrate your receptiveness by visibly adjusting initiatives based on weaknesses employees identified and publicly attribute updated iterations of strategies directly to those who provided constructive feedback challenging the status quo. Course correct transparently so no one believes themselves above re-examination or feedback. This cements for the entire organization that the market needs—not individual ego—and ultimately steers all decisions and choices.

Driving Change Through Transparent Leader-Team Collaboration

When you decree seismic changes in a black box—sealing off inputs or visibility into decision drivers—the confusion and lack of context breeds silent sabotage. By not illuminating the full rationale and bringing teams along each step of the journey, you foster begrudging compliance at best and passive-aggressive resistance at worst.

Without transparency into intended goals or defined impact metrics, people feel whipsawed by arbitrary directives dropped from above that seem misaligned with on-the-ground realities. This information vacuum gets filled with rumor mills and speculative carved-out communications, guessing true motivations—severely eroding trust and belief in the vision.

CHAPTER 5 FOSTERING GROWTH AND INNOVATION

Sidelined and excluded from collaborating on change design conceptually, most people default to a wait-and-see hostage mentality of minimum viable effort rather than taking true ownership. They take on the role of chess pieces moved arbitrarily instead of drivers steering transformations meant to empower their potential. This mindset breeds a culture focused more on navigating internal politics of opaque processes versus championing progress.

However, avoid considering transparency a box checked, and prioritize regular two-way interactions with your team. Establish recurring touchpoints through quarterly skip-level meetings to broaden perspectives and bond directly with frontline change agents. This avoids blind spots distorted by intermediate filtering, allows direct context-sharing about company goals and business direction, and provides an opportunity to clarify any hidden misconception about decision drivers. Additionally, implement open office hours where any employee can join to discuss suggestions or concerns transparently, sending a message that all voices deserve time with leadership and cementing belonging to business across team members. Also, execute anonymous pulse surveys every two months assessing rollout effectiveness, culture shifts, refinement areas, and resource gaps delaying progress. But quantify dissent anonymously so people feel psychologically safe candidly evaluating sensitive initiatives.

Finally, you must ensure transparency flows in the other direction through consistent evidence sharing. Spotlight early proof points where new initiatives gain traction and exposures requiring recalibration. If targets slide, explain external issues faced while outlining the next steps. Rather than finger-pointing, conduct collaborative analysis to uncover root causes. Distill and review processes to remove unnecessary bureaucracy and proactively recognize missteps, even amid pressure for optics wins.

CHAPTER 5   FOSTERING GROWTH AND INNOVATION

Squandering Seeds of Innovation

Companies best able to capitalize on emerging opportunities are often those who empower teams closest to evolving market challenges to inform responsive innovation tailored to shifting customer needs. However, outmoded legacy structures across most organizations severely constrain contributors from bringing potentially cutting-edge visions to fruition—blocking adaptive progress in the process by disempowering change agents.

Opaque decision paradigms grant influence solely to senior leaders, shielding them from on-the-ground frustrations and signaling necessary transformations. Simultaneously, suggestion systems that capture frontline insights often lack pathways to evolve promising ideas into scaled impact. People thus learn raising objections risks irritating managers demanding rigid adherence to the status quo with no repercussions for stifling progress.

These dynamics persist because often, the same senior leaders with disproportionate influence to shift systems cling most stubbornly to the legacy comfort zones that initially brought their career success. Having built reputations and followers through mastering past-optimal operating models rather than driving cutting-edge reinvention aligned to emerging competitive realities, they feel psychological safety in enforcing rigid structures. However, perpetuating the dated status quo reduces the air supply to those best positioned to envision the future. Rather than prioritizing tough cultural transformations paving the way for internal innovators across levels to thrive, these entrenched leaders devote more energy to constraining creativity counter to new directions.

Even organizations seeking modernization through updated models fail to provide backing resources or rewards that could spark the type of conviction and ownership needed for concepts cultivated from within to take root across operating structures fully. Without developmental space for the most promising change agents to thrive, their vulnerable seedlings of progress get devoured by formidable bureaucracy thickets and incentives still predominantly aligned to systems that no longer fit market demands.

Elevating Innovation by Creating Dedicated Roles

Beyond rhetoric extolling innovation, if you are serious about embedding it within your engineering team culture, you should formalize responsibilities through dedicated roles at both individual and team levels.

At the individual level, identify likely change agents across domains who demonstrate high creative IQs and passport them into supplemental 20% time innovation shaper capacities. Counteract the temptation to monopolize their talents solely for immediate project priorities by ensuring protected hours for exploring ideas and forming cross-functional collaborations outside their core assignments. Make shaping the vision and developing working prototypes for efficiency improvement part of their formal Individual Development Plan, and set specific goals to drive innovative attitude. Establish specialist mentorship guides from your best design thinking coaches, providing startup-like rapid consultation support in translating raw ideas into Minimum Viable Product experiments, and evaluate opportunities to compensate shapers via bonuses tied directly to net savings successfully pioneered.

At the team level, launch six to twelve-month innovation squad rotations, granting high-potential managers stretch assignments for analyzing processes outside their functions to unearth friction points and human-centered solutions. Grant them latitude to question orthodoxies other domains take for granted and normalize the undoing of outdated assumptions while lifting up modernizers. For example, Spotify's culture of perpetual improvement is driven by Hack Days and Hack Weeks, where employees self-organize around exploring creative ideas.

Innovation left as an informal endeavor risks being dismissed as an accessory rather than an essential capacity. But leaders who elevate it through dedicated roles infuse focus and resources and influence structurally into unlocking critical progress immediately and proactively anticipating future-aligned evolutions.

Connecting Change Agents to Drive Innovation

While formalizing innovation through dedicated roles empowers individuals and teams, the ultimate multiplier effect emerges as you deliberately connect promising change agents across disparate initiatives before scale-up. You must facilitate this collaboration because pockets of creative progress often live isolated in certain units, unaware that similar efforts are happening elsewhere.

This siloed redundancy threatens innovation velocity as solutions get endlessly recreated in parallel rather than collectively advanced. However, intentional leader intervention connecting pockets of progress already underway unlocks dormant potential through building bridges across key change agents pursuing complementary modernization efforts. By directing emerging talent to spearhead fragmented initiatives and team up, scaling the most promising cross-cutting proposals, you further empower these force multipliers to accelerate explorations beyond what any individual can achieve. Guide disparate innovators toward enterprise synergies greater than their isolated sums. Bridge your changemakers, enabling them to share discoveries, explore synergistic prototypes leveraging combined strengths, and unlock significant impact on the organization and product.

However, the collective intelligence transcending isolated gains gets lost until you initiate cross-pollination. Once aware of intersecting priorities, your innovators can integrate solutions holistically addressing issues enterprise-wide versus just departmental angles.

CHAPTER 5   FOSTERING GROWTH AND INNOVATION

First, implement a required goals-sharing forum each quarter where emerging top innovators selected across business units present five-minute overviews of initiatives they are pioneering. These include technologies leveraged, progress milestones met, and upcoming goals. Encouraging visibility into distributed pockets of innovation helps leaders spot potential intersecting priorities for exploration and collaboration, avoiding duplicated efforts while accelerating innovations through partnership.

Second, curate an online internal innovations portal allowing anyone piloting new projects to voluntarily share concepts in incubator phases, seeking skillsets from other groups to advance efforts. Displaying exposures helps changemakers find potential collaborators to progress initiatives further and faster through partnership versus isolated slog. Develop a simple intake form for posts with initiative abstract, known skillset needs, and contact info. Community upvote traction helps surface posts showing the greatest collaborative potential for staff browsing potential projects.

Finally, develop a quarterly executive advisory council consisting of director-level respected veterans of transformation programs across business units. Challenge perspectives on the proposed processes or technological solutions already in market testing with honest, uncensored critique analyzing which carry the most disruptive promise versus dilutive distraction. Distill focus around 3–5 most critical priorities thoroughly inspected from all angles, providing tailwind momentum to the innovations warranting scale allocation.

CHAPTER 5   FOSTERING GROWTH AND INNOVATION

Shepherding Growth and Innovation-Oriented Cultures

As an engineering leader, your central purpose involves shepherding people-centric cultures where empowered teams feel inspired to sustain innovation matching the accelerating pace of technological revolution and market demands. You drive transformation through mutual trust and collective wisdom by demonstrating genuine adaptability, transparency, and willingness to refine directions based on critical feedback.

You must focus on nourishing individual growth, a sense of purpose, and psychological safety across teams to spark creative breakthroughs. Study after study proves that placing human fulfillment on par with business ambitions unlocks the discretionary passion and willingness to take risks that enable game-changing inventions. Engineering pioneers need confidence that bold ideas will get heard and refined versus swatted down by short-sighted bureaucratic forces.

Yet, even though establishing a strategic vision and priorities is crucial for alignment, it also leaves room for groups across the company to reimagine solutions unconstrained by conventions. Keep funneling resources toward the most promising concepts organically cultivated by internal change agents striving to uplift customers and peers through their ingenious resolutions. Then, further, guide these autonomous explorations toward enterprise synergies and compounding gains by deliberately connecting complementary innovators for mutual inspiration.

Make innovation intrinsic beyond formal new organizational roles by weaving creative expectations into everyday behaviors and cultural rituals. Reinforce desired invention mindsets through recurring ceremonies, from frequent design jams steeping proposals in customer truths to collaboratively autopsying failures to extract lessons that inoculate downstream efforts. Imprint the belief across teams that creativity and ingenuity represent the ultimate drivers of sustainable excellence, without which no company can remain sufficiently relevant amid constantly evolving user needs.

The ingredients for embedding enduring innovation across engineering already live within your teams, though current constraints obscure their visibility. As an influencer seeking cultural transformation, your leading role involves deliberately catalyzing, connecting, and unleashing these latent sparks into full flame.

Begin by laying stronger psychological foundations that instill safety and care as fundamental priorities across the employee experience. Help people feel confident that proposed ideas will undergo thoughtful consideration and refinement rather than snap judgments or reprisal. When this sheltering trust settles organization-wide, the innovation velocity previously bottled up by hesitation starts flowing freely.

Once your people feel confident in their ability to try new approaches without the risk of ridicule or penalty, step back as the driver and let the collective brilliance manifest ahead of imagined limits. Grant autonomy for teams closest to evolving market challenges to reinvent solutions tailored to users' shifting needs. Connect internal change agents pursuing modernization efforts parallel to compound thinking and amplify impacts through collaboration.

In essence, your central responsibility becomes nurturing emergent greatness by supporting explorative journeys over prescribing fixed outcomes. Let ingenuity become this generation's Sputnik moment when your people channel generative genius into launching their own transformations, reinforcing your culture's dedication to sustained, fearless innovation as the ultimate driver of excellence. The fuel is already present; it just needs sparked release.

Takeaways

1. Innovation starts with people. Nurture their growth and creativity above all.

2. Craft strategic visions focused on maximizing human potential over dictating outcomes.

3. Use vivid narratives in vision storytelling so teams imagine outcomes.

4. Set near-term milestones, so teams participate in strategic direction.

5. Foster psychological safety for teams to speak openly about ideas and concerns.

6. Personally role model vulnerability and nonjudgmental responses.

7. Conduct blameless failure retrospectives focused on process learnings.

8. Allow anonymous idea inputs to bypass inhibitions around speaking up.

9. Build cross-functional teams to interlock complementary expertise.

10. Rotate members between product domains to expand perspectives.

11. Create inner source models for code/asset reuse across teams.

12. Form communities of practice for informal knowledge sharing between specialists.

CHAPTER 5   FOSTERING GROWTH AND INNOVATION

13. Champion a growth mindset focused on continuous learning.
14. Make helping teammates upgrade skills a key performance metric.
15. Allow regular self-directed learning days for passion projects.
16. Frame change as an innovation opportunity rather than a threat.
17. Personally model the adaptive behaviors you want teams to embrace.
18. Solicit contrarian input to refine change initiatives based on feedback.
19. Spotlight early proof points where change drives positive outcomes.
20. Foster inclusive hiring processes seeking cultural add over status quo fit.
21. Mitigate bias through structured interviews calibrated by consistent guides.
22. Onboard new hires with peer mentors invested in their smooth immersion.
23. Set 30-60-90 day ramp-up plans guiding new engineers along growth trajectories.
24. Spark creativity through recurring hackathons encouraging bold ideas.
25. Embed customer obsession through collaborative design thinking sprints.

CHAPTER 5   FOSTERING GROWTH AND INNOVATION

26. Extract key learnings from failed initiatives without blame through retrospectives.

27. Centralize knowledge and insights from past projects into accessible repositories.

28. Provide online portals for teams to submit promising ideas for exploration.

29. Construct innovation sandboxes with simulated environments for safe experimentation.

30. Align governance policies to fuel innovation by providing safe guardrails over restrictions.

31. Make innovation intrinsic through cultural rituals like hackathons and design jams.

32. Spotlight teams whose ingenuity and collaboration achieved impactful outcomes.

33. Quantify engineering success through clear business metrics proving value.

34. Connect internal innovators across units to compound solutions holistically.

35. Formalize innovation responsibilities through supplemental shaper roles and rotations.

Time to Practice

1. Do the narratives in your current engineering vision story effectively inspire teams toward a human-centric purpose focused on improving lives? Or do they feel disconnected from tangible outcomes?

CHAPTER 5   FOSTERING GROWTH AND INNOVATION

2. What existing spaces demonstrate psychological safety where engineers can comfortably debate controversial ideas or share sensitive concerns without judgment? How might you thoughtfully expand this environment of safety?

3. How often do ceremonies like hackathons and learning days allow teams to exercise creativity by pursuing passion projects outside delivery pressures? Should you institute regular innovation-focused events each quarter to drive empowerment? If so, how would you design them to broaden team and business impact?

4. Have you consciously assessed talent practices to mitigate biases in sourcing and screening processes that could hamper building diverse, innovative teams? What inclusivity metrics would you need to track?

5. Does your onboarding process proactively invest in smooth immersion for new hires through peer mentors and defined 30-60-90 development plans? If gaps exist, what initial improvements can positively shape this experience?

6. When engineering attempts to stall, what rituals support conducting collaborative, blameless retrospectives focused on extracting process lessons learned? What ceremony could make this continuous?

CHAPTER 5   FOSTERING GROWTH AND INNOVATION

7. What channels exist in your business for engineers across levels to safely submit promising ideas or sensitive concerns? How might you increase psychological safety for speaking up?

8. How often do engineers currently inform planning cycles or self-organize teams around opportunities matching strengths and passions? How can you expand bottom-up initiation?

9. While project insights create value, they often languish locally. How might you facilitate company-wide reuse by centralizing knowledge assets into accessible repositories?

10. How might you better spotlight isolated pockets of innovation progress across units to allow complementary teams to synergize solutions? What voluntary forums could compound potential?

CHAPTER 6

Evaluating and Developing Your Team

If you have reached this final chapter, you are now equipped with crucial skills to adapt your leadership style and create an environment where people can thrive. However, even the most cohesive teams will only succeed with an efficient talent evaluation system. Why is it so essential? Because relying on vague notions of *"success"* obscures individuals' accurate contributions. Without formal feedback processes, poor performers go unaddressed, top talent becomes frustrated, and leaves and mediocre work are rewarded—even experienced leaders at all levels struggle with this.

Defining accomplishment through generic concepts like *"works hard"* or *"good team player"* hides more than it reveals. Relying on vague notions of success, metrics without context, and *"gut feelings"* leads well-intentioned leaders down problematic paths. Roles become misaligned to strengths. Promotions are handled poorly based on tenure rather than contributions. Top talent feels undervalued and demotivated. Teams stagnate. Dysfunction festers. The most dedicated employees burn out unnoticed.

CHAPTER 6   EVALUATING AND DEVELOPING YOUR TEAM

These pitfalls have quantifiable consequences. A recent global study by the Work Institute of over 4000 workers uncovered the top reasons for resignation.[1] More than 40% of the respondents cited the lack of feeling appreciated as the primary cause for their resignation. In contrast, the lack of trust and transparency with leadership ranked as the second most common reason for leaving the company. Most impressive, only 10% felt aligned with the company's direction.

The link between high turnover and poor people management is undeniable, especially in IT companies. For engineering leaders, success often narrowly translates to metrics like delivery times, deployment frequency, velocity, commits versus deliveries, and other quantitative indicators. But this is a selfish definition of care and achievement. It prioritizes results first and people second.

Yet, the real meaning of care recognizes behaviors, motivations, innovations, interests, family life, collaborations, and aspirations. It seeks to understand the human stories behind accomplishments and obstacles. Caring with your people means having the courage to share constructive feedback, even when difficult. It involves getting in others' shoes rather than judging from a distance. Once you understand this broader definition of caring for others, results become a consequence of this level of care, not the cause. Ignoring this perception, you fail to see how loneliness breeds mediocrity and how inspiration fuels excellence.

This human-centric mindset toward care and achievement is more than just conceptual. A 2020 analysis by Gallup examined the effect of high-empathy managers on team performance.[2] They surveyed over 15,000 employees to classify managers on their level of compassion and understanding. Workers with the most caring leaders showed 21% greater

---

[1] Work Institute. (2022). Annual retention report
[2] Harter, J., & Adkins, A. (2020). What great managers do to engage employees. Gallup.

productivity and 48% higher retention rates. They also ranked their lives 13% higher in *"thriving"* metrics like relationships, financial security, and sense of purpose.

Recognize that nurturing human strengths beyond metrics increases performance, morale, and well-being. Your people will feel valued as people, not just roles. You create purpose and provide meaning, driving higher discretionary effort for the team's collective success. As the researchers stated, *"When managers create great workplaces where employees can thrive, the profits follow."*

It's a fact: without implementing processes to align roles, give constructive feedback, and reward contributions, leaders at all levels struggle with turnover and disengagement. Top talent leaves to find appreciation elsewhere. Disengaged employees become noninnovators. Customer satisfaction declines. As organizations expand, misaligned roles and fuzzy responsibilities lead to duplication, gaps, and infighting. A lack of structure makes high performers feel underutilized and undervalued.

The risks are too great to ignore rigorous yet compassionate talent evaluation; you must nail it to succeed. This chapter provides a human-centric system to support some of the most significant and overlooked practices for evaluating and developing your team: techniques to assess strengths, share meaningful employee reviews, address underperformance with empathy, and manage terminations.

Using the 9-Box Model to Support Talent Calibration

Evaluating talent objectively is incredibly challenging. Even experienced leaders rely on subjective notions of *"top performer"* and *"high potential"* when assessing individuals. But what the hell do these terms mean in practice? How do you measure a *"high potential"*? Is it possible to make such a statement grounded in less intuition and more observations?

CHAPTER 6   EVALUATING AND DEVELOPING YOUR TEAM

The answer is yes. The 9-box model is an effective tool to support you in addressing these pitfalls. This simple matrix transitions vague concepts into clearly defined, observable criteria customized to your team. Plotting team members onto the grid enables insightful discussion and allows you to introspect each member's readiness level in a given function.

At its core, the traditional 9-box model has two axes: Performance and Potential. Each axis has three levels: Low, Medium, and High. Plotting team members on this 3x3 grid generates nine boxes with unique implications. For example, an inexperienced newcomer may rank *"High"* in potential due to raw skills and eagerness to learn but *"Low"* in performance because they are still building capabilities. In contrast, a seasoned team member with a track record of results may rank *"High"* in performance but *"Medium"* or *"Low"* in potential if their skills are becoming outdated.

Despite the model providing a helpful structure to evaluate talents, customizing the axes and levels to match your team's needs and traits is highly recommended to get the best result from this model. This section will provide an optimized approach that best suits engineering teams, where you replace the *"Potential"* axis with *"Agility,"* and the scoring model transitions to *"Developing," "Accomplished,"* and *"Outstanding"* instead of the original *"Low," "Medium,"* and *"High."* Remember, the idea is to make the criteria tangible and not abstract. Let's untangle this definition.

Performance and Agility: A Customized Approach to the 9-Box Model

For fast-paced engineering teams, the axes of Performance and Agility enable optimal talent evaluation. Traditional frameworks fixate too heavily on past accomplishments, neglecting future capability. However, in software engineering, relying solely on laurels is a liability. Agility—continuous learning, flexibility, and drive to improve—empowers organizations to adapt and lead. Likewise, well-rounded Performance measures expertise and impact holistically, beyond isolated metrics. With customized definitions grounded in specifics, the 9-box model transitions from generic theory to tailored application. Reviews evolve into catalysts for development, not rote ranking.

Defining Performance

Defining Performance requires a profound introspection of your expectations as a leader versus the company requirements for a given position. The outcome produced by this process contributes directly to your definition of Performance and must be grounded in qualitative and quantitative information. However, before aligning your expectations and sharing how success looks like for you with your reports, it's vital to demystify the industry association between performance and quantity. Suppose a product development team delivers all the commitments and some stretch goals for a given quarter. When you look at the team's dashboard, you see incredible numbers related to lead time, deployment rates, committed versus delivered, and others.

However, over time, you notice increased defects resulting from these accomplishments. Divergences about technical decisions come to the surface. People don't feel confident discussing team deliverables due to knowledge silos. Engineers have led the projects with minimum collaboration among them. The lack of engagement and empathy with the product is evident. The team spends too much time finding the guilty instead of finding the solution. In your opinion, despite all the positive results, would this team be operating at a high performance?

Despite all the great metrics, many leaders fall into the trap of sticking to numbers without further context and forget about how the individual impacts success—losing the human aspect of the evaluation process. It's crucial to look at performance holistically and include individual behavior in this definition. While velocity, quality, and delivery metrics provide data, the full picture also includes collaboration, communication, mentorship, and modeling company values. Balancing individual results and team cohesion is paramount to make Performance tangible.

For instance, for a junior engineer excelling in Performance, this could mean rapidly gaining proficiency to contribute independently. It involves eagerly learning processes, absorbing the codebase, adhering to coding standards, and embodying company values like transparency. Furthermore, they may show a hunger for proactively seeking feedback and self-improvement, demonstrating commitment beyond assignments. For an engineering leader, strong Performance may involve aligning team efforts to the product roadmap through cross-functional partnerships and facilitating other functional areas at the company to grow—sales, product marketing, customer success, and others. It entails encouraging insightful technical discussions, providing prompt performance feedback, setting realistic estimations, and being a role model.

Defining Agility

Defining Agility requires a growth mindset focused on potential through demonstrated behaviors. For individuals, the Agility axis represents the ability to improve continuously, sense change and respond effectively, move with speed to action, pursue continuous learning and self-reflection, apply creative problem-solving, adapt quickly, innovate, and handle ambiguity. These behaviors directly influence an individual's efficiency and effectiveness levels. Moreover, they empower organizations to pivot quickly, meet new challenges intelligently, and create breakthroughs proactively.

Continuous improvement and learning entail proactively seeking new skills, absorbing feedback, and constantly seeking self-improvement opportunities. Agile individuals stay on top of industry trends and eagerly expand their knowledge. They reflect critically on strengths, weaknesses, and biases that may limit perspectives. Even experts remain students in challenging comfort zones. Staying static is never an option—the focus is always on becoming better and maximizing one's potential.

Furthermore, sensing change and responding effectively instills vigilance—continually scanning for technological shifts, user needs, market dynamics, and new product improvement opportunities. It moves the needle to stay on the pulse of industry trends, customers' needs, and emerging innovations. Equally valuable is the judgment to respond appropriately. This means pivoting efforts and priorities swiftly while mitigating risks when changes warrant action.

The Agility axis also entails moving with speed to action when opportunities arise. Whether commercializing new ideas or addressing issues, agile individuals mobilize quickly rather than getting bogged down in analysis paralysis. They balance pragmatism and vision to keep pace with rapid evolutions.

Moreover, equally important is to demonstrate an attitude to handle ambiguity. An engineering team rarely works with static requirements and projects for long. Assumptions that are relevant today may be obsolete tomorrow. Agile engineers embrace this fluidity as the norm, demonstrate calm and critical thinking when requirements are unclear, and collaborate with stakeholders to find optimal solutions promptly. When plans change or initiatives pivot, they adapt quickly rather than getting frustrated. People with a high level of Agility thrive in uncertainty and focus energy on delivering value, not resisting necessary change. They are role models for team resilience. Finally, agile engineers effortlessly absorb business needs beyond superb technical skills, translating them into tangible product value and aligning decisions with overarching objectives.

CHAPTER 6   EVALUATING AND DEVELOPING YOUR TEAM

Assessment Definitions: Unlocking the Essence of Performance and Agility

The next step is measuring success along the axes of Performance and Agility. This process is crucial for gaining a tangible perspective on individual and team capabilities. The framework divides the scores into Developing, Accomplished, and Outstanding categories. Your grasp of the nuanced definitions of these categories is pivotal. It lays the foundation for clear expectations and accurately appraises each team member's contributions.

Let's start with the **Developing** rating. This score signifies minimal evidence, both observed by you and reported by others, of the team member manifesting the desired level of Performance or Agility. This assessment suggests that the individual's achievements and behaviors may not align with the expectations set for their role; in fact, they might fall below the established standards. It implies a phase where the employee is still in the early stages of mastering the necessary skills and adapting to the required mindset. A *Developing* rating signals an opportunity for focused guidance, constructive feedback, and targeted development plans to nurture the employee's potential and elevate their contributions to the expected level.

Moving forward, the **Accomplished** rating in talent assessment indicates compelling and firm evidence, confirmed by your observations and the consensus of others, that the employee performs their duties within the expected level of Performance or Agility. This professional consistently exceeds established standards, leaving a lasting impact well-aligned with their role. The *Accomplished* category paints a picture of an individual who meets expectations and consistently exceeds them, contributing significantly to the team and organization. This classification affirms a successful integration of essential skills and mindset while maintaining a solid level of excellence. Furthermore, this level highlights the fundamental role of the individual as a valuable asset to the team, displaying a history of impactful contributions worthy of acknowledgment and recognition.

Lastly, the **Outstanding** scoring highlights significant evidence illustrating the employee's extraordinary demonstration of Performance or Agility. This individual meets your expectations and significantly surpasses them, consistently delivering an impact far exceeding the norm for their role. The *Outstanding* category represents a professional who sets a new benchmark for eminence, contributing at an unparalleled level to the team and organization. This rating affirms an effective and efficient integration of crucial skills and an impact-driven mindset, sustaining high excellence. Additionally, it underscores the individual's indispensable role as an exemplary asset to the team, showcasing a track record of transformative contributions deserving the highest recognition and commendation.

Putting It All Together: Evaluating Talent with the 9-Box Model

You now have the cornerstones needed to effectively evaluate your team members' talents using the 9-box model. By defining Performance and Agility in tangible, customized ways, identifying observable behaviors for each assessment level, and grasping the nuanced scoring system, you can have insightful discussions calibrated to your engineers' realities.

The next step is putting these pieces together into an actionable framework. Based on their Performance and Agility ratings, plotting team members on the 9-box grid generates nine distinct segments. Each quadrant indicates clear strengths, growth needs, and recommendations so you can make talent decisions tailored to each individual.

However, it's crucial to remember that the evaluations must align with the expectations and needs of your specific team and company. For example, Accomplished Performance and Agility may be ideal for some organizations, while others may see it as complacency. Stay aware of your team's context, and avoid rigid definitions of success and failure. The goal is maximizing fit and potential, not enforcing uniformity in your judgment.

Outstanding Performance and Outstanding Agility: The Leading Edge

This elite talent quadrant demands priority retention and motivation efforts. Losing top professionals inflicts immense setbacks—their differentiated capabilities and knowledge are challenging to replace. Sustaining excellence requires understanding their aspirations beyond immediate incentives. Regularly connect on career goals, challenges, and passions. Provide tailored opportunities to deepen impact, like stretching assignments, high-exposure projects, and mentoring roles. Inspire them to lead initiatives and develop management muscles to unlock further potential. Avoid complacency by continually pushing for growth.

While bonuses, promotions, and recognition matter, purpose is their ultimate driver. Help them see how their contributions impact others and connect to company values. Foster an environment where they direct strategy and develop people. Spotlight their accomplishments publicly to reinforce their value. They earned preferential treatment—expedited promotions quickly with aligned roles and challenges. Delay risks frustration. However, avoid perceptions of favoritism by ensuring opportunities remain merit-based.

With greatness comes responsibility—their capabilities demand consistent modeling of culture and principles. Coach them to share knowledge, collaborate across silos, and grow others. Exceptional technical expertise left unbalanced by empathy and teamwork has limited impact. Guide them to strengthen versatile leadership abilities that lift collectives. Remain aware of disengagement signs like diminished citizenship, lack of care for teams, or ethical breaches—no one is irreplaceable.

Accomplished Performance and Outstanding Agility: Develop to Excel

This segment represents emerging talents—dependable delivery accelerated by adaptability. They already contribute high value through consistent results and a growth mindset. With nurturing, their balanced potential can amplify team-wide impact exponentially. You must view professionals in this segment as your organization's next generation of excellence.

Growth should be the top priority for those embracing improvement despite technical proficiency. Inspire continued self-development by providing visible stretch assignments and projects that broaden their impact. Offer opportunities for higher learning aligned with their aspirations, like conferences, certifications, and intensive training programs. Dedicate time for self-directed study and support them in crafting personal development plans. Communicate promotion criteria focused on diversifying skills, not just domain delivery. Work closely with them to avoid potential stagnation proactively.

Even though technically independent, their adaptability must be guided toward positive ends. Coach them to synthesize speed with quality when driving change and leverage their comfort with ambiguity to facilitate challenging discussions. Guide them to share knowledge, mentor others, and lead by example. With support channeling their agility into collaborative decisions, they will thrive in uncertainty as a role model for teams.

Finally, proactively consider those in this segment for opportunities to formally expand influence, such as leading key cross-functional initiatives or mentoring newer engineers. They have much to teach others through their experience. Provide a venue to hone versatile management abilities and contribute higher-level strategic thinking to team direction. They earned consideration for promotion but still require seasoning through diverse assignments before moving to the next level.

CHAPTER 6   EVALUATING AND DEVELOPING YOUR TEAM

Outstanding Performance and Accomplished Agility: High-Performing Pro

Professionals in this segment exemplify excellence in Performance, consistently exceeding expectations and serving as role models within their teams and company. However, their Accomplished Agility indicates room to enhance adaptability and comfort with change. With guidance expanding their agile capabilities, their talents can transform uncertain situations into solid wins.

Their pragmatic approach yields superb outcomes yet resists rapid changes that introduce ambiguity or risks beyond their control. Although undeniably capable, pressure and ambiguity can overwhelm when navigating requirements alone. Risk-taking rarely will come naturally to these high performers. Thus, you must practice compassion and patience to nurture their courage and mindset change—experimentation with calculated risks must become second nature. Create opportunities where you can guide them toward the prioritization process and promote innovative thinking.

Ask for different solutions for the same problem, and help them identify the pitfalls between quality and pace. Once they find it, participate in the decisions and planning, but let them walk on their legs. Show how their strengths applied to unfamiliar assignments and constituencies can elevate whole collectives. Next, recognize smaller wins to instill the mindset change and confirm what success looks like. Then, facing uncertainty, preset mileposts help reinforce concrete progress. Then creativity has space to emerge safely. Reinforce expanding potential by ensuring they apply their powerhouse strengths to new assignments and diverse constituencies.

Accomplished Performance and Accomplished Agility: Solid and Steady

Even though they are Accomplished all around, their potential requires proactive nurturing.

Professionals in this segment deliver consistent quality, meeting all expectations. They precisely execute the requirements *"by the book"* and are reliable assets. However, steadiness should not be confused with excellence. Why? Because with only Accomplished Performance and Agility, they execute well in their comfort zone but rarely stretch their capabilities or think strategically beyond direction.

While stability is crucial for organizations and teams to operate smoothly, well-rounded excellence requires more than just reliable delivery of expectations. True excellence involves proactively enhancing one's skills, innovating processes beyond the status quo, and demonstrating versatility and improvement as organizational priorities shift. It requires a growth mindset focused on constant betterment. Without active nurturing, a mentality of complacency can develop where past accomplishments are sufficient. Consequently, it incentivizes coasting on existing capabilities rather than continual improvement, and your staff will stagnate to meet current demands rather than rise to the challenges of tomorrow.

However, you are pivotal in inspiring integrated performance, personal growth, and driving higher goals. With supportive guidance and accountability, professionals in this segment can expand their perseverant performance to new areas. Their consistency makes them ideal candidates for roles developing newer team members through mentorship. Stretch them through leading key initiatives beyond their functional domain as well. Position them to disrupt the status quo positively and invent processes and solutions for future scale, define clear standards focused on reaching beyond stability into positive disruption, creative problem-solving, expanding teamwork, and nurturing talent through hands-on development opportunities.

CHAPTER 6   EVALUATING AND DEVELOPING YOUR TEAM

Developing Performance and Outstanding Agility: Strong Potential

Professionals in this quadrant exhibit outstanding adaptability while requiring development on consistent delivery. When nurtured through a layered coaching approach addressing root causes—not just behaviors—their responsiveness is an asset.

In their drive to make rapid progress, professionals in this segment often focus heavily on execution speed while completing iterative cycles to the detriment of quality and stability. Their responsiveness leads them to pivot based on continuously shifting priorities. Each minor change unintentionally sparks tangents, moving them further from the central goal. Their agile and innovative nature ironically becomes counterproductive to the team's mission without sufficient structure. Consequently, great ideas fail to reach fruition due to continual disruption.

Creating a collaborative performance plan is crucial for nurturing mutual understanding between execution-focused and agile team members prone to tangents. Consider scheduling an open discussion focused solely on listening to their frustrations and exploring root motivations nonjudgmentally—often, anxiety due to uncertainty sparks coping through hyperactivity. Then, recognize and provide empathy that their core nature is enthusiasm and inventiveness, not harm. Jointly assess how establishing clear deliverable expectations across an agreed timeline reduces anxiety. Define what conditions warrant plan adjustments versus pushing forward, and help them see how their role impacts customers by supporting team goals and inspiring purposeful excellence beyond task completion.

This understanding enables self-correction through co-created accountability channels focused on positive reinforcement and celebrating small successes. Compassionately reinforce gaps in finishing cycles while ensuring necessary support systems are available. Taking time to align expectations and accountability to vision is fundamental to allowing patience and guidance that will later transform raw agility into consistent performance.

Outstanding Performance and Developing Agility: Performing Without Innovating

These individuals deliver exceptional results but must be more comfortable responding to change and ambiguity. Their pragmatic approach centers on quality ownership and framing solutions as personal signatures. However, they are reluctant to adapt, which risks losing relevance amid evolving business landscapes requiring more dynamism.

With deep expertise, they happily immerse themselves in technical details, iterating until they achieve excellence. But this diligence also invites tension when facing pivots or urgency requiring trade-offs. They demonstrate hesitation in rushing or compromising the hard-won quality standards they uphold. So unexpected pivots or urgency spark resentment at change. Still, their reliability consistently exceeding expectations, especially on the most complex assignments, makes them indispensable assets if nurtured.

Respect their wisdom by proactively consulting them on changes that may disrupt workflow. Despite facing initial resistance, efforts to earn their trust and meet them where they stand yield compounding returns over forcing change through decree alone. Their strengths remain vital for performance advancement if paired with guidance developing comfort responding to fluid requirements. Unlocking adaptability amplifies capabilities to match their reliability excellence.

Accomplished Performance and Developing Agility: Limited Progress

While accomplishing formal expectations reliably in the short term, professionals in this quadrant often face capability stagnation as needs shift. Their avoidance of risk causes initial steadiness to transform into barriers stifling critical progress. Over time, an overdependence on outdated tools or unwillingness to evolve methodologies also emerges.

Beyond individual sluggishness, accomplished performers with developmental agility can negatively impact teams over time if unattended. Reliant on past practices, they dismiss newer member initiatives as naive or superfluous. Insecurity masked as wisdom breeds resentment, costing collaboration opportunities. Moreover, they may get behind criticisms to justify their unwillingness to update skills and define ambitions narrowly to rationalize plateaus.

Initially, their technical proficiency earns the benefit of the doubt while assigned responsibilities are accomplished adequately. However, a deeper analysis may reveal fear of irrelevance eclipsing mission focus. Verbose excuses exhibit an unwillingness to take ownership. Less visible in early periods are rising opportunities and progress lost from multiplying downstream effects quarter after quarter. Toxicity is already deeply rooted before problems become apparent. Complacency rules and makes rote expectations alone insufficient to transform rigid perspectives into fuel for progress. They lack self-awareness connecting behaviors to consequences, requiring your effort to identify the gaps obstructing potential.

To support people with this profile, you must help them transform discussed commitments into tangible ones to reinforce accountability and follow-through. But, given development lags, coaching plans often prove insufficient to course correct reliably, and you must consider establishing formal performance improvement plans to fast-track capability building by outlining measurable milestones aligned to needs.

Interestingly, due to the serious nature and message of formal Performance Improvement Plans (PIP), individuals in this segment often respond positively to the gravity of the situation and use it as motivation to surpass obstacles through improved discipline once properly supported— *we will cover PIP processes to balance clarity with empathy later in this chapter.*

Lastly, concurrently identify and amplify niche strengths that are already exhibiting momentum outside formal plans. Even small wins validate the effort's viability when mired in stagnation. They display latent potential, nascent resiliency, and a desire to contribute. It is worth the price of investing in their recovery.

Developing Performance and Accomplished Agility: Evaluate Further

Professionals exhibiting Accomplished Agility yet Developing Performance require attentive nurturing to mitigate underperformance risks. They display openness, embrace change initiatives, and mobilize quickly. At times, outcomes meet expectations. But compliance lacks reliability—quality assurance barriers catch preventable defects. Short-term wins give way to stretched milestones requiring rework and excuses, staling team progress and business growth. They act responsively without conscious risk-taking. At the same time, their agile actions may catalyze unexpected adverse domino effects.

If unrestrained, their undisciplined working styles jeopardize team cohesion, as rework caused by sloppy deliveries spreads tension among members. Impacts compound—their careless interruptions stall collaborative workflows, while excuses erode collective accountability. Confusion arises about potential and actual capabilities—especially if it's related to a senior team member. What was supposed to be the light for success became the anchor for stagnation.

Beyond cascading consequences, daily frictions also emerge. In collaboration contexts, accomplished agility individuals paradoxically often perform better when working solo than in tightly coupled groups. They rush pivotal decisions without connecting details to overarching rationale. While responsive to business needs, the focus centers more on reactive and short-term solution shaping rather than proactive co-creation aligned with strategic priorities.

CHAPTER 6   EVALUATING AND DEVELOPING YOUR TEAM

Intervention mandates close observation paired with clear directive guidance focused squarely on closing performance gaps through formalized coaching plans. They require frequent proactive and candid feedback and conversations that continually redefine how success looks at each phase. Also, it's beneficial to meet formally to evaluate plan effectiveness, celebrate small wins, and discuss barriers requiring recalibration.

Yet, recognize that without an urgent course correction, the accomplished Agility, aligned with their lackluster performance, may quickly escalate to a score Developed in both areas. It's paramount to seek root causes to justify this evaluation—frustration from role stagnation, lack of skills to perform the job, or leadership conflicts often catalyze disengagement. Then, demonstrate developmental support.

Collaboratively design milestone-based talent recovery plans they help structure. Exercise nonjudgmental listening to frustration sources. Routinely evaluate plan effectiveness—continuously revisit alignments to their passions. Adapting fluidly as motivations shift rebuilds buy-in through trust in your dedicated partnership. With patient guidance, such dormant potential reignites, lifting individual and collective growth trajectories.

Furthermore, if formal mentoring programs fail to ignite accountability and ownership, you must consider enacting formal performance improvement plans adds gravity, clarifying outcomes for continued nonconformance. Avoid making it your second nature, but recognize that firm foundations aligned with rigid guidance empower higher performance activated through accountability and a sense of urgency.

Developing Performance and Agility: Low Impact

Few leadership conversations feel more daunting than confronting clear delivery underperformance coupled with stagnating capability. Yet, the Developing/Developing quadrant leaves little ambiguity—their attitude and behaviors are disconnected from the expectations aligned to their role and exhibit neither impactful results nor future upside potential indicative of excellence, growth trajectory, or team enablement.

The professionals in this section often externalize blame habitually to rationalize poor outcomes instead of seeking shared understanding. Their outdated mindsets perceive constructive feedback as attacks rather than developmental opportunities. They default to passive disengagement or active disruption when experiencing friction. Short-term wins worsen inflated self-appraisals and require realignment to actual accomplishments. They demonstrate a low level of self-awareness. Additionally, they forgo commitments made absent consequences, requiring constant supervision and wasting high-potential talent better reallocated toward those embracing growth.

When the matter is growth, including them in mentoring programs may be insufficient, and they are reluctant to dent their developmental inertia. They habitually avoid recommended resources, adamantly claiming sufficient expertise to perform their role. Unteachable rigidity rejects the constructive feedback necessary for growth. Hopes for progress and recovery slowly give way to countless uncomfortable conversations—which sign their job may be at risk.

Unconcerned with preserving mediocrity, their troubling patterns cascade into systematically eroding team trust and cultural contamination. They start losing trust and benefits and are progressively labeled low-impact assets, and you start getting questions about their presence—termination sounds imminent.

However, you are the catalyst to help them to overcome such a critical situation. To become a people-centric leader, termination must be an option, but not the first. You must fight back and resist the pressure and the temptation to get shortcuts to solve the dysfunctional behavior. You must formalize a Performance Improvement Plan.

CHAPTER 6   EVALUATING AND DEVELOPING YOUR TEAM

Performance Reviews: The Arc for Success

For many professionals, performance reviews represent yearlong culminating moments to align feedback, celebrate accomplishments, and shape new development areas through self-reflection. Yet, receiving such high-quality reviews has become a luxury due to many leaders' chronic overlooking and avoidance.

But why the negligence? First, some lack fluency in translating organizational strategy into required behaviors for their teams to enable and cascade priorities through helpful feedback. Second, being vulnerable is difficult. By avoiding reviews altogether, some conceal their own shortcomings, receiving developmental feedback themselves. They focus elsewhere rather than modeling growth for team members through accountability. Another reason is that many leaders underestimate the relationship-building value and make performance reviews a low priority when compared to operational demands competing for bandwidth. Finally, the absence of structured frameworks and perceived unpreparedness heighten discomfort in facilitating authentic conversations.

A 2016 analysis published in the *Academy of Management Journal* investigated quantitatively the connection between performance review quality and productivity gains.[3] Over 8 months, the study analyzed survey data from 244 employees in China across subjective measures—supervisory coaching, trust in leadership, role clarity, and objective performance metrics—and found that higher quality reviews correlated significantly to multiple improved organizational outcomes. Employees felt their leaders delivered constructive feedback and built greater working trust and understanding, directly driving engagement gains upwards of 20% and discretionary output gains of 15% over control groups.

---

[3] Qian, J., Song, B., Wang, B., Shi, J., & Wu, H. (2016). High-quality workplace relationships as substitute for task-oriented leadership in predicting employee job crafting. Academy of Management Journal, 59(6), 2169-2192.

CHAPTER 6 EVALUATING AND DEVELOPING YOUR TEAM

However, developing robust evaluation muscles through consistent reviews also unlocks interpersonal and calibration advantages beyond quantifiable output gains. Performance reviews empower employees at all levels to self-reflect deeply on their recent accomplishments and assess blind spots they may harbor in how their behaviors deliver value. Instead of limiting goal setting to universal company metrics, you can provide additional qualitative examples of success extended to each individual, matching their role and capabilities.

Over successive reviews, standards expand from narrow delivery key performance indicators into more holistic quality considerations like team contributions, customer orientation, and capability building. Reviews become regular channels to shape more ambitious definitions of excellence tailored to nurture potential and accelerate skill development in a continuous loop. The ethos is to contribute to your reports' growth so they can, level by level, achieve an Outstanding Performance and Agility indicator in your 9-box model. The path is complex yet rewarding for both sides if embraced with an open mind and bravery.

In the following sections, you will learn a simple and powerful system to have performance conversations and focus your energy on what matters.

Cadence: As Important As the Structure

Establishing review rhythms matters tremendously for performance and consistent leadership habit-building. Beyond enabling progress milestones, recurrent conversations hone lifelong empathy and candor capacities more than episodic meetings alone could. You level up your partnering abilities with each tension-filled coaching or vulnerable reflection.

Yet, confusion still abounds on ideal periodicity despite agreement that sustained dialogue unlocks potential otherwise untapped between sporadic check-ins. More significant than prescribing cadences is considering the trade-offs. Frequent performance conversations offer continuity gains yet require preparation cycles that may divert operational capacity, for example. Let's explore the ups and downs of delivering this review quarterly, semesterly, and annually.

Quarterly Performance Reviews

Quarterly reviews are constantly surrounded by arguments around their advantages and downsides—often legitimate. When structured appropriately, more recurring conversations better support continuous improvement with tighter feedback loops, enabling course correction promptly as priorities shift. Communicative quality also heightens through clear expectation revisiting and achievement recognition in weeks.

Upsides to quarterly reviews start with boosting morale when used for constructive means, not control mechanisms exerting undue pressure. Timely acknowledgment of significant achievements offers intrinsic rewards catalyzing motivation. Younger team members especially appreciate promptly setting updated goals after past cycle objective attainment. Additionally, more frequent discussions promote responsively defining how success looks amid changing landscapes.

However, imposing overly rigid quarterly reviews without considering supportive processes has downsides. Firstly, an excessive emphasis on short-term demands often happens at the expense of broader competency advancements that deliver impact over quarters, not just weeks—it's vital to maintain balance between. Further, making quarterly reviews meaningful demands nontrivial hours of introspection and preparation, frequently conflicting with other essential initiatives without proper support—exponentially increased with the number of direct reports you lead. Finally, unrealistic quarterly pressures could incent toxicity in the absence of psychological safety valves and empathetic flexibility in reassessing strained situations.

CHAPTER 6   EVALUATING AND DEVELOPING YOUR TEAM

Semesterly Performance Reviews

Semester cadence reviews balance both sustaining engagement through midyear touchpoints with latitude enabling strategy absorption before realignment. Leaders valuing extended goal-setting consideration find six-month rhythms accord more planning bandwidth where objectives and milestones see proper initiation before reassessment.

Upsides include facilitating comprehensive achievement analysis with room for in-depth feedback exchange that is less rushed than quarterly appraisals. Additionally, with business priorities constantly in motion, semester reviews afford employees improved opportunities to make progress, applying effort against both immediate and longer-term ambitions. The extended interval also promotes thoughtful performance planning aligned to broader organizational targets. Finally, freeing up your hours from quarterly demands allows better focus on other mission-critical activities when managed seamlessly.

However, while offering engagement continuity and strategic planning latitudes, semester review downsides center on delays in adapting support when needs pivot quickly. With only two touchpoints annually, modifying personalized success criteria or realigning veered-off objectives encounters longer turnaround times compared to quarterly catch-ups. Likewise, the extended period without formal evaluation heightens the employee's anxiety about receiving a formal evaluation, often paralyzing the capacity for self-evaluation and impacting job satisfaction.

Annual Performance Review

Annual performance cycles enable you to accentuate extended strategic developments that transpire gradually and then reach pivotal milestones, eventually warranting holistic examination. Ultimately, when studying the previous year's enterprise accomplishments, you identify that maximizing organizational synergies through individual objective setting proves far easier.

Additional upsides abound. Streamlined yearly processes conserve time and resources otherwise consumed, perpetually tracking incremental progress. Annual cycles also enable stabilizing functions through consistent long-term targets—guardrails providing welcome certainty as growth volatility churns. Through whole-cloth reexamination, you effectively recognize outstanding cross-functional contributions that seemingly surfaced through interdependent enterprise successes.

Conversely, prioritizing long reviews risks downplaying acute contributor frustrations absent outlets airing concerns promptly. Infrequent sit-downs also severely limit nimble responses to unforeseen impediments or pace layer changes, undesirably allowing temporary roadblocks cementing permanent setbacks. Further, the prolonged suspense awaiting annual reviews exacerbates the anxiety of some personalities who thrive on receiving positive reinforcement regularly. Ironically, critiques feel more crushing without recent wins counterbalancing areas needing improvement spotlighted harshly in the rearview. Ultimately, balancing trade-offs remains critical.

A Pro Tip

Regardless of the cadence you choose to execute, it's vital to implement supportive guardrails around review rhythms to mitigate downside risks through sustained connectivity channels beyond formal occasions. Use and abuse your one-on-one alignment discussions to uphold relationship continuity and deliver prompt feedback. The definition of success is dynamic and frequently adapts to business mutation. Avoid waiting for a review cycle to calibrate—it may become too late.

Structure: A Blueprint for Performance Reviews

Performance reviews are often overlooked and grounded in the misconception that oral delivery is enough. However, many people need time to digest feedback, especially when it's critical. Therefore, your performance review must be an artifact—searchable and lifelong—where your report can revisit, review, and introspect as many times as needed and wished.

Having a written review allows your employees to comprehend the feedback fully and allows them to reference it long after your discussion. It also shows that you took the time and care to consider their contributions and areas for improvement thoughtfully. Here, a simple conversation fails to provide the depth and permanence that a tangible review offers. So, craft your written review intentionally, being comprehensive yet concise, balancing achievements and opportunities with an eye toward the future. The document must spark self-reflection long after your meeting ends.

However, dropping your evaluation thoughts in a disjointed, sloppy document is insufficient and ineffective. You must thoughtfully organize your review into clear sections that logically build upon each other. This artifact may be simple yet meaningful. Still, you can evolve it into a more robust evaluation system over time.

Begin by having employees conduct self-reviews, assessing their own accomplishments and growth areas. Next, create a manager evaluation dashboard to discuss their placement in the 9-box performance/agility model and ensure shared definitions of those axes. Moving forward, provide your own assessment grounded in specific observations, highlighting achievements and development needs. Set clear expectations for the next period and recommend how they can meet them. Finally, you can also incorporate 360-degree feedback from peers to provide multiple lenses.

Let's discuss each of these sections.

CHAPTER 6   EVALUATING AND DEVELOPING YOUR TEAM

Self-evaluation: A Temperature Check for Self-awareness

The self-evaluation section establishes employee self-awareness as your review's cornerstone. Before receiving any external feedback, your team introspects on achievements, lessons, strengths, and areas of improvement from their lens. Rather than worrying about structure compliance, they mainly focus on their definitions of success and standards for criticism.

Truthfully, people often dislike writing self-reviews because many companies adopt standardized evaluation models that focus on the same repetitive questions review after review, which fails to spark introspection or curiosity. Additionally, some frameworks overwhelm employees with an excessive number of prompts stretched over too many pages.

Instead, keep your self-evaluations simple, open-ended, and dynamic. Limit yourself to three to five thoughtful questions that unpack key areas of reflection. Further, enhance engagement by varying these prompts across review cycles to uncover fresh perspectives. For instance, in one review period, ask, *"What key accomplishments did you achieve?"* *"What were your pivotal learnings?"* and *"What could you do differently next time?"* Then, in the next cycle, inquire, *"What new capabilities did you gain during this period?"* *"Describe your proudest overcome challenge and how you tackled it,"* and *"Suppose you are a bug in the wall observing you daily this period; what behaviors you would see?"* Remember, quantity is not a synonym of quality. Less often is more!

The Manager Review: Anchoring in Observations

This section can make or break your relationship and leadership. Empty statements are inefficient in driving introspection and often reverse progress, as reports see you as irrelevant to their growth when failing to provide meaningful reflections.

CHAPTER 6   EVALUATING AND DEVELOPING YOUR TEAM

Nowadays, many leaders utilize AI tools to generate reviews and avoid difficult conversations. However, for now, these generative algorithms produce overly generic feedback disconnected from reality. They lack the nuanced qualitative insights demonstrating a deep understanding of an employee's accomplishments. As leaders increasingly experiment with emerging technologies like ChatGPT to draft reviews, ensure your evaluation stems from direct engagement rather than solely relying on AI approximations. While convenient, computer-generated language risks damaging rapport and trust when replaced entirely for human discernment grounded in observational evidence.

Another common issue is that many leaders struggle to balance emotion with reason. Consequently, they deliver biased reviews of their reports, misaligned with the current performance within the period. For example, if a leader feels frustrated by an employee consistently missing deadlines, they may provide overly harsh criticism that skews negative. However, if they objectively assessed the review period, perhaps the employee took on extra responsibilities that led them to deprioritize certain tasks. Or they demonstrated initiative that benefited other projects. Leaders paint a subjective picture by letting emotions override facts, demotivating teams instead of giving constructive feedback grounded in reality. Make active efforts to separate feelings from observations so reviews accurately reflect demonstrated achievements and improvement areas over a defined timeframe.

The solution lies in grounding assessments in clear observations instead of labeling subjective evaluations. Additionally, adopt inclusive language like *"we"* and *"us"* to reinforce partnerships in growth. For example, consider the feedback, *"Your code quality is bad."* This offers little analysis to act upon. Instead, reframe it into an observation—*"While reviewing your pull requests, I've noticed you aren't using our defined code standards, consequently increasing complexity and review times beyond expectations. Despite several comments on adopting these practices, there is still room to improve consistency in applying standards moving forward."*

CHAPTER 6   EVALUATING AND DEVELOPING YOUR TEAM

This grounds the critique in objective examples while framing standards alignment as a partnership for efficiency.

Structuring recognitions with observable evidence is as crucial as doing so for constructive criticism. Simply sharing *"You did a good job on Project X"* lacks contextual meaning. Instead, highlight specific observations such as: *"You demonstrated an outstanding commitment to understanding Project X's customer pain points by asking insightful questions from multiple lenses. This allowed our team to deeply grasp requirements and design an innovative solution, which we delivered ahead of schedule, reducing client churn risks."*

Grounding praise in recent behavioral examples provides a tangible impact they created while reinforcing productive practices to continue. Vague applause risks ringing hollow without evidence tied to outcomes. Structure achievements with rich qualitative details, too—not just quantitative results.

Setting Expectations: Defining How Success Will Look Like

The expectations section empowers you to define focused development areas for the next review cycle, grounded in their motivations, role requirements, and your insights on growth opportunities. Avoid setting numbers as a default outcome for this section, and establish aligned objectives spanning capabilities to upgrade—whether behaviors, attitudes, collaboration abilities, communication styles, technical proficiencies, leadership capabilities, or key performance indicators. This section is responsible for defining what success will look like, and there is no room for ambiguity—clarity matters!

However, even though initial measures provide direction for the upcoming review cycle, it's critical to recognize that business priorities and personal goals evolve naturally, so your expectations and alignment. Priorities may change to better position the company in the market.

Project requirements may uncover hidden necessities and potential new strategies. Skill development needs could necessitate capability-based performance indicator recalibration. And that is fine! Yet, you must ensure that you communicate whatever changes in the previously defined expectation, enabling a responsive reconfiguration. As important as communicating these changes promptly is providing the reasons behind the mutation, potential impacts, and how to mitigate them.

Recommendation: A Guide to Support Growth

Once focused expectations are set, recommendations suggest supportive avenues for achieving development areas while empowering employee ownership of growth trajectories. Still, you must consider this section informative guidance, not prescriptive requirements.

Recommendations demonstrate investment through caring advice. Suggest training programs, books, mentors in your network, job shadowing, or new rotational assignments that could enrich skills. Connect employees to internal experts that ease their learning curves and signpost external resources like conferences, certifications, or networking groups to engage with.

Still, avoid directly imposing directives, as it feels like a top-down intervention. You must frame recommendations as optional guideposts equipping self-direction fueled by autonomy. Clarify as well that not applying recommendations will not impact formal performance evaluations if expectations are otherwise met. This section solely exists to scaffold support structures toward maximum potential through influence, not authority.

360-Feedback: An Outside Look In

360-degree feedback enhances review robustness through outside perspectives by inquiring peers and cross-functional partners about their experiences working with your employees. Feedback consists

CHAPTER 6 EVALUATING AND DEVELOPING YOUR TEAM

of demonstrated capabilities, communication styles, vision setting, leadership behaviors, and more—illuminating blind spots and escaping any pre-existing bias.

This method purposely expands inputs beyond the manager-employee axis to increase objectivity, mirror areas for improvement, and spotlight strengths that are harnessed further. It works best when participants span diverse operational scopes, granting exposure to the individual's multifaceted contributions. Yet, avoid limiting the survey solely to direct peers. The fuller the picture, the richer the insights.

Despite all the benefits, this process is time-consuming to become meaningful; once you need to select a group of people and request feedback in specific areas, they need to fit your request into their priorities, answer, and finally, you can analyze and compile. Although heavily rewarding if conducted thoroughly, limit formal 360-feedback cycles to annual or semester gatherings, delving into deep versus superficial ongoing queries burdening participants and delaying holistic comprehension.

Time is an expensive resource. Thus, it's imperative that your questions are simplified and to the point. Select two or three areas in which you want external evaluation and move forward. Still, it's important that you use the same set of questions for all the participants of the process. Other than facilitating the analysis overall, it mitigates significant bias from the process.

Therefore, to encourage open sharing, craft messages emphasizing no-judgment zones, defining the sense of urgency with an expected date, but keeping it comfortable for declines. Also, provide options to ensure anonymity and ways of delivery. Let's see the following message example:

> Hello,
>
> *In preparation for a performance review for John, and considering you've worked closely with him during this review cycle, I want to ask you to provide feedback in the following areas:*

CHAPTER 6   EVALUATING AND DEVELOPING YOUR TEAM

- *Where does John brighten in his role as an Engineering Manager?*
- *How does John impact your growth at the company?*
- *In which areas could John improve to be a more efficient and effective Engineering Manager?*

Here are a few additional thoughts I'd like you to know:

- *I'll need that feedback by January 22. If you can't provide it by then—that's fine, but please let me know quickly so I can ask someone else.*

Please let me know your preferred way for me to share the feedback with John. Here are the options:

- *You will send the feedback to me and forward it yourself to John;*
- *You are OK with me forwarding the feedback verbatim;*
- *You want me to use the feedback in a way that does not reveal who provided it.*

Thanks in advance for your time.

Recognize that providing 360-degree feedback stretches people's comfort zones. After getting the inputs you asked for, show gratitude for their vulnerability and courage to enrich excellence, not critique failures. Especially for making time to participate in someone's growth!

Finally, understand it's not your function to filter what your report will digest from the feedback. Respect confidentiality requests by adapting identifiable details. Additionally, remove any disrespectful statements. Otherwise, provide all feedback verbatim—let your employee assess what's most beneficial for their growth.

CHAPTER 6   EVALUATING AND DEVELOPING YOUR TEAM

While you may feel impulses to shelter your employees from painful materials, filtering risks playing false god rather than partner. Your role lies not in judging message validity but rather in showcasing the diversity of inputs to shape their perception. Through this brave exposure to transparency, awareness expands on all sides and collaborates directly to growth and performance.

Performance Improvement Plan: Revitalizing Potential

Implementing a Performance Improvement Plan (PIP) is one of the trickiest processes in management. There is often a lack of clarity in defining what successful performance looks like and outlining actionable steps for improvement. Additionally, when facing an underperforming team member, the default reaction is to avoid the issue or pursue termination rather than recovery. As a result, PIPs frequently lead to ending the employment relationship rather than unlocking talent.

As a leader, you must view performance improvement and terminations holistically, beyond the individual employee. Firing someone affects team morale and often feeds negative organizational gossip. The costs of hiring a replacement in terms of company money, time, and other resources also tend to exceed investments in talent recovery. A loss of knowledge and capacity also departs with the individual.

However, investing in Performance Improvement Plans (PIPs) does not always work well either. An unsuccessful PIP can open the door to a toxic environment, spread disengagement, hinder achieving milestones, and ultimately contribute to a dysfunctional team. Therefore, you must approach PIPs strategically—balancing compassion with accountability. The key is communicating the reason for starting this process, setting clear expectations, providing abundant support, maintaining open communication, and allowing sufficient time for meaningful change.

What Exactly Is a Performance Improvement Plan (PIP)?

A Performance Improvement Plan (PIP) is a multifaceted process implemented by managers to address the underperformance of an individual employee. It consists of a formal notification of the performance gaps, structured coaching sessions, clear success benchmarks, and periodic progress evaluations over a predetermined period—typically 30, 60, or 90 days. When executed effectively, a PIP aims to provide transparency, support, and accountability to align employee output and behaviors with team and company expectations.

Yet, this is not a one-size-fits-all process. Managing employee underperformance can look substantially different depending on a variety of factors. These variables include the degree of the performance gaps, whether the issues are skills-based or attitude/behavioral, the employee's role and responsibilities, their tenure and contributions to date, alignment with company values, openness to coaching, response to feedback so far, and the team/manager dynamics.

An underperforming intern requiring enhanced supervision may need a different approach than a veteran team lead displaying unacceptable behavioral patterns. While the documentation, transparency, goal setting, and progress evaluations remain constant, the support strategies, resources provided, and even duration of the PIP should align with the specific context of the situation and individuals involved. You must assess each case independently and implement personalized improvement plans tailored to the needs at hand.

CHAPTER 6   EVALUATING AND DEVELOPING YOUR TEAM

Why Should I Adopt a Performance Improvement Plan?

Implementing a well-constructed PIP decreases the latency between identifying and resolving performance issues through either improved employee capability or transition. This process enables you to promptly address performance gaps before minor productivity issues cascade into more considerable team dysfunction that threatens critical goals. Taking timely action preserves team dynamics, prevents impact on milestones, and maintains operational excellence.

Furthermore, a PIP equips managers to independently navigate complex employee situations, including documentation, structured feedback, measurable goal setting, progress tracking, and final determinations. You improve your coaching, mentoring, and performance management competencies through this process, increasing your skills to lead teams effectively through uncertainty.

At an individual level, a PIP provides underperforming employees full transparency into the specific areas where their work product or behaviors fall short of expectations. The documented performance gaps, structured action plan, clear success metrics, mandated check-ins, and provided learning resources create focus, support, and accountability around improvement. This process strengthens capabilities for motivated employees by addressing development areas, refocusing efforts on the most critical goals, revealing hidden potential, and often deepening the working relationship with the manager through dedicated coaching. When done compassionately, an adequately executed PIP catalyzes positive personal and professional growth.

Significantly, a PIP also benefits the company legally if the employment relationship ultimately has to be terminated. The detailed documentation shows that you communicated the performance issues, established measurable improvement goals aligned to the gaps, provided abundant resources and support, conducted progress check-ins, and the employee was granted adequate—even generous—time to demonstrate commitment and capabilities to meet expectations. These records and artifacts can protect the company against wrongful termination lawsuits—having proof that you took thoughtful steps to set up the employee for success reinforces termination decisions. Even though a PIP aims to recover and develop talent, the process also generates relevant documentation and evidence in case the employee is unwilling or unable to improve.

Setting the Foundation for Performance Improvement

Before executing a formal Performance Improvement Plan (PIP), you must demonstrate you have attempted regular coaching and feedback opportunities with the employee over an extended timeframe. PIPs should only be considered a last resort option after genuine efforts through check-ins, clearly set expectations, and performance dialogs have failed to resolve deficiencies over a reasonable period.

Even then, you must continue building a foundation of support and seek to understand the root causes behind behavior changes before taking formal action. Context matters deeply here—life happens. A personal crisis, health matters, family loss, or other personal situations could temporarily impact someone's work capacity and output. Have compassion to recognize tough situations before judging performance through a formal PIP program.

Still, key prerequisites before implementing a formal PIP include the following:

Consistent One-on-One Meetings: Hold regular 1:1s with each direct report to build personal connections, understand the whole person, and provide a safe space to discuss sensitive matters. During these conversations, address what's going well and areas for improvement to promote transparency.

Clear Expectations: Set realistic, attainable key performance indicators and success definitions for every employee based on their role. Well-defined goals and guardrails provide clarity for meeting standards.

Ongoing Feedback: Give regular praise and constructive criticism relative to the established goals so people understand when they are off track. Frequent, caring feedback is key for development and to help evaluate a potential performance crisis.

Regular Performance Reviews: Ensure you deliver formal and meaningful reviews. Refer to the previous section and craft all the necessary components to have a performance conversation.

Engaged Leadership: Actively engage with your team. Passive, absent leaders allow issues to remain unaddressed until they escalate beyond repair. Employees need your presence and commitment.

CHAPTER 6   EVALUATING AND DEVELOPING YOUR TEAM

A Blueprint for Performance Improvement Plan

A Performance Improvement Plan necessitates a clearly defined structure for consistency and accountability in the improvement process. Without owners, objectives, proper support resources, and agreed-upon actions tied to designated deadlines, too much room is left for mismatched expectations and diverging interpretations of progress. Employees require an explicit roadmap while facing the stress and uncertainty of fundamental professional development under a compressed timeline. Meanwhile, managers need standardized documentation to assess commitment to growth and capability improvement relatively at fixed evaluation points. A sturdy PIP framework also benefits HR and company leadership to justify final rulings around employment continuance or termination later.

The foundational FOSA template serves as a starting point to ensure proper scoping of the PIP structure—defining the Facts around lagging contributions, stipulating minimum improvement Objectives, outlining helpful Solutions for building skills, and transparently conveying the Actions that management commits to taking in the event of progress or persistent struggles.

With the end goals clarified using a FOSA lens, a comprehensive PIP blueprint should be expanded to contain additional components.

Objectives: Setting the Stage

The objectives section serves as the foundation of a Performance Improvement Plan by clearly stating the purpose and expected outcomes behind entering a formal improvement process with an employee. Also, this section should state the intended goals for the employee coming out of the PIP, getting them back on track to minimum performance thresholds and supporting growth into an exemplary contributor. It must set the stage to highlight the need to acquire specific skills or competencies demonstrated.

CHAPTER 6   EVALUATING AND DEVELOPING YOUR TEAM

Finally, the objectives section should transparently declare potential ramifications if performance does not improve over the course of the structured coaching and development plan. This might span probationary action, position loss, or termination of their employment. Employees deserve transparency into the severity and sensitivity of their performance deficiencies relative to continued job security should issues remain unresolved through the performance improvement process.

Here, you can review a potential definition for this section:

> The primary purpose of this Performance Improvement Plan is to formally address ongoing performance gaps and provide clear expectations paired with support to improve your contributions to the team.
>
> Over the past six months, through both one-on-one discussions and formal performance reviews, concerns have been consistently voiced regarding your quality of work, adherence to processes, and lack of capacity to take on additional responsibilities, as examples. These issues have had tangible impacts on team productivity and goal attainment.
>
> This PIP intends to convey clear guidelines for job expectations and offer resources, coaching, skills development opportunities, and management support to facilitate improvement. By outlining key areas needing improvement, quantifying goals, committing to weekly check-ins, and providing various learning tools, this plan aims to set you up for success and assess progress at the 60-day milestone.

Please be aware that failure to achieve and sustain meaningful improvement across all facets documented here may ultimately result in additional performance management escalation, including probationary status or termination of your employment. The intent is for you to maintain employment and boost your contributions, but demonstrable commitment, effort, and results will be mandatory.

Let's move forward in partnership to pave a path for your growth and strengthened delivery to the team. I'm committed to seeing you succeed, but I need that same dedication to leveling up output. Please thoroughly review this plan and set up a meeting to further discuss details and launch engagement.

The Improvement Plan: The Path to Recovery

The Improvement Plan is the prescriptive core of the Performance Improvement Plan. This comprehensive section links current performance deficiencies to tangible goals, mapped actions, and timed evaluations required to turn performance around. Moreover, this section should define specific observed examples where an employee's contributions, work quality, behaviors, or engagement falls short of expectations, illustrating concretely substantiating the performance gaps to be addressed.

This section comprises the areas for improvement, performance concerns, expectations and specific actions, status, and the status narrative on the PIP end date.

Areas for Improvement

The Areas for Improvement component should directly specify performance gaps observed and documented by you or broader leadership over time. These observations must lean on the SBI model of relaying the Situation or example that highlighted the deficiency, elaborating on the detrimental Behavior, and clearly stating the Impact that resulted—whether missed deadline, low-quality outcomes, unaccepted behavior, and others. Areas for improvement must transcend general criticisms to incorporate concrete illustrations grounded in recent work examples. The details substantiate the performance deficiencies, while the SBI framing connects poor behaviors to meaningful business impacts. Employees with clear situational examples tying their contributions to tangible outcome shortfalls are likelier to take ownership of the issues and engage wholeheartedly in the improvement plan.

Performance Concerns

The Performance Concerns section connects directly to each Area of Improvement mentioned previously. For example, if *"Quality Assurance Process Adherence"* is a stipulated area needing attention, this section would provide recent illustrations tied to dates and work samples that showcase breaches of QA protocols. If the concern is *"Leadership Engagement"* or *"Ramp Productivity,"* the examples would point to a lack of participation in team building activities, absence of constructive feedback during one-on-one peer reviews, or disengagement from collaborative sessions to improve cross-team coordination and adopt new processes.

Painting in-depth word pictures citing data, stakeholders impacted, and tracing the employee behaviors back to business outcomes clarifies why these issues are now severe enough to warrant PIP-level intervention. By stating precise performance concerns, there is little room left for subjectivity or self-preservation.

Lastly, specifying Performance Concerns directly tied to Improvement Areas establishes indisputable evidence of consistent shortcomings. While uncomfortable for both manager and employee, confronting substandard behaviors or work products head-on inspires change in a way that vague criticisms do not. The transparency around the severity of these concerns intends to elicit acknowledged failure modes by the employee. This admission then enables a shared mental model to scaffold systemic changes. Without airing precise grievances, there is little impetus for the hard work ahead. The documentation also protects the organization if performance recovery does not ultimately materialize, even when good faith efforts are made during the Performance Improvement Plan.

Expectations and Specific Actions

With performance deficiencies and concerns established, the Expectations and Specific Actions section outlines corrective measures. For each stipulated Area of Improvement, you must define the next discrete steps that will purportedly close the gaps highlighted.

This definition includes prescribing training programs to build requisite skills, defining success measures for assignment completion excellence, providing sample work products that exemplify excellence to support a reset to quality standards, offering mentor partnerships that expose employees to current high performers, and whatever modes the manager feels best facilitates growth.

Furthermore, the transparency around exact expectations—whether output quality samples from high performers, mandatory training milestones, or deadlines for assignment completion—erases any obscurity around what success looks like versus mediocrity. When both parties vocalize standards in tangible detail and align on action plans, accountability follows. Once enabled with clear guidelines and access to helpers, you can accurately evaluate the employee's commitment at intervals.

This section transforms good intent into executable roadmaps.

Status on the PIP End Date

The Status on the PIP End Date represents the final assessment of whether an employee met prescribed expectations for improvement. While the designation itself contains only a few brief words like Complete, In Progress, or Incomplete, this component carries tremendous weight.

That is because the determination dictates the next steps post-PIP—restoring the employee in good standing, extending the PIP timeline, taking additional performance management actions, or terminating employment altogether. Especially after dedicating months to the intensive PIP process of coaching, checking in, working shoulder to shoulder, and providing various development resources, distilling down to a Complete, In Progress, or Incomplete label may seem overly simplistic.

However, that pivot point either preserves organizational faith in the individual's willingness and ability to reform or confirms that deficiencies likely require structural change beyond the repair of the existing work relationship. As such, properly evaluating and assigning this concluding PIP status must be done objectively, compassionately, and decisively to serve all interests.

Status Narrative on PIP End Date

The Status Narrative after a Performance Improvement Plan timeline serves to qualify the one-word designation of Complete, In Progress, or Incomplete.

You will log holistic commentary on demonstrated wins, observed gaps, the pace of improvement over time, receptiveness to support resources, and other qualitative insights that shaped the decision on whether expectations were ultimately satisfied by the employee. References to specific coaching conversations, milestone check-ins on assigned work products, and participation in community events or training programs help substantiate subjective impressions.

Both positive advancements and deficiencies should feature in this closing narrative. The aim is to provide an accurate, well-rounded perspective on why the employee landed at their designated status, including evidence points when reasonable doubt may exist on either side. In essence, this documentation protects all parties after an emotional process.

Specifying the Support Team: A Collective Effort for Recovery

A Performance Improvement Plan does not happen in isolation between manager and employee alone. Instead, carefully selecting additional people to participate, such as managers, peers, mentors, and HR partners, can provide guidance, accountability, third-party objectivity, and operational coverage when the road gets rocky.

Explicitly listing ancillary players' names, roles, responsibilities, and commitments demonstrates organizational investment in an employee beyond just your efforts. It also signals that objective outside perspectives will factor into evaluations, not just a solitary subjective review from a single manager frustrated by persistent deficiencies pre-PIP. Formalizing a support team role assignment ensures complete coverage across skills coaching, behavioral adjustments, and administrative policy compliance across the PIP timeline.

Assigning accountability to specific line managers, HR advisors, senior technical mentors, and other hand-selected contributors creates a safety net around the employee. It conveys care for the individual and a steadfast resolve to overcome hurdles impeding their success.

CHAPTER 6   EVALUATING AND DEVELOPING YOUR TEAM

Logging Ongoing Check-In Sessions

Once a Performance Improvement Plan launches, close monitoring and consistent coaching check-ins provide valuable support mechanisms for keeping engagement and momentum high. You should schedule weekly one-on-one sessions explicitly addressing PIP items, including shifting support as new needs emerge across the tightly orchestrated recovery plan.

All these meetings must be captured with standard templates outlining attendees, discussion notes on key topics reviewed, action items and commitments established, blockers raised by the employee, mitigation strategies, and candid verbal feedback when course correcting. Additionally, any failure by the employee to attend has implications, and you must also log them along with the explanations or notable inferences on hesitancy provided.

Thoroughly tracking these check-in interactions over time provides a qualitative record that complements the more prescriptive improvement plan. Together, they offer a clear overview of milestones achieved or missed, extended supplemental resources demonstrating organizational support for change, and pivotal behavioral moments fueling confidence in eventual success or final termination decisions. Ultimately, the logs enable undeniable clarity around exactly where contributors elevated commitment to expectations versus continued deficiency trends.

Making the Final Call: The Path Forward

After the concentrated effort of an intensive Performance Improvement Plan lifecycle, you must make a demanding yet mission-critical determination on the future state. You must assess current capability and project future potential and decide if further investment in the employee is prudent given team needs and alternate talent pipelines.

In some instances, demonstrable turnaround catalyzed by the PIP warrants restored organizational trust and opportunity expansion. In other cases, revelations of persistent gaps call for probationary actions or permanent separation. While painful after so much one-on-one work, you must interpret the entirety of the process outcomes relative to the business context, avoiding letting personal advocacy attachments cloud impartial judgment. Moreover, consulting the assembled support team for additional perspectives would be helpful before finalizing conclusions. Reviewing logs and time-based progress narratives also informs important calls balancing an individual's improvement pace against team dependencies and goals.

Even though challenging, you must not allow unfavorable PIP outcomes to spur guilt, regret, or self-doubt when sound support systems are provided. You plot the course like navigators charting the recovery route in painstaking detail, but employees steer daily choices. As long as one upholds their duties, organizational decisions become byproducts of the employee's willingness and capability to close gaps. By focusing on consistent coaching processes versus fixation on unrealistic transformational expectations, you recognize that occasionally, termination serves all interests despite best intentions. Distinguishing process integrity from outcome accountability alleviates emotional drains when tough calls serve the team's greater purpose. You must be brave!

Ultimately, a Performance Improvement Plan intends to recover and maximize talent. But it occasionally surfaces unpleasant realities that performance and cultural deficiencies run too deep for cost-effective remediation. This section equips you to make those excruciating yet necessary determinations with compassion and conscience.

Terminations: A Necessary Evil

Despite intensive efforts to set clear expectations, provide developmental resources, conduct engaged coaching, and allow sufficient time for progress, some Performance Improvement Plans ultimately end with the difficult decision to terminate employment. Especially in highly regulated labor markets, engineering leaders must ensure they have undertaken proper protocol and documentation trials demonstrating good faith personal efforts while protecting the broader organization if an individual remains misaligned with role accountabilities.

The Role of Performance Improvement Plans on Terminations

When performance deficiencies or behavioral gaps reveal themselves as engrained and unresponsive to structured improvement interventions, you may have to make the call to part ways.

Firing people is hard, and it ought to be hard. People's livelihoods are at stake, often with families depending on them. However difficult it is, you have an equal responsibility to the broader team and its mandates serving customer needs. You must objectively assess when an individual's contributions—despite intentional enablement attempts—threaten group cohesion, progress, reliability, and other foundational dynamics that uphold standards.

In these solemn situations, Performance Improvement Plans provide the documentation trails that justify employment terminations stemming from sustained performance gaps. The plans demonstrate your efforts to thoroughly communicate shortcomings, establish reasonable goals for improvement, provide developmental resources and access to helpers, conduct consistent check-ins, and grant more than adequate time to demonstrate commitment to positive change.

While incredibly hard conversations, making termination decisions grounded in ethical support processes can find solace that you personally invested in struggling employees while also upholding their duty to foster high-functioning teams. The PIP serves as the record of good faith efforts to improve and retain talent, even when deficiencies proved too technically or culturally ingrained for remediation.

Don't Wait Too Long

As discussed throughout this chapter, implementing a Performance Improvement Plan is emotionally and operationally intensive for all involved. Once launched, these structured remediation programs divert immense focus, energy, and resources toward progress check-ins, skills coaching, documenting issues, and weighing termination decisions if warranted. You must resist the natural temptation to indefinitely postpone formal post-PIP intervention when signals first surface that an employee is unwilling to change their behavior and attitude.

Even after conducting an intensive PIP process, leaders face a tough decision on whether additional performance management cycles are beneficial or if severing employment is necessary. The temptation is high to offer another round of support to a likable individual now equipped with more skills, deeper relationships, and heightened accountability after initial investments. However, tolerating sustained gaps outside reasonable guardrails is equally disruptive after formal attempts to facilitate improvement through structured plans. At some point, leadership must make the call on whether deficiencies indicate motivational issues that you can't influence or capability ceilings within a role. There are no easy answers, but teams suffer without decisions, so objective determinations become acts of compassion across the board.

Have the courage to make tough decisions so the entire flywheel propels rather than isolated parts spin. Promote those willing to change, guide strugglers toward roles better fitting their strengths, but don't wait too long clinging to sunk potential. In the end, that benefits no one.

Don't Make the Call Unilaterally

While you are accountable for performance and personnel decisions within your teams, unilaterally determining employment termination can backfire without careful consultation and consensus building.

CHAPTER 6   EVALUATING AND DEVELOPING YOUR TEAM

Even in at-will employment arrangements giving you discretion, abruptly firing individuals risk allegations of unfair treatment, discrimination, or dismissal from personality conflicts versus performance necessity. Seeking broader leadership validation, HR guidance, and legal review aims to secure alignment on process integrity, documentation accuracy, and organizational readiness for separation.

This group consultation admittedly elongates difficult choices and introduces some emotional influencing. However, few organization-wide decisions with legal, financial, staffing, and operations implications should rest solely on the subjective perspectives of an individual contributor, frontline manager, or even mid-level department lead. Input from the interconnected support team you have assembled during the Performance Improvement Plan itself ensures well-rounded considerations of capability gaps that are unable to be addressed even after formal attempts. Convening this group builds invaluable perspective, for example, from

- **HR Partners:** They ensure proper protocols are followed, appropriate documentation is gathered, and legal risks are mitigated.

- **Senior Engineering Leaders:** They assess technical or operational impact relative to broader initiatives if a termination occurs.

- **Finance Stakeholders:** They detail replacement hiring, buyout, or transition costs to validate decisions.

- **Other Invested Leaders:** They share any additional improvement cycles the employee completed under guidance, demonstrating consistent deficiencies.

- **Legal Counsel:** They outline risks and precedents for claims if behavior traces to protected class status and support building airtight cases.

Ultimately, you retain authority to execute chosen talent actions. But gathering supportive consensus rather than wielding unilateral judgments protects both credibility and conscience when employment separations become simply unavoidable. The broader inputs compensate for your blind spots and bias under emotional duress while handling painful choices.

Lead with Heart During Hard Goodbyes

Pouring countless hours into Performance Improvement Plans, you will invariably develop personal connections with struggling employees. So, when the time comes, and you decide that separation is the best option for all involved, conducting termination meetings ranks among the most angst-ridden conversations imaginable. Maintaining empathy, compassion, and support during these situations facilitates notifying the employee about what is coming next.

Also, consider the grieving individual's perspective upon losing a job after receiving genuine support and pursuing alternate paths forward. You poured immense personal energy into avoiding the pain these decisions inevitably inflict. While accountability drives choices after windows expire sans meaningful change, exercise compassion guiding transitions.

Reinforce that necessary separations only proceed after careful attempts at counsel, development, and realigned opportunities. Underscore it became apparent that the employment relationship could not continue, not that human value ever diminished. Then, shape upcoming interactions with empathy, heightening sensitivity around fractured income, purpose, and stability through little direct fault. Finally, demonstrate sadness over potential loss, hope better settings may catalyze strengths, and lead heart-first amid hard goodbyes.

Care for humans behind roles!

CHAPTER 6   EVALUATING AND DEVELOPING YOUR TEAM

Takeaways

1. Lead with empathy, compassion, and care while evaluating people—uplift human dignity and potential.

2. Adopt a human-centric approach focused on nurturing strengths and motivations when assessing talent.

3. Implement models like 9-Box grounded in observing evidence before judging people's potential.

4. Set ambitious yet realistic expectations rooted in the interpersonal context beyond delivery metrics alone.

5. Conduct consistent performance reviews focused on recent specific evidence and outcomes.

6. Balance constructive feedback with acknowledgment of accomplishments and strengths.

7. Customize developmental plans and PIP structures to individual situations.

8. Provide developmental resources before formal improvement procedures where possible.

9. Communicate precise improvement areas tied to transparent examples when addressing gaps.

10. Outline actions, targets, and milestones to resolve deficiencies during improvement plans.

11. Select a support team of cross-functional partners to enable struggling employees through care structures.

CHAPTER 6   EVALUATING AND DEVELOPING YOUR TEAM

12. Log all improvement plan check-ins, successes, and barriers to resolve for evidence-based calls.

13. Make employment decisions tied to improvement plans self-compassionately but head-on.

14. Lead any necessary terminations with empathy, transitional support, and compassion.

15. Evaluate holistic performance spanning technical skills, soft skills, and team contributions.

16. Champion accountability focused on human progress over impatient perfection-seeking.

17. Priority #1 is nurturing personal esteem and potential over processes when managing people.

18. Seek root causes with empathy when facing subpar contributions.

19. Feedback is a continuous process outside formal reviews to maintain responsive support.

20. Separate roles from humanity during hard conversations—candor with care lifts all.

21. People-first leadership builds durable trust and loyalty amid turbulence through consistent caring.

22. Progress over perfection—celebrate small improvements while sustaining encouragement structures.

23. Lead with the heart and develop with empathy—that is the path to engineering leadership greatness.

24. Become less techie and more people-centric to drive your team to success.

CHAPTER 6   EVALUATING AND DEVELOPING YOUR TEAM

Time to Practice

1. Reflecting on your engineering team, which 1-2 members would you classify as "Accomplished" in Performance but "Outstanding" in Agility on the 9-box matrix? What specific evidence exemplifies their strengths and achievements in those classifications?

2. When providing constructive feedback to struggling engineers, how do you balance clearly communicating performance gaps with showing empathy on situational contexts impacting their output?

3. What coaching, training, or mentorship resources exist currently that you could leverage more to nurture promising talents with high potential but developing skills?

4. If you needed to implement a Performance Improvement Plan for a struggling report, who would you recruit as their support system for skills building, objective input, and empathy? How would they contribute to the recovery plan?

5. When providing tough feedback to engineers, how do you balance candor with care to uphold their dignity as people beyond just their functional roles?

6. Imagine you have taken an employee through a Performance Improvement Plan, and they could not improve meaningfully. What structures could you establish to guide a compassionate termination decision aligned to business needs?

Index

A

ABCs mindset, 252, 254
Accomplished rating, 302–303
Accomplished agility
    and accomplished performance (solid and steady), 307
    and developing performance (evaluate further), 311, 312
    and outstanding performance (high-performing pro), 306
Accomplished performance
    and accomplished agility (solid and steady), 307
    and developing agility (limited progress), 309–311
    and outstanding agility (develop to excel), 305
Accountability, 6–7, 91, 127–128, 337
Adaptative leadership, 98
AfroTech, 262
Agile team formation, 242–243
Agility, 253
    accomplished
        evaluate further, 311, 312
        high-performing pro, 306
        solid and steady, 307
    definition, 300, 301
    developing
        limited progress, 309–311
        performance (low impact), 312, 313
        performing without innovating, 309
    outstanding
        develop to excel, 305
        leading edge, 304
        strong potential, 308
Agricultural practices, 243
Annual performance review, 317–318
Anonymity, 235, 324
Assessment
    accomplished rating, 302, 303
    definitions, 302, 303
    developing rating, 302
    outstanding scoring, 303
Authenticity, 2, 3, 6, 8, 9, 12, 67, 279
Authentic leadership
    communication mediums, 116
    dreams, 118, 119
    ground rules and expectations, 116
    life story, 117, 118
    setting expectations, 120

INDEX

Autocratic leadership
    autocratic control and selective inclusive leadership, 59
    benefits, 53, 54
    breeding resentment, 55
    burdening the leader, 56
    cutting-edge AI products, 58
    decisions and operations, 60
    delaying awareness, 55
    delivery process and plan execution, 59
    vs. democratic leadership, 57, 84
    historical oppressiveness, 52
    impeding development, 55
    vs. laissez-faire leadership, 57, 94
    risks of diminished morale, 59
    roots, 52
    Sarah's journey, 58
    vs. servant leadership, 56, 73
    stifling innovation and motivation, 54
    team's pace and strategy, 56
    vs. transformational leadership, 57, 63
Autonomy and empowerment
    agile team formation, 242, 243
    decentralized decision-making environment, 241
    execution and converting ideas, 241
    planning, 241, 242

B

Balancing priorities, 233
Be positive, 253
Big Hairy Audacious Goals (BHAG), 203
Build cross-functional teams, 238–239
Business direction, 282
Business goal, 82, 142, 221
Business mutation, 318
Business-oriented approach, 225
Business units, 231, 266, 286

C

Candidate evaluation, 261
Caring, definition of, 296
Celebrate customer-obsessed teams, 230
ChatGPT, 321
Cloud architecture principles, 257
Coaching, 23, 101–102, 183–185
Collaboration, 136
    and knowledge sharing
        build cross-functional teams, 238, 239
        communities of practice, 236, 237
        inner model philosophy, 237, 238
        modern business age, 236
    skills, 264
Collaboration with product teams

business impact, 151
consistency, 153
customer-centric
    products, 146
dispelling ownership
    misconceptions, 148–151
establish regular
    ceremonies, 152
ideation and definition, new
    capabilities, 151
individual features, 152
individual limitations, 147
institute ceremonies, 153
language, 152
product and engineering roles,
    147, 148
structured models, 152
teams—approach roadmap
    planning, 153
technical constraints risks, 147
Communication, 155
    empathic listening role, 43, 44
    impact, leadership, 41, 42
    misaligned, 41
    practical strategies, 45, 46
    skills, 22
    structure and design,
        message, 42
    verbal, 43
    well-structured *vs.*
        comprehensive
        message, 43
Communities of practice, 236–238
Community upvote traction, 286

Company goals, 282
Compelling communication, 41
Compliance-driven models, 258
Computer architects, 230
Conducting blameless
    postmortems, 234
Conflict management
    avoid responsibility and
        blaming behaviors, 131
    engineering teams, 130
    facilitation, 133–136
    interpersonal
        conflicts, 131, 132
    lack of enthusiasm/
        engagement, collaborative
        work, 131
    mediation, 133–136
    open communication, 132
    resource allocation
        conflicts, 131
    team disruptions, 131
    technical debates and
        disagreements, 131
    unconstructive criticism,
        feedback, 131
Constructive feedback, 5,
    19, 47, 334
COVID-19 pandemic, 154
Craft phenomenal candidate
    experiences, 253
Creativity, 3, 6, 46, 53, 54, 65, 76,
    226, 239, 262
Critical feedback, 27–29
CRM notes, 140–141

INDEX

Cross-functional collaboration, 122, 138–139, 144, 146, 150, 284
Cross-team mentoring, 120
Cultural add, 260, 265
Culture transforms, 77, 231
Curiosity, 30, 119, 123, 199, 239, 240, 250
Customer-centricity, engineering teams
    balance customer needs with business/technical priorities, 142, 143
    collaboration
        cross-functional, 138, 139, 144
        customer-facing roles, 145
    customer-centric engineering culture, 146
    customer feedback, 140–142
    customer perspective, 137
    engineering leader, 137
    inward-looking perspective, 137
    product development, 137
    resistance to cultural/mindset shift, 144, 145
    set customer service goals, 139, 140
    siloed departments, 145
Customer-centric KPIs, 139
Customized IDPs, 207
Cutting-edge AI products, 58

D

Data Team, 237, 238
Debugging techniques, 264
Decisive direction, benefits, 53, 54
Delegation, 39–40, 53, 57, 106
Democratic leadership, 107
    vs. autocratic leadership, 57, 84
    business requirements, 87
    characteristics, 79, 80
    collective intelligence and cooperation, 88
    constructive feedback, 88
    core traits and principles, 86
    decision-making processes, 83
    "dividing to conquer" approach, 87
    embrace solid ethics and moral responsibility, 82
    empowered and collaborative team culture, 78
    encourage active participation, 81
    engineering teams, 79
    group dynamics and harmony, 81
    inclusive communication, 81
    vs. laissez-faire leadership, 85, 95
    make collaborative decision-making the norm, not the exception, 82
    prioritize continuous development, 82

promote a sense of shared responsibility among the group, 81
rich history in Ancient Greece, 78
risks and pitfalls, 82–84
vs. servant leadership, 75, 86
stress mounted and progress lagged, 87
toolbox, 79, 80
vs. transformational leadership, 64, 85
unravel or backfire, 82
Developing rating, 302
Developing agility
and accomplished performance (limited progress), 309–311
and outstanding performance (performing without innovating), 309
Developing performance
and accomplished agility (evaluate further), 311, 312
and agility (low impact), 312, 313
and outstanding agility (strong potential), 308
Development life cycle, 239
Digital disruptions, 160
Digital economy, 227
Disengaged employees, 297
Diversity and profitability, 249
Dysfunction festers, 295

E

Embedding innovation
collaborative design
challenge perceptions, 269
empathize with people, 269
guide participants, 269
prototype concepts, 270
redefine problems, 270
test and refine, 270
demo sessions, 274
early feedback, 273, 274
hackathons, 267, 268
quarterly all-hands meetings
incremental/execution level, 271
open networking, 272
quantify value in business terms, 272
shared objectives *vs.* siloed efforts, 271
spotlight launches accelerating product vision, 271
spotlight values in action, 272
reaching new heights
engineering cultures, 276
failing-forward attitude, 276, 277
failures to extract the learnings, 278
humanize triumphs, 277
team growth through learning days, 274, 275

INDEX

Emotional conflicts, 133
Emotional intelligence (EQ), 1
  components, 11
  empathy, 11, 15–17
  engineering leadership, 10, 11
  leader, 11
  motivation, 11, 15
  practical strategies
    comfort and growth zones, 18
    empathy, 21
    motivation, 20, 21
    resilience and persistence, 17
    self-awareness, 18, 19
    self-regulation, 19, 20
    social skills, 22
  self-awareness, 11–13
  self-regulation, 11, 13, 14
  social skills, 11, 17
Empathic listening, 43–45
Empathy, 11, 15–17, 21, 68–69, 262
Employee experience, 161, 226, 232, 288
Employee growth and customer experience, 224
Employee well-being, 162, 222
Empowerment-fueled innovation, 227
Engineering autocracy, 149
Engineering cultures
  autonomy and empowerment, 241–243
  collaboration and knowledge sharing, 236–239
  empowerment-fueled innovation, 227
  growth mindset, 239–241
  human ingenuity *vs.* dictating outcomes, 228
  psychological safety, 232–235
  strategic visions
    adapt and reinforce, 231, 232
    foundation, 228
    lead with actions, 230, 231
    milestones to invite participation, 229, 230
    tell compelling narratives, 228, 229
  task-oriented, 221, 227
Engineering leadership, 1, 10, 11, 15, 40, 163, 223, 268, 296
Engineer-led formation, 243
Environmental elements
  agricultural practices, 243
  centralize knowledge to avoid reinvention, 244, 245
  creativity with processes and governance, 247, 248
  cultivate creativity through idea portals, 245, 246
  diverse and unbiased hiring, 248–266
  sandboxes, 246, 247
  soil lacking, 243

INDEX

Envision software, 229
Escalation platforms, 280
Evaluating and developing your team
    9-box model, 298–314
    performance reviews, 314–326
    PIP, 326–339
    terminations, 340–344
Executive audience, 42
Exit interviews, 141
Extrinsic motivation, 15

F

Facilitation, 80, 83, 86, 133–136, 267, 268
Facilitator, 102, 128, 133, 134
Feasibility, 17, 138, 148, 151, 152, 238, 246, 268, 269
Feedback, 19, 45, 46
    bidirectional interactions, 26
    constructive conversations, 27, 28
    critical, 27–29
    culture, 2
    leaders *vs.* team members, 26
    personal and professional growth, 26
    positive feedback, 26, 27
    self-reflection, 29, 30
Fixed mindsets, 30–31, 239
FOSA, 331
Fuel innovation velocity, 241

G

Genuine positivity, 5
Goals, Reality, Options, Way Forward (GROW), 203
Goals-sharing forum, 286
Good team player, 295
Google, 225, 255
Grant autonomy, 92–94, 288
Growth and innovation
    change agents to drive innovation, 285, 286
    creating dedicated roles, 284, 285
    customer expectations, 278
    dynamics persist, 283
    engineering cultures (*see* Engineering cultures)
    environmental elements (*see* Environmental elements)
    forward-thinking leader, 278
    fruition—blocking adaptive progress, 283
    Individual Development Plan, 284
    individual level, 284
    innovation-oriented cultures, 287, 288
    Microsoft, 225–227
    modeling adaptability, 279–281
    opaque decision paradigms, 283
    people-centric culture, 223–225
    psychological safety, 283
    re-examination/feedback, 281

INDEX

Growth and innovation (*cont.*)
    shepherding growth, 287, 288
    skill growth, 222
    team level, 284
    transparent leader-team
        collaboration, 281, 282
    type of conviction and
        ownership, 283
    unrealistic deadlines and
        unempathetic
        demands, 222
Growth mindset, 47
    curiosity, 240
    fixed mindset, 30, 31
    potential, 30
    practical strategies, 34–36
    proactive approach, 30
    process over outcome, 33
    professional development, 239
    reciprocal team development,
        240, 241
    reflection, sustainable
        growth, 31, 32
    SBI model, 239
    unlearning, 32, 33
Gut feelings, 295

H

Hackathons, 231, 267–268, 292
Healthcare, 230
Hiring process
    ABCs mindset, 252, 254
    constraining beliefs, 250–252
    culture add, 251
    good culture fit, 251
    HR policy, 249
    perfect candidate profile, 251
    qualities, 250
    recalibration, 257–266
    system design discussions and
        code challenges, 250
    unconscious bias
        cloud architecture
            principles, 257
        first impressions, 254, 255
        halo/horn effect, 256
        and innovative hiring, 254
        nonverbal cues, 256
        skills downplayed, 255
        stereotyping, 255
HR policy, 249
Human-centric mindset, 296
Human-centric narratives, 277
Human-centric system
    evaluating and developing your
        team (*see* Evaluating and
        developing your team)

I

Idealized influence, 61, 63, 109
Ignoring listening, 43
Incident Management process, 280
Inclusive leadership, 59, 224
Individual Development Plan, 284
    goal-setting framework, 209
    informal coaching, 208

OKR and SMART goal-setting
frameworks, 209–211
long-term visions, 212
objectives, 213–216
technical mentoring
competencies, 216
technical skills, 215
trust and psychological
safety, 216
one-off document, 209
Individuality
business needs, 114
cross-functional
collaboration, 122
external behaviors, 121
leadership style, 115
self-awareness, 122
values, 121–123
Individualized consideration, 61,
62, 66, 109
Inner model philosophy, 237–238
Innovation
and decision-making, 249
embedding, 266–278
roots of, 249
soundboards, 235
Inspirational motivation, 61, 74,
103, 109
Integrity, 1, 2, 6, 9–11, 47, 63, 70, 77,
82, 124–125, 129, 339, 342
Intellectual stimulation, 62
Intensive PIP process, 336, 341
Interpersonal conflicts, 131, 132,
164, 198

Intrinsic motivation, 4, 15, 21, 54,
73, 82, 93, 97, 237, 246

J

Job descriptions and
qualifications, 258–260

K

Kubernetes expertise, 251

L

Laissez-faire leadership, 107
accountability with
autonomy, 91
vs. autocratic leadership, 57, 94
autonomy, 94
case study, 95–97
complacency from reduced
oversight, 93
vs. democratic leadership, 85, 95
empowerment over control, 90
empowerment through
autonomy, 89
engaged detachment, 91
freedom and authority, 89
hands-off approach, 94
high-level guidance, 90
imbalanced distribution of
workload, 93
lack of direction and
coherence, 92

INDEX

Laissez-faire leadership (*cont.*)
    lower morale from reduced guidance, 93
    perceptions of indifference and indecisiveness, 93
    principles, 90–93
    risks and navigate, 92
    selective intervention, 91
    vs. servant leadership, 74, 75, 95
    vs. transformational leadership, 64, 95

Laughter, 157

Lead by example, 46
    accountability, 6, 7
    integrity, 9, 10
    promote positivity, 5, 6
    role modeling, 3, 4
    setting standards, 4, 5
    trust, 126
    walking the talk, 8, 9

Leadership, 1, 2, 49
    engagement, 334
    skills, 241
    styles, 107, 108, 113, 114

Light-touch processes, 242

LinkedIn, 226

Long-term innovation, 222

M

Machine learning, 86, 225, 230, 243

Manager review, 320–322

Matching and Orientation phase, 194–198

Mediation, 133–136

Mediator, 133, 134

Meditation/yoga, 19

Mentees
    benefits, 186–189
    life story, 199

Mentoring
    benefits, 186–189
    vs. coaching, 183–185
    empathy, 181
    ethical obligation, 183
    genuine care, 181
    growth, 185
    leadership principles, 181
    reward, 185
    self-awareness, 183
    superficial knowledge, 181
    vulnerability, 182

Mentor mindset
    comfort zone, 190
    cultures and beliefs, 192, 193
    domain and interpersonal skills as quality indicators, 190
    mentee's motivations and needs, 190
    mentorship program, 191
    personalities and behaviors, 192
    role, 191
    selflessness posture, 191

Mentorship program structure
    closing and celebrating phase, 194, 207, 208
    developing and learning phase, 194

feedback, 204, 205
network, 206, 207
profiling outcome to drive objectives, 202, 203
setting goals, 203, 204
share resources, 205, 206
Matching and Orientation phase, 194
  ambitions, 195
  backgrounds, 195, 196
  career journey, 196
  knowledge and approach, 196
  mentees' aspirations, 195
  open discussion to align, boundaries, 197
  program structure, 196
  transparency, 195
  typical meeting cadence, 197
multi-phase program flow, 193
profiling phase, 194
  mentee's life story, 199
  roles and scaling exercise, 200–202
  unlocking others' potential, 198
Microsoft
  cultural shift, 225
  cultural transformation, 225
  digital economy, 227
  employee experience, 226
  genuine employee care, 226
  revenue growth, 225

revolutionize culture and leadership strategy, 227
stock price, 226
transformation, 227
Mutual inspiration, 287

N

9-box model
  agility, 300, 301
  assessment, 302, 303
  fast-paced engineering teams, 298
  high potential, 297
  performance, 298–300
  potential, 298
  talent evaluation (*see* Talent evaluation with 9-box model)
  top performer, 297
Nonjudgmental dialogue, 14, 34
Nonjudgmental listening, 189, 312
Nourishing individual growth, 287

O

Objectives and Key Results (OKRs), 203, 204, 209–213, 215
Onboarding process, 265–266
One-on-one discussion, 117, 332
One-on-one meetings
  avoid detrimental pitfalls, 171, 172
  benefits, 163–165

357

INDEX

One-on-one meetings (*cont.*)
    collaborative note-taking, 166
    engineering leadership, 163
    framework, 170, 171
    frequency, 168, 169
    note-taking platform, 166
    preparation, 165, 167
    team members, 167
    team values, 167
Online internal innovations portal, 286
Open-ended mentoring, 184
Out in Tech, 262
Outstanding scoring, 303
Outstanding agility
    and accomplished performance (develop to excel), 305
    and developing performance (strong potential), 308
    and outstanding performance (leading edge), 304
Outstanding performance
    and accomplished agility (high-performing pro), 306
    and developing agility (performing without innovating), 309
    and outstanding agility (leading edge), 304

P

Panic and blame, 13
Passive-aggressive resistance, 281
People-centric culture, 223–225
People-centric engineering leadership, 223
People-centric foundations, 279
People come last mentality, 221
People feel confident, 224, 288
Performance
    accomplished
        develop to excel, 305
        limited progress, 309–311
        solid and steady, 307
    concerns, 334, 335
    definition, 299, 300
    developing
        evaluate further, 311, 312
        low impact, 312, 313
        strong potential, 308
    outstanding
        high-performing pro, 306
        leading edge, 304
        performing without innovating, 309
Performance Improvement Plan (PIP), 310
    areas for improvement, 334
    benefits, 328
    check-in sessions, 338
    clear expectations, 330
    coaching processes *vs.* fixation, 339
    consistent one-on-one meetings, 330
    defined, 331
    employees require, 331

engaged leadership, 330
expectations and specific
 actions, 335
FOSA, 331
foundation, 329, 330
framework, 331
identifying and resolving, 328
individual level, 328
investing, 326
lifecycle, 338
in management, 326
managing employee, 327
notification of performance
 gaps, 327
objectives section, 331–333
ongoing feedback, 330
Performance Concerns,
 334, 335
PIP End Date, 336, 337
probationary actions/
 permanent separation, 339
recovery, 337
 and develop talent, 329
 and maximize talent, 339
regular performance
 reviews, 330
supervision, 327
support team, 337
and terminations, 326, 340
Performance reviews
 annual, 317, 318
 and consistent leadership
  habit-building, 315
 empower employees, 315

high-quality reviews, 314
negligence, 314
quality and productivity
 gains, 314
quarterly, 316
and relationship-building
 value, 314
semesterly, 317
structure
 balancing achievements and
  opportunities, 319
 digest feedback, 319
 expectations, 322, 323
 manager review, 320–322
 recommendations, 323
 self-evaluation, 320
 self-reviews, 319
 360-degree
  feedback, 323–326
successive reviews, 315
Perspective-taking, 189
PIP End Date
 Status Narrative, 336, 337
 Status on, 336
Pointless statements, 245
Policy experts, 230
Positive feedback, 26, 27
Power breaks, 48
Pretending listening, 44
Product and engineering
 roles, 147–148
Product dictatorship myth, 149
Product/feature feedback, 142
Productivity policies, 223

INDEX

Product managers, 42, 146–152, 238
Product-oriented audience, 42
Profiling phase, 194, 198–199, 202
Project Development Units
    (PDUs), 210, 213
Project Management Professional
    (PMP), 210–215
Psychological foundations, 288
Psychological safety
    anonymity, 235
    change by role modeling,
        233, 234
    conducting blameless
        postmortems, 234
    failure risks criticism, 233
    self-censorship, 233

Q

Quality assurance, 230, 236, 267,
    277, 311
Quarterly performance
    reviews, 316

R

Ramp Productivity, 334
Recalibrate hiring process
    in assumptions and
        convenience, 257
    expanding sourcing
        pipelines, 260–262
    job descriptions and
        qualifications, 258–260

    reframing interview
        processes, 262–266
Reframing interview processes
    assessment, 263
    cross-functional hiring
        committees, 263, 264
    forming balanced, 263
    interview guides to calibrate
        assessments, 264, 265
    onboarding process, 265, 266
    product and design
        partners, 264
    technical skills, 262
Remote asynchronous
    contributions, 235
Remote engineering teams
    challenges
        build trust, virtual
            relationship, 157, 158
        communication and
            collaboration, 155–157
        company cultures, virtual
            teams, 154
        COVID-19 pandemic, 154
        growth mindset, 154
        office *vs.* remote employees,
            161, 162
    transparency, goals and
        expectations
        employee engagement and
            well-being, 159
        in-person contact, 158
        taming remote work
            distractions, 160, 161

INDEX

Remote leadership, 155
Resource allocation conflicts, 131
Role modeling, 3–4, 159, 233–234

S

Sandboxes to safe experimentation, 246–247
Selective listening, 44
Self-awareness, 11–13, 18, 19, 35, 122, 200
Self-direction, 89, 95, 237, 323
Self-doubt, 13, 16, 100, 105, 106, 159, 187, 192, 276, 339
Self-driven development, 240
Self-evaluation, 317, 320
Self-expression, 18, 119
Self-realization, 145
Self-reflection, 8, 18, 29, 30, 32, 45, 46, 134, 193, 300, 314, 319
Self-regulation, 11–14, 19–20, 49
Sell your values, 254
Semesterly performance reviews, 317
Servant leadership, 107
    vs. autocratic leadership, 56, 73
    broken culture, 76–78
    criticisms and challenges
        balancing authority with servitude, 71
        counterarguments and misconceptions, 72
        empowerment risks, 71
        misconceptions, 71
    risk of inefficiency, 72
    vs. democratic leadership, 75, 86
    empathy, 68
    foresight, 69
    humility, 69
    vs. laissez-faire leadership, 74, 75, 95
    listen deeply, 69
    principles, 70, 71
    team's growth, 68
    vs. transformational leadership, 64, 73
Shepherding people-centric cultures, 287
Short-term milestones, 230
Siloed redundancy, 285
Situational leadership, 51, 108
    case study, 104–106
    challenges, 103, 104
    coaching (S2—for Level 2), 101
    competence encompasses, 99
    delegating (S4—for Level 4), 102
    directing (S1—for Level 1), 101
    distinct stages of development, 101
    inaccurate assessments, 104
    limitations, 98
    model champions, 98
    optimal leadership style, 104
    perform tasks and roles, 99
    readiness level, 99, 100
    relentless evaluation, 103
    supporting (S3—for Level 3), 102
    toolkit, 103

INDEX

Situation-Behavior-Impact (SBI) model, 204, 205, 207, 239, 334
Skill development, 40, 192, 197, 199, 274, 315, 323
Social skills, 11, 17, 18, 22
Specific, Measurable, Achievable, Relevant, Time-bound (SMART) goals, 203, 210, 211
Sponsor regular cycles, 243
Static mindset, 30, 55
Support tickets, 138–140
Sustainability, 70, 230, 248
Systems design patterns, 264

T

Tactical and exclusionary approach, 258
Talent evaluation with 9-box model
    accomplished performance
        and accomplished agility (solid and steady), 307
        and developing agility (limited progress), 309–311
        and outstanding agility (develop to excel), 305
    developing performance
        and accomplished agility (evaluate further), 311, 312
        and agility (low impact), 312, 313
        and outstanding agility (strong potential), 308
    outstanding performance
        and accomplished agility (high-performing pro), 306
        and developing agility (performing without innovating), 309
        and outstanding agility (leading edge), 304
Team culture, 20, 21, 77, 78, 128, 284
Team development, 240–241
Team empowerment
    feedback, 24
    frequent communication, 24
    fundamental level, 23
    granting autonomy, 25
    positivity, 25
    unlock potential, 23, 24
Team player, 29, 258, 264, 295
Team's motto, 248
Technological evolution, 237
Tell compelling narratives, 228–229
Tense all-hands meeting, 96
Terminations
    don't wait too long, 341
    labor markets, 340
    PIP, 340
Test automation approaches, 264
Test-driven development (TDD), 184
30-60-90 plan, 266
360-degree feedback, 319, 323–326

Thriving metrics, 297
Time blocking, 38, 48
Time-bound coaching, 185, 210
Time management
    delegation and elevation, 39, 40
    engineering leadership, 40
    leader, responsibilities, 36, 40
    mental bandwidth, 36
    power breaks restoration, 40
    responsibilities, 36
    strategic "no", 38, 39
    strategic scheduling, 38
    time and effort, 37
    time beyond money, 36, 37
Toxicity, 310, 316
Transformational leadership, 98, 107
    authenticity, 67
    vs. autocratic leadership, 57, 63
    complacency represents, 65
    components, 61
    culture of bold innovation, 60
    vs. democratic leadership, 64, 85
    idealized influence, 63
    individualized consideration, 62
    innovative algorithm, 66
    inspirational motivation, 61
    intellectual stimulation, 62
    vs. laissez-faire leadership, 64, 95
    journey, 67
    maintaining momentum, 65
    managing overwhelming expectations, 65
    preventing organizational fragmentation, 65
    vs. servant leadership, 64, 73
    struggling tech company, 65-67
Transparent leader-team collaboration, 281-282
Trust
    accountability, 127, 128
    lead by example, 126
    leadership character, 124
    rebuild broken trust, 129, 130
    vulnerabilities, 125

U

Unconscious bias, 252, 254-257, 260, 261
Unlearning, 32-33
User feedback, 148

V

Verbal communication, 43, 45

W, X, Y, Z

Women Who Code, 262
Works hard, 295

GPSR Compliance

The European Union's (EU) General Product Safety Regulation (GPSR) is a set of rules that requires consumer products to be safe and our obligations to ensure this.

If you have any concerns about our products, you can contact us on

ProductSafety@springernature.com

In case Publisher is established outside the EU, the EU authorized representative is:

Springer Nature Customer Service Center GmbH
Europaplatz 3
69115 Heidelberg, Germany

www.ingramcontent.com/pod-product-compliance
Lightning Source LLC
LaVergne TN
LVHW010334260326
834688LV00036B/707